Coruscated Confabulations

Oh! The humanity!

Kalikiano Kalei

Aeolian Flights Press

SACRAMENTO, CALIFORNIA

Kalikiano Kalei/Aeolian Flights Press
5960 South Land Park Drive, #256
Sacramento, California 95922
www.authorsden.com/kalikianokalei

Publisher's Note: This is a work of fiction. Names, characters, places, and incidents are a product of the author's imagination. Locales and public names are sometimes used for atmospheric purposes. Any resemblance to actual people, living or dead, or to businesses, companies, events, institutions, or locales is completely coincidental.

Coruscated Confabulations: Oh! The Humanity! / Kalikiano Kalei. -- 1st ed.
ISBN 978-0-692-96286-2

Dedicated to all the wonderful Siberian Husky dogs that have shared my life and made it bearable, despite the myriad and frustrating idiosyncrasies of my fellow humans, who seem metaphorically bent on crapping prodigiously in their own kennels.

"If dogs don't go to Heaven, I want to go where they go when I die.".

—SAMUEL CLEMENS

Contents

"When you touch a man's body, he will enjoy the moment; when you touch a man's heart he will remember it forever." -Dixie Waters

(Above: LF in 1969)

THE POINT OF IT ALL

The wind was strong. It gusted fiercely under the heavily clouded skies, sweeping all before it with a disregard as ancient as the land itself.

Above the lush green of the hill's thicket of tangled growth, the sky was hidden by a vast jungle canopy of interconnected tendrils. Except for the small circular break in the uppermost layer of the matted vegetation, the impression from below was one of an enormous green tent, growing translucent as the apex of the womb-like space soared above the disturbed soil directly below it.

Standing beneath the ragged opening in the roof of this silent natural cathedral, Nguyen could see the fringes of the gap shiver as the draughts of wind passed above. Her tall, slender figure paused at the edge of the dome's living wall. After a moment of silent contemplation, sensing the powerful indifference of the torrent of air beyond the uppermost treetops, she allowed her gaze to fall back upon the hollow's blackened crater.

A violent intrusion, at once unnatural and out of place, had occurred here nearly 18 years ago. The thick, palpable feeling of it seemed to fill the empty space before her and seized her imagination with ghostly hands. Even the animals and birds, normally oblivious to any disturbance after the merest of brief pauses in their noisy activity, remained unseen and unheard in this strange place. Nguyen thought she could detect the faint odor of burnt oil, but it was at best nothing more than the hint of an aroma blended into the rich mix of earthy smells produced by the jungle's growth and rot.

She had been told of this place by her mother for as many years as she could recollect. From the moment she had been capable of understanding anything at all with her childish awareness, she could recall the disapproving conversations of her aunties and the strange way they had of looking at her mother when she repeated these things in front of her only child. Their looks, she remembered, had seemed curiously to reflect both sadness and condemnation.

Nguyen was tall for her age, with large curious eyes and a disturbing way of gazing questioningly at people. With her lustrous, dark hair braided into the long queue that her mother wove for her, at such times she appeared deceptively youthful and willowy in the simple *Ao Dai* she dressed in. As if expressive of her serious, reflective inner nature, she had a habit of hugging her arms to her chest when considering something. To some, her gesture suggested an instinctive need to reassure herself that she was physically *here* and not somewhere else. Now, confronted by the objects enclosed within this silent cone of jungle tendrils, she gripped herself in this unconscious manner as she surveyed the scene, eyes wide and hardly daring to break the absolute silence with the small sounds of her breathing.

In the center of the hollow, all but completely covered by 17 years of jungle growth, were the mangled remains of some large war machine. Nguyen had seen enough airplanes flying over her village to recognize the remnants of an aircraft fuselage, its smoothly rounded sides split open like a burst winter-melon to reveal twisted internal structural members. Contorted beyond recognition by the violence of a crash, scattered bits and pieces of it were dark with stains and oxidation, but sections of the original faded camouflage paint were still visible here and there in the subdued sunlight. What fire there had been on impact had apparently blown itself out shortly after the explosion, but the flash- blackened area, though small, remained barren. Nothing now grew upon that part of the jungle floor which had been scorched by this man-made fallen star, after its fiery descent from the heavens.

Stepping closer, delicately, Nguyen studied the quiet scene. If her mother's story were to be believed as something more substantial than mere fable, this wreck was the only *other* remaining trace of her father's earthly existence....an all but forgotten relic of his fleeting presence in this jungle, long gone. Her wide eyes softly drank in every detail of the sight confronting her as she brought back the details of the story her mother had so reluctantly told her in the past.

The front part of the airplane (or what had once been one) was somewhat more intact than the rear of it and her gaze was drawn to the large, empty space on its upper surface which was surrounded by shards of yellowed Plexiglas canopy. There were cables hanging from it now, intermixing so strangely with creeper vines and other natural growth that it was nearly impossible to tell one from the other. The explosion's flame had not touched this area from what she could see. Directly above this part of the wreck hung the circular entrance to the air spaces above the jungle, through which the plane had originally come screaming in, *18 years ago.* She tried to form a mental image of that moment, when the broken machine had had wings, a tail, and had flown through the air like a metal bird of prey, bearing her father in its sharply pointed beak.

Her father, so her mother had said, had been a pilot. Not just a pilot, but an *American* pilot, tall and well-proportioned and also...her mother had told her, somewhat oddly...a *handsome* pilot. Thinking about this, Nguyen remembered that her grandmother had also found the pilots of the great Asian War very attractive, during the early years of the Viet Minh resistance. *Dashing* was the word grandmother had used.

Nguyen stepped back from the metallic wreckage and squatted down so that she could gaze across the whole clearing. *A handsome American pilot*... What must he have looked like, she wondered? How had his voice sounded? Did he smile with his face, or was his face set harshly? Did he smile at all? The questions crowded each other, pouring into her thoughts like the heavy Monsoon rain as she strained to recall the conflicting details of the stories told her by her mother and her aunties.

Her mother had said he was a good man, a wonderful man. She said that she had even seen him cry once--although Nguyen could not even *imagine* such a thing as *tears* coming from face of one of the rough and sternly domineering men of her own village. She sighed, wrestling with the contradictory thought. He must have been a most unusual man, for her mother had hastened to tell her that this had not been a display of weakness in him, but rather that he had seemed stricken with grief over his involvement in the war, 18 years ago--a burden of terrible sorrow which she had never explained further or gone into.

Nguyen meditated upon this. First about her mother and then about *the story*. A mother who would become with each retelling, filled with obvious emotion, expecting her daughter to attend without demanding deeper explanation--as if the tale were something which revealed itself in the listening. A mother who the other villagers told her she took after so much in appearance, thought and gesture. The mother her aunties had clucked their tongues about and waggled fingers at so frequently when she began telling Nguyen the story, starting off as if it were new and had never been told before. And a mother who she knew had always been so quietly proud of both her beauty and her Chinese ancestry.

Squatting on her thighs, sandals jammed into the soft jungle loam, Nguyen reflected on the melancholy enigma who was her mother. She had once been a very beautiful woman, everyone had said, with long, slender and shapely limbs joined to a figure that was the envy of all the village women. She could have easily had her choice of any man in the village, according to gossip. Her hair, as dark and silky as the soft fur of the panther's underbelly, she habitually wore in a single long braid down her back as she worked in the village paddies. Her battered *Kalashnikov* automatic rifle slung in the crook of a nearby tree, she always pulled the straw hat carefully down over her eyes to protect her face from the hot noonday sun, according to Mother's Third Auntie. With her fair face and comely bottom, many an idle village man found an excuse to pass by while she bent low over the rice and rudely speculate on the charms which the shapeless, worn cloth of her garments did not manage to hide well enough.

There had been many things about her which had set her off from the rest of the villagers. Not the least of these had been her education in the missionary school. Precious enough among the people of the village, where any education at all was usually rare and costly, she had impressed the teachers with her keen mind and quick grasp of subjects. Working under the hot sun in the village paddies she stood out, with her tall, willowy gracefulness and long legs, from the other, drabber women.

At that time, the Viet Cong had been operating more actively in the province and one day her silhouette had caught the eye of a young NLF cadre passing through the village. He had returned later, inquiring about her. Upon learning of her exceptional abilities, he had arranged with her family to recruit her for political education and training--despite her being a mere woman--and had taken her up north with him to Hanoi for 6 months. The trip had been hazardous, but her mother had finally returned to the village fit, healthy, and browned by the sun, possessed of a serious new look on her face after her studies of the 'people's struggle.' Second Auntie had said you could see the unnatural flames of *National Liberation Front* idealism burning in her intense eyes, where before there had been only peaceful reflections of *Wah* with the simple village routines.

Nguyen paused in her ruminations to wonder what this looked like, for she had never seen *anything* at all in the dully glazed eyes of the dreary village women but weariness, as they labored to take care of their families and the endless field work. Her aunties had said that education, *for a woman*, could be a dangerous thing, but Nguyen had her doubts.

Not long after their return from Hanoi, the young cadre, who had helped cultivate these new political awarenesses in her mother, had been caught in an ambush by a squad of ARVN rangers some kilometers east of the village and Nguyen's mother had thereafter taken over his work as the village's political educational officer. Sometime after this she had learned of his death under questioning by the ARVN soldiers, but had banded her heart with the steely strength of her belief in the cause of liberation. Like the soldier she now supposed herself to be, she had not shown any emotion at all upon hearing the news of his torture and death.

Thus, had her life progressed, submerged within the senseless savageries engaged in by both sides. As the war progressed, the village passed back and forth between the NLF guerrillas and the ARVN like a worthless prize zealously fought over by fanatical gamblers in a crazed lottery, rewarding both victor and loser with nothing but misery and intense suffering. For years the war continued in this manner, as did the ageless rural routines of the village, interrupted only by the pointless battles which punctuated their coexisting rhythms. There was no such thing then as concern for past, or future. Only the present had even remote meaning for any of the villagers. Most had merely regarded Nguyen's mother as an unavoidable nuisance--a politically ‘emotional’ person who they usually ignored in the midst of their more pragmatic daily struggles for food and shelter. All except the men, however...who even burdened as they were with the terrible deprivations of the war, could still smirk at each other over her more obvious attractions. The irony of such exceptional beauty, managing to survive amidst the horror and ugliness which surrounded the village, was utterly lost on their lustful thoughts.

Finally, Mother's Fourth Auntie had told Nguyen, the long-anticipated Tet Offensive had struck with vicious surprise against the Americans, rising like a great poisonous snake from the jungle depths. The NLF had come out into the open for the first time in waves, supported by regular NVA soldiers, to sweep through the countryside. But after the shock of their offensive had diminished they had ultimately been beaten back, leaving only *more* death and desolation in their wake and an all-but-broken VC resistance. With the subsidence of their initial victories, the village had been plunged into a thicket of skirmishes as the reeling ARVN forces responded with a new threat: the introduction of American aircraft to strafe and bomb the countryside in support of the South Vietnamese troops.

* * *

It was on one such day, when Nguyen’s mother, alone and at some distance from the village in the aftermath of the Tet, heard the distant scream of planes approaching. Unslinging her AK, she quickly crouched among the growth at the edge of the paddies to take cover from the danger. Gazing out beyond the line of trees, she managed to catch sight of a group of 4 *Intruder* aircraft coming in at low level, wings laden with the horrible eggs of the liquid death that was *Napalm*. Seized with fury, she wildly fired off the whole clip of her AK at the center aircraft as it passed directly over her, giving vent to a surge of impotent outrage. That it was a hollow, futile gesture was certain, but at least it had been a positive response of *some* kind and better that than enduring the exhausting emptiness of helpless inaction. She knew instinctively that it was little more than the act of a defiant mouse cornered by a large and hungry cat, and yet she had fired at these *demon planes* with a murderous rage that surged forth from sources deep within her which were primal and beyond her understanding.

As the planes screamed overhead she had ducked back into the thicket, but not before noting, thunder-struck, that her bullets had apparently *hit* something! The center airplane was streaming a thick black plume of smoke from one of its two exhaust pipes, its turbines howling with mechanical indignation as it streaked away from her. Almost immediately after it disappeared from sight she heard a strangely muffled explosion, followed closely by another larger booming sound. The watery verge under her sandals shook briefly as the earth heaved from the detonations, then subsided.

Since there were no more airplanes to be heard or seen, she had carefully emerged from the growth and peered in the direction the planes had departed in. Not too far from her, a roiling, greasy column of smoke was visible emerging from the trees on the low hill-side a thousand meters distant. Just beyond her vantage a whole section of the paddy fields was covered with a blazing sheet of flame, and a hundred meters above it, and still borne on the wind, a small figure hung suspended under a large camouflaged parachute canopy! She had actually *managed* to shoot an American plane down with little more than a *popgun*, armed with her raging indignation! The American pilot had ejected and was coming down almost directly on top of her!

Her intellect vaguely resisted acceptance of the reality of what had happened, but her body's reflexes had already leaped beyond mere thought. Leveling the gun, she slapped the spare clip taped to the AK's magazine into its action and ran forward to capture the *Yankee air pirate* who now symbolized everything she hated about the enemy's imperialistic war.

The updrafts created by the blazing napalm had blown him away from its inferno and a few seconds later the pilot thudded heavily to earth beneath the chute, struggling with the shroud that covered him and hid Nguyen's mother from his sight. A firestorm of emotions briefly shook her, but taking a second to reassert control, she stood with the AK aimed at the center of the nylon shrouded mass, believing herself fully prepared to kill this *dog* at the slightest provocation. Recognizing the bizarre contrast of her outwardly brave behavior with her undeniably nervous inner state of anxiety, she wondered what the pilot would look like. A brute? A murderer? A monster? What sort of ogre would meet her eye? What kind of demon would thoughtlessly incinerate whole villages of helpless people on the ground with liquid fire? The sweat on her hand made her finger slippery on the crude metal trigger of the heavy Kalashnikov as she confronted her fears.

The pilot managed at last to cut through the entrapping parachute fabric and emerged awkwardly from the canopy's folds like a monstrous silkworm from its cocoon. That part of his face not hidden by his helmet was bloody and he staggered forward almost into the muzzle of her weapon. Shock registered in his unsteady posture, and he held his right hand absently to his helmet, as if checking to see whether his head was intact and still on his shoulders.

Wiping the blood from his eyes and seeing the gun aimed at him, he sat back stupidly, snared by the parachute harness that had ironically delivered him safely to earth only to hold him firmly captive when confronted with imminent capture. The surprise of their encounter lingered only a split second before Nguyen's mother reacted, yelling at him to get on his feet while gesturing menacingly with the gun. When he complied slowly, still trapped in the nylon shrouds, she signaled with a flick of the AK-47's barrel for him to free the harness, indicating that he was to turn and walk away from the discarded parachute with his hands over his head. Motioning him roughly to walk in the opposite direction of the wrecked aircraft's column of black smoke, the muzzle of the AK pointing all the while at his back, they were safely away from the site before the first enemy aircraft came rolling in from the east in an attempt to locate the downed pilot

For some time, they traveled in this manner, he stumbling forward over the uneven ground, her following grimly, resolute, determined, but also wary and considerably frightened. After an hour, they stopped: he had indicated that he could go no further without a rest, and they had encountered no others, neither villagers or VC. They were by this time near the shade of some hillside trees on the edge of the jungle growth, though still far from the village. As he sat, she watched him with restrained hostility, squatting somewhat apart from where he rested. After observing him in this manner for several minutes, she threw her corked bottle at his feet with some water in it for him to wash the blood from his eyes and off his face. It was an afterthought which she came automatically to her and which she really couldn't explain...he was, after all, a *murderer...*

As he swabbed some of the clotted blood away, she was shocked to find that he was not much more than a boy...tall, large, and strong...but a barely grown-up boy, not much older than she. He was speaking what she decided must be English to her, and of course she did not understand. After he had cleaned up his face somewhat and put a bandage from his survival vest on the scalp wound, she found to her further amazement that he was a very handsome boy, despite the bloody superficial cuts and gashes. His features were *Chinese*, and his dark hair and eyes, though disheveled and still bearing some bloody residue, were *striking*, she reflected with some surprise.

The shock of the crash was obviously wearing off, leaving the American pilot once more in possession of his senses and therefore--she reminded herself--doubly dangerous. *Still*, this was not the image of a blood-thirsty vandal she had expected to find...*and possibly to kill.* Immediately upon thinking this, the political inappropriateness of these thoughts overcame her with a flash of brief shame and once more she leveled the gun at him, grunting for him to rise. Confronting this moment of womanly weakness with the admonishment of her confused emotions did not quell the feeling, and she tried very hard to regain her former sense of anger as they made to move out.

She was about to motion him on again when he turned to face her and asked calmly in a rough but recognizable Cantonese dialect, *"Are you Chinese?"* She was stunned! He was speaking words she clearly understood, but it was *not possible* for a Yankee to say what he had said! She glanced quickly down at his feet, as if the sight of them would help reassure her that she *had* heard what her ears *thought* they had heard. His scuffed black boots, braced on the solid earth beneath his undeniably real presence, were not much help in convincing her that this was in fact actually happening. It was a *trick*!

He spoke again, *"Do you speak Chinese?"* This time there was no denying it. He was speaking fair Cantonese dialect, although with a peculiar accent. Was it not a dream?

Still numbly disbelieving the evidence of her own ears, she shook her head slightly to indicate she had heard him, but kept the AK's ugly muzzle aimed at his stomach.

"Where are we going?" he asked. Still confused but determined not to let this cloud her thinking, she decided finally not to speak to him and motioned him on again. It was a trick he was playing on her, surely, this knowledge of Chinese! She could not help but wonder abstractly about his use of a language she understood all too well.

Gun at his back, she poked its barrel at him to move again and was about to follow him, expecting him to comply. Suddenly his hand shot out, grabbing the muzzle of the AK and swiftly twisting it away from his back, wrenching her wrist as he did so. With his greater strength, now recovered from the crash, he had disarmed her in a moment of catastrophic indecision! Shocked to find herself *his* prisoner now, she glared at him with disbelief clearly etching the handsome lines of her determined face. Her moment of pause had been her undoing! She had been trapped by her own careless breech of emotional discipline.

"Sit," he now commanded her in Chinese. She squatted as he ordered, no longer in control. Slinging the weapon muzzle down over his shoulder, he squatted across from her at a safe distance of several feet. *"I am not going to hurt you,"* the American said, again in Chinese, *"but I need your help. Are you Vietnamese? You look Chinese."*

Nguyen's mother, still dumbfounded to hear this American speaking understandable Cantonese dialect, finally responded: first to her senses, then reluctantly to his questions. *"Yes, I am Vietnamese, but my family are Chinese. How is it that you speak as you do?"* she ventured, her training and caution momentarily overcome by irrepressible curiosity. He was *not* the image of the horrible demon she had expected to meet--but then, she reflected quickly and with some irony, she was *not* a typical VC woman, either. Swallowing this thought, she studied him, *his* prisoner now.

"My family also came from China....from Hong Kong. I was raised there. We moved to the US just before I started college." He had been watching her carefully, appraising her as he spoke, alert to any sudden move but confident and calm in his manner and not betraying his fatigue. He had already decided that she was no *ordinary* Vietnamese villager, and had also guessed that she was *not just* an unexpectedly pretty woman but an *intelligent and educated* one...*not* the sort of peasant he had expected to find at the trigger end of a gun, despite her soiled black outfit and careful absence of expression.

His hand probed his left temple. *"My head still aches a bit. It's too far from the crash site now to expect a quick rescue and we need a rest before continuing. Just before the crash I caught a single string of tracers coming up from below the plane; they must have hit one of my engines...blind luck! How many more of you are out there?"*

Nguyen's mother hesitated, sensing that she might successfully employ a lie to help her situation; imaginary VC might be as valuable to have around her as real ones and she had *nothing* to lose. *"I think it was my gun that brought you down, but the others are very close. They know where you came down and they are searching for you as we speak."*

The American looked at her with a clear look of cynicism in his expression. *"Well....there's little choice but to..."* He let the statement dangle, unfinished. Shifting the Kalashnikov into his left hand, he motioned to her with it. *"Come closer, turn around and kneel down."* An electric tingle of alarm shot through her at this and she stared hard at his face to read the meaning of these words, her heart fluttering slightly with fresh new fear.

"Relax." He read her anxiety in the brief slip of her composure. *"I don't intend to hurt you."* She glanced at his face. His look was hard to decipher.

He had brought a length of nylon cord out of his vest then and tied her hands together, lashing her ankles in a similar manner and joining them to the wrist bonds before running a line around her neck and fixing one end to his left wrist. *"You might as well relax, we're going to rest here for a while. It won't be comfortable, but I can't leave you loose, obviously enough."* The bonds he placed on her wrists weren't tight but there was not enough slack in them to permit thoughts of slipping free of their constraints. It took a great effort not to let her mind run loose with worry and she lay quietly for the moment, scrutinizing him.

Shifting the AK across his lap, he gazed across the few feet of clearing beneath the overgrowth at her, the look of fatigue now showing more clearly on his face. She watched as he brought out his emergency rescue radio and attempted to call out on it, noting that it appeared to be visibly damaged. It failed to elicit a response. Reaching into another pocket on the survival vest, he pulled out a bar of tropical chocolate, glancing about in all directions to reassure himself of their temporary safety. Finally, he turned back to gaze at her, noting her eyes as they followed the candy bar to his mouth. *"You're a damn beautiful woman for a VC. What's your name?"*

She hadn't answered, but rather stared blankly back at him, her frustration over being captured by an American she herself had shot down embarrassing her as she sat helpless and bound before him. His question had sounded harmless enough but she felt an increasingly chill surge of fear rising from her gut to her throat as his eyes roamed frankly over her body. The precious chocolate was forgotten in an instant.

Without expecting a reply, the American continued, more to himself than to her, *"Fucking-A lousy, stinking little war this is.... I didn't come over here to kill civilians and simple peasants, and yet here I am, brought to earth in the middle it by a gorgeous VC woman who obviously regards me as some kind of a mass murderer. Back in the States I have a family...probably not too much unlike yours here...brothers, sisters, mother, father, lots of cousins, uncles, aunties. Believe me, it wasn't my idea to come here and drop bombs on your people! I just want to fly. Flying's my passion, not killing. I would have had my commercial airline ticket by now if it hadn't been my lousy luck to get caught up in this worthless fucking war."* He paused, listening to the sounds in the dense thicket before turning back to her and continuing. *"You really hate me, don't you? Can you understand what I'm saying to you, woman? It wasn't my idea to come here."*

Separated from him by the few feet of the clearing in the thick undergrowth, Nguyen's mother was indeed listening to him carefully, wary of his Asian appearance and uncertain of this unpredictable *American* pilot in a blood-stained flight suit who spoke Chinese. She reflected on it for a moment, struck queerly by the fact that it was *his own blood* on his hands. As he continued to talk, the slight chill of her fear subsided a bit and she took a closer look at him. His face was *very* Chinese, his eyes, skin, his dark hair...she reflected on the irony of a war that placed two people of similar ancestry at bitter ends of a horrible contest of wills. For what purpose? He could be her older brother, she thought, or...and she paused again...*her lover*...if it were not for the powerful political struggle that swept all personal considerations aside. Leaving that ironic, somewhat shocking thought suspended in her mind, shaken for even considering it, she caught him saying once more, *"You really are a beautiful woman...I wish you would tell me your name."* The thrill of fear floated through her again as she noted the look on his face. It was a mix of things: a residue of shock, fatigue, hunger, frustration, and what? A suggestion of *lust*?

The long night finally passed, with the first rays of the dawn glowing pink in a narrow band of sky that separated earth and the grey clouds overhead. Each of the two had drifted off from time to time during the night out of sheer weariness, but the rest had been brief and elusive as the thick vegetation's nocturnal population of small animals, snakes and birds came alive in the black depths of the small, close hollow, creating an uncomfortable background quotient of additional anxiety. At least there didn't seem to be any of the woman's VC companions nearby, the American had satisfied himself with some relief. Nguyen's mother, for her part, felt he had suspected her lie about the others from the onset. Before the sun was fully up, he rose, shaking off the remnant of the fitful night. It struck her that he was watching her carefully, conserving his motion the way a mongoose might while fixating a cobra before seizing it.

Alarmed, she concentrated on his movements as the morning sun filtered through the heavy undergrowth, outlining his form. Was he really such a depraved person, she wondered? Was her political indoctrination correct in insisting that the enemy had *no* human scruples whatsoever? She had long since had a suspicion that all *was not* as it had been made to seem to her, once the enemy had been revealed and reduced to a personal encounter of some intimacy such as this. He seemed intelligent, gentle; he was obviously educated, *and* he shared her ancestral heritage...even though he was a person she *should* have hated. Again, the futility of the war with all its incomprehensible madness flooded in upon her, drenching her with the nauseous awareness of its conflicting paradoxes and insoluble contradictions.

The humid night had left her hot and sticky, her garments wet and uncomfortable from being unable to move throughout the long darkness. He caught the intensity of her gazing at him and spoke to her in Chinese. *"Look, I'm going to untie you, but I want you to agree not to try to escape. Do you understand?"* He placed his hand on the Kalashnikov to emphasize his meaning.

Nguyen's mother stared doubtfully at him. Some hidden sense filled her with renewed anxiety as he moved towards her across the small cleared area in the foliage.

He crossed around so that he was kneeling just behind her. The moist warmth of the Vietnamese night had pressed her thin garments to her body, revealing the swell of her breasts and hips. She sensed him behind her, studying her body. Momentarily fascinated by her long dark braid of hair, he hesitated before gently grasping the sinuously thick braid at its root. His other hand reached around her waist and came to rest on the bonds which joined her wrists. Despite the heat of the jungle, she felt the warmth of his hand upon the soft, protected skin of her inner wrist and then the strength of his grip upon her upper arms. *"You are so beautiful...,"* he murmured. Once more, as it had when she had lost the gun to him, her heart began to flutter. Bound and tied up like this...all of her NLF political strength and resolution were now doubly cursed, betrayed by her 'gift' of exceptional beauty, and reduced by it to a graceless jelly of primitive fear and helpless apprehension.

Her brief feeling of intense self-disgust dissolved instantly as he slowly turned her to face him. She saw, glittering without pretense in his eyes, what she had feared ever since she had become his prisoner: *she was going to be raped.* The knowledge washed over her with the shock of a cold torrent.

As he pulled her head back toward his she caught the scent of his sour-sweaty maleness and felt a dread, unreasonable sorrow for this person who has going to *do this* to her. It occurred to her that if she were very lucky, she *might* survive the assault, although she *knew* what the outcome of such an attack would be had it been a common ARVN soldier who took her in this way. It was, however, only a *fain*t hope, for she had heard all the stories about what the enemy did to captured women...

And then, maintaining his grip on the thick braid of her hair, he cut the cord binding her ankles. Using the braid as a sort of harness, he forced her knees apart and pushed her bound arms out in front of her. A fleeting urge to resist surged within her, but what good would it do...out here...alone...and tied? Weakly, her spirit utterly drained, she sagged to her knees, aware of his hands as they untied her shirt, then pulled her pants down around her knees. It amazed her that he was strangely gentle in doing this--not ripping her clothes from her body in preparation of doing violence, but undoing them carefully, almost reverently. The preposterous nature of this thought flickered insanely through her mind and then guttered as his hand cupped her breast.

From behind, as her pants fell free, she felt the heavy warm morning air bathe the heart-shaped cheeks of her vulnerable and exposed rear. Her small but firmly rounded breasts, revealed and sweaty beneath her chest, stood free. Absurdly, in front of her, she noticed a brilliant purple flower standing by itself among the growth. A large bee was darting in and out of its succulent, crescent-shaped orifice. She felt his hand cup itself again around one of her breasts. Then a brief wave of hysteria swept over her, and she trembled, waiting in this position for her fate to overwhelm her.

Pushing her head down and forward, legs splayed widely, the American took her from behind, thrusting himself into her utter dryness with shocking fullness. But not rudely, not violently, not brutally. She gasped at his enormity as he gripped her buttocks with gentle force and penetrated her, finding to his amazement that she had never been touched by a man before in *this* manner...or any other. He seemed to overcome his momentary surprise at her maidenhood then, and oblivious of her sweat and dirt, he had actually *kissed* her neck and caressed her body with what felt to her like *tenderness*. Wordlessly, he continued, seemingly unmindful of the potential danger surrounding them. His rape of her seemed the rape of a vigorous lover, as she might imagine it, not that of a rutting animal.

Although she had tried to feel nothing--summoning up the paper courage of political, idealistic convictions to distance herself from the shame of his forced intrusions--she found herself, for more than a fraction of the moment, swept up in feelings and emotions never before guessed at or even *imagined*. It was no good, she found herself thinking, to deny that there had not been some insanely delirious hint of dangerous pleasure mixed in with all her fear. It was an exotic, fantastic mixture of wildly contrasting emotions which coursed through her mind and body throughout his insistently forceful mounting of her. Before long, after enduring long minutes of his thrusting, she strangely found herself losing some of her fear and abandoning herself sacrificially to ancient instincts and emotional urges utterly beyond her ken.

Finally, she felt him shudder, his hot flood of explosive wetness filling her. She slumped, still impaled upon him and aching greatly. He had finished with her and *now* she must prepare to die; with any grace she could summon, *if that were possible...*

Waiting for the feel of his sharp blade upon her throat, she tensed, all her senses suddenly alive and the adrenaline rushing within her once more. She *knew* what the chances of surviving a rape were for a woman who had been used this way by the enemy...gentle or not. A captured woman was abused and then destroyed...there could be no alternative, and certainly no mercy from the hated enemy. Not even from one who was so strange and different. It had been the Japanese way during the earlier war; why should it be any different with this new enemy?

She felt his hands release their steel grip on her thighs, shivered as he withdrew himself, dripping and still engorged, from her now moist recess. Determined to turn and confront her death, however it might come, she dared to look at his face. She was startled to find him squatting beside her, spent, sweating, but with a strangely soft look illuminating his familiar-but-foreign eyes. "*You are so beautiful.*" He spoke the words quietly, with a low, gentle quality in his tone which was a shocking thing to discover coexisting within the terrible threat of death that his act of domination represented to her. *"Do you hate me for this, beautiful woman?"*

He placed his hand on her face, and caressed the smudges of dirt from it. She was stunned by the wholly unnatural experience of it. It seemed a dream, truly. Could this really be happening? Was she dead and in another universe? It could not have seemed stranger...yet not *entirely* disagreeable. *"You will not kill me?"* She managed finally to eject the words that struggled to form on her lips...

He laughed with a consuming foreign humor that was apparent on his face, *"No, my pretty one, I will not kill you.*

How could I kill something so beautiful? Would I kill my own mother? Or my sister? Or my lover? No, I told you I wouldn't hurt you. Have I been so hurtful?"

The cold grip of raw fear had left Nguyen's mother just enough to allow her a flash of rational reflection that he had *not* hurt her much after all--except for some tears and painful moments upon his forced entry into her unprepared maidenly parts. It had not been *painful* as much as it had *stirred her* with strange, dangerously primitive feelings, long smothered and repressed by the brutal realities of this war, with its constant reminders of ever present death.

She contrived to force the vestige of a shy smile, still uncertain of his motives. *"That's better,"* he said. *"And now I need your help to find my own people. It's long past time to get the hell out of here and return to safety."* Reaching out, he inspected her freed ankles but left her wrists bound. Cramped from the long hours of being bound and thrown off by the unreal tumult of sensations which had smothered her wits during his taking of her, she struggled to rise, falling briefly back to the ground. Seeing this, he helped her up, having refastened her clothes about her, and almost tenderly brushed back a few dusty strands of hair from her face. *"My god...you are a lovely creature,"* she heard him say.

It was then, as he looked searchingly into her unreadable eyes and holding her at arm's length, that she reacted. It was the work of a second to grab his unsnapped survival knife from its sheath on his vest with both her hands and swing wildly out at his face. An anguished scream, welling from deep within her, cut the stillness as sharply as the steel blade bit the air.

The surprise written on his face was immense as the sharp point of the carbon steel knife connected by pure chance with his throat. The blade caught him just below his chin and cut far into the windpipe, ripping the carotid arteries on both flanks as the stroke finished its slashing arc through his trachea. The blood that sprayed out drenched her fully with a horrible, sticky rain of his crimson life fluid. As he staggered backwards, propelled by the tiny dynamo of her pent-up power stroke with the knife, his eyes bulged with disbelief.

It was all over in a flicker of the eye, *and he had not even made a sound*. The shock was upon her then, as she saw what she had done. He lay sprawled on the ground at her feet, the blood still pumping out of the frightful gash in his throat. Exhausted, stricken with horror, she fell nearby, releasing the knife as she tumbled down and quivering with a mixture of rage, passion and pure adrenaline. Shortly afterwards she collapsed completely, wrists still bound, and fell into unconsciousness.

It was some time later before she awakened. Finding the strength to saw through the bonds on her wrists, she searched absently about for something with which to remove some of the thick, dark clots of blood which coated her. Finally, she left the American pilot where he had fallen, his flight suit covered with his own blackly coagulated blood and the ancient, red *An Nam* soil. The tawny Chinese features of his face were amazingly unstained as the jungle midges swarmed upon the gaping wound in his throat. Wiping the knife's blade clean on the pilot's flight suit and gathering up her strength, she set out to find her village with the AK-47 slung in place over her slim shoulder. With a last blank gaze at the grotesque ruin below his handsome, boyish face, she swung about unsteadily for home. As the tall grass of the fields parted before her with each step, a single disjointed thought burned itself stupidly into her mind: *his eyes had had tears in them!*

* * *

Nguyen's thoughts were distracted from her meditation on her mother's story by a single ray of random sunlight, as it chanced down through the dense green foliage overhead, illuminating part of the ruinous metallic wreck before her. She stood, scrutinizing it carefully. There appeared to be some faint and weathered writing below the shards of Plexiglas on the forward, upper part of the overgrown fuselage. Standing, she ventured towards the sunlit metal panel, the shuffle of her footfalls the only sound breaking the heavy silence.

There were indeed words there, although written in something other than her familiar native language: *Jason Wong, 1Lt.* A name in English? According to her mother, this had been her father's airplane long ago. Was this *his* name? She wondered about this as she looked toward the rear of the shadowed relic. Her mother had said she had loved her father very much, that he had been a kind, gentle and sensitive man. And a *handsome* American pilot, as well. Nguyen remembered the silent tears which would always come into her mother's dark, empty eyes whenever she repeated these things to her daughter.

Puzzled greatly by all of this, and no closer to being able to understand any of what she had been told by either her mother, or her aunties, Nguyen glanced up again at the hazy grey clouds which swept over the hole in the foliage above. She meditated a minute on her own self, the meaning of her life and her being here. What was the *point* of it all? Who could possibly understand any of this, let alone what the whole world of experience which surrounded her own life was all about? She decided the Buddhist priests of the nearby retreat were correct after all...there was *no meaning* in any of these things. It was simply all a darkly humorous and very strange riddle to which there was no apparent meaning. The only thing she was *certain* of was the fact that she had herself been born some nine months after her mother had returned from some duties outside the village, and that her mother had--from what she had been told--never been quite the same ever again. Even her forever-disagreeing aunties had *agreed* upon *that* fact.

That, she told herself, was over 17 years ago, during a war which was now history. All she was left with now were the stories of her mother and her aunties, this relic of an metal bird that must once have brought her father here, and the uncertainty of her private thoughts. *Nothing* she knew about them seemed to make the slightest sense whatsoever, in combination.

Pausing by the cockpit of the aircraft to take a last look at the overgrown tangle of wreckage before her, Nguyen pulled the rusty old survival knife from her waistband and placed it carefully on the instrument panel behind the yellowed canopy shards. With a start, she saw the rusted blade of the knife seem to become dark and red, and glancing upwards, felt the first heavy drops of rain cascade through the gap in the trees overhead. *'Buddha's tears'*, the bonz would tell her.

Nguyen stared at the knife for a moment as the moist rust changed the blade to a sinister ochre shape on the wreck's exposed console. Then, with a brief shiver, she turned her slender, youthful woman's form away from the wreckage. Hugging her arms to her maidenly breasts, she absently retraced her foot prints through the humid maze of jungle and back towards the entrance to the hollow, as the deluge of warm Monsoon rain began to pour from the ruptured clouds above.

"*Good-bye, Father,*" she whispered to the stormy winds sweeping above the silent grove. Looking up at the gray expanse of clouded sky, she added: "*My mother loved you.......*"

THE DOODAH ROOM

In the slanting rays of the late afternoon sun, the twig cast an odd shadow across the dull rust of the undisturbed sand. Protruding only an inch or so from the wind-swept crescents of the striated dunes, it did not seem at first glance to be anything remarkable from Joachim's vantage by the Toyota.

As he leaned back on the truck's fender, holding the black cigarette thoughtfully between right thumb and forefinger, Joachim continued to stare at the distant spires of the Kuwait City television tower. Something about the twig in the sand kept drawing his attention back to the sandy piles of drifted sand which lay some 50 yards ahead of him. Distracted from the golden shimmer of the sun's reflection on the towers, he turned his full attention on the twig.

The thought suddenly came to him, as he gazed bemusedly in its direction, that it might not be a twig after all, since no natural growth--certainly nothing resembling a bush--could be supported in the perpetually desiccated waste of endless sands that stretched in all directions. With one last deep drag on the cigarette, he flicked the butt away and decided to walk over to examine the enigma.

Savoring the strong Balkan tobacco's bite in his mouth, he covered the short distance on his stocky, sunburned legs with an unconcerned languidity, scattering the wind-smoothed grains of sand with each scuff of his sandals. Within a few moments he was standing over the curious twig and stared down at it for a second before hunkering down to examine it at closer proximity. Joachim was a Bavarian, and Bavarians never did anything without affecting a studied irreverence. But Joachim was also an engineer by profession, and the natural motivation of a scientific background usually overcame the provincial habits of his regional origins, and confronted by the strange twig his natural instincts yielded to the analytical habits acquired through his training.

Pulling his knife out of its sheath, he sank the blade into the sand around the projection and swept the grains aside so as to fully expose the object which had captured his attention. The twig suddenly took on a more familiar form in the fading light as it stood revealed as a mummified vestige of bone, heat-shrunk, incinerated tissue baked onto it like the bark of a weathered tree. Joachim felt a mild uneasiness as he continued to scrape away the sand. It could be anything, he found himself musing--the long dead remains of a camel, possibly a sheep. But...and the thought lingered with a delicious distastefulness...might it also be part of a human remain? This was, after all, an area in which heavy fighting had occurred during the retreat of the Iraqi Army Republican Guards, *en route* to Basrah, in the Gulf War.

The bone was not coming free and remained fixed, apparently deeply rooted in the dunes. In the east, the sun was now very low on the horizon, and the spires of Kuwait City were starkly outlined by the feeble rays of sun which strained to penetrate the eternal background filter of airborne dust. Shrugging off the brief reflection, Joachim took a closer look at the object slowly revealing itself as the sands parted around it. There was no longer any doubt. It was a human finger bone, attached still to the rest of the hand, and it pointed upward towards the sky as if flinging a futile, silent and long-dead accusation toward the heavens.

The gathering dusk by that time had rapidly made any further discoveries near-impossible. Glancing across the sand at the Toyota truck, Joachim stood up, replaced his knife in its sheath and retraced his steps back across the wind-riffled eddies of dune. Standing once more by the truck's door, he could barely make out the stark outline of the pleading, skeletal arm in the thickening gloom of the desert twilight.

With only the merest residual thought of his discovery left, and already abstractly filed away in that scientific part of his mind wherein such findings were deposited, Joachim quickly turned towards the more immediate matter of preparing something to eat from the box of food which lay in the Toyota's bed. More importantly, in a separate box nearby, a large 20-liter plastic jerry can held the latest batch of home-brewed, dark Bavarian style beer. Lighting a Bluet Gaz-fueled camp light, Joachim was in the process of cutting up some schnitzel to eat with the beer when he heard the loud hail that came some distance beyond the illuminated circle of the camp.

"Achtung, y'all!" Joachim cringed slightly, vaguely resenting the attempt at humor, as his American companion advanced into the light. Putting the glass of strong beer down, he surveyed the figure beaming naively before him.

The American, Arnold Sawyer by name, was at first glance an interesting study in contrasts--even by the relatively weak light of the gas lamp. A full six feet tall, sturdily built, and projecting an air of still somewhat gawky openness, Arnold was the blonde, blue-eyed offspring of Swedish immigrants who had settled in the state of Alabama some hundred years ago. Standing before Joachim, Arnold's youthful eyes moved animatedly from food to beer and back again. Hunger and thirst were clearly on his mind after the trek out across the dunes, from which he had just returned. *"How about some of that stuff you brewed, bud?"* he asked in his curiously atypical Southern American accent.

Regarding Arnold with a gaze which one normally reserves for an inspection of one's effluent after a successfully brief 'reign' on the throne of human necessity, Joachim gestured towards the jerry can. *"Help yourself. Did you get lost out there?"*

"Naw, I wasn't that far away. And besides, I figured you'd have a fire lit to steer back to, anyways." Arnold had his small daypack slung over his shoulder and as he spoke deposited it into the bed of the truck, close to the beer jug. He was wearing faded US Army desert camo pants and a T-shirt. The T-shirt, also somewhat faded, carried a slogan that said: *"Eat right, stay fit, die anyway..."* The irony of the statement was completely lost on Arnold, who wore it simply because his girlfriend had given it to him.

The beer, a product of the last week's batch prepared in the bathroom, at Joachim's accommodation on the Siemens compound, was excellent. It was far from being anywhere near a true, commercial quality *Bayerische Dunklebrau*, but as an example of the expedient brewing methods employed out of geographic and cultural necessity it was strong and smooth and very potent. Joachim was quite proud of it and complimented himself briefly after hoisting another glass of it to his bearded mouth. Savoring the pungent flavor of the dark fluid as the draught coursed down his throat, he regarded Arnold again, who was by this time pouring himself a glass of the brew.

Arnold was one of those exasperating Americans--*sehr typisch*, in Joachim's view--who, despite having left the insular boundaries of their native country, persisted naively in maintaining a world-view which was clearly the product of that characteristic, near-institutionalized ignorance of the world beyond those borders that obtains in the United States. Moreover, he was still painfully young--23 years old in contrast to Joachim's 50--and appeared to be afflicted with that great American tendency to feel the rest of the world views life through American filters. For Joachim, it was the most unfortunate combination of characteristics possible--youthful naiveté and cultural ignorance. And although philosophically he knew that a figuratively lobotimised individual was probably a better companion (after a fashion) than a deeply sensitive, culturally aware one, the thought didn't make his being stuck out here in the depths of the desert with a *Kasekuche* any easier. Leaving this reflective fragment abruptly, Joachim took another gulp of the beer and mused pleasantly that it was starting to run its fingers around his brain more discernably, as fumes from the frying meat brought him back to matters at hand.

The *schnitzel* had burned, but there was cheese, Egyptian flat-bread, and other food to consume. Arnold, by now already into his 3rd glass of the beer, was similarly unconcerned with the quality of the meat and had discovered the peaches and grapes--their juicy qualities especially pleasing in the desert dryness. Turning to the German, he asked, *"What were you up to this afternoon, Sidiyk?"*

Joachim had lit another of his special Black Russian cigarettes. He puffed deeply, amid gulps of the beer, and regarded Arnold with indifference. *"I? I was looking at the sand."* That was the extent of his response, which by the look on Arnold's face was clearly insufficient for purposes of starting or maintaining a conversation. Arnold's expression brightened, however, as Joachim continued, after a pregnant pause, *"I found something interesting, not far from the truck. Can you guess what it was?"* Joachim's eyes seemed briefly to loom brighter from of the shadows on his face as they caught the reflected glare from the *gaz* lamp.

"No, what? A Bedouin humping a sheep? An olympic-sized swimming pool? Adolph Hitler's burned corpse?" Joachim started for a brief second at the mention of Hitler,

took another puff on his Balkan Sobranie Black Russian, and focused on Arnold.

"Almost correct. It was, at any rate, a burned human body."

This time it was Arnold's turn to glance up at Joachim, his youthful lack of subtlety suddenly piqued, despite the strong effects of the beer. *"You're shittin' me! You didn't really find some stiff out there, did you?"* Arnold put the glass of beer down for a second as he waited for Joachim's reply, open-mouthed.

The night had deepened and the only light aside from the vast canopy of faint stars, which filled the clear sky overhead, came from the direction of Kuwait City; its dull glow merely a suggestion of some human habitation in the desert landscape of sand to their east. The silence which prevailed, attending the stygian dark of the wastes perfectly, was otherwise vast and complete. Joachim, for his part, took a moment to glance around their site before answering.

"No, I am not shitting you, and yes, it appeared to be the body of someone who had been incinerated...someone whose body has apparently been there for a long time now, and possibly that of a soldier killed in the Gulf War. It is, in fact, just a few meters from where we sit, and if it were not so dark you could see part of it, which sticks up out of the sand." Joachim did not reflect upon his use of the word "it" instead of a more personal pronoun, in referring to the corpse, possibly betraying his cold, scientific preference for objectifying phenomena in his choice of words.

"I don't have any more idea of what it is than that, and we shall have to wait until morning to look more closely...if that is what you wish to do."

"Damn," muttered Arnold, arms now propped up on his knees and glass of beer drained. *"Must be some Iraqi, do you think? There could be a whole slew of 'em out here, since this is near where they blasted the shit out of that Republican Guards regiment that was making a breakout to Basrah, back in 1991."*

Arnold was caught up in some fanciful speculation for a moment, doubtless confusingly related to an internal contextual conflict between his own fondness for Alabama squirrel hunting, gun adulation, and the events of the 1991 Desert Storm action which took Kuwait City back from Saddam. His eyes glazed, then he turned back to Joachim.

"Was it gruesome?"

"Couldn't tell...only a hand that's visible, but the hand is very badly incinerated. It has been sitting out here for some time, as I said and I am not interested in investigating further." Joachim was thinking of some other badly fire-damaged remains he had once viewed as a child, when an American airlift transport had crashed short of the Templehoff runway and practically in his family's front yard.

"At any rate, dead is dead, whether it is someone we know or not, and who knows whether or not it is better to be where that unfortunate creature is now than where we are here."

Who knew, indeed! But more to the point, he surmised, what did it matter? Joachim personally had no fear of death. Rather it was, he had determined, the fear of dying that gave him most pause for thought. Death was merely another state of being or nonbeing. The dying phase, the 'translation' from life however, was marked by pain (usually) and was something that the physical body's senses were poorly structured to conceptualising. Joachim hated pain. Dying, he reminded himself, is simply a natural part of human experience, but preferably it did not come horribly. Thoughts of Goya's tortuous depictions of (undoubtedly) agonizing impalement surfaced, simultaneous with his imagination's recreation of how the Auschwitz victims had died...or possibly the Japanese Hiroshima casualties...the possibilities for a horribly painful death were certainly endless, given mankind's ingenious capabilities for violence among its own kind. He allowed himself a fractional second of rueful awareness that his own father had been responsible for some of those deaths, under the Hitler regime.

Arnold, seated across a short expanse of lighted sand from Joachim, looked out into the darkened vicinity of the burned corpse.

"Hell, he must have been napalmed. The Air Cav guys in the Blackhawks just liberally wasted those Iraqis when they got bottled up on Route 5. That must have been quite a sight to see, from up there in the choppers. I saw some pictures of it, but I sure would have enjoyed being in on that squirrel shoot from the git-go!"

Joachim, himself feeling quite well lubricated after several glasses of the dark home- brewed malt fermentation, considered half-heartedly the arduous difficulty of attempting to fathom the populist, southern-styled reactionary wellsprings of Arnold's *Americanismus* for a brief moment before mentally shrugging the subject off entirely. It was probably beyond his ability to understand, he decided, mindful of the obvious aspects of Arnold's age and national origin. Further, after the beer and horrible mish-mash of food that they had had with it, such thoughts mattered little by any reckoning, and he leaned back, suddenly aware of the almost fluid coolness of the sands upon which he sat.

With the sensation of coolness under his butt came a cold awareness of the utter futility of human life, of pathetic human attempts to reconcile the unreconcilable, of even trying to regard the whole chaos of human experience rationally.

Quite suddenly, Joachim felt very much older than his 50 years. Fortunately, the rough Bavarian part of his dual nature stepped forward out of his consciousness to rudely remind the scientist in him to shut the hell up! Just in time, too, he reflected, patting his full stomach with some contentment, noting that Arnold, now quiescent and feeling the powerful effect of the beer, was starting to nod. Getting up briefly, to get the bedrolls, he pitched Arnold's at him and turned the *gaz* lamp off.

Overhead the stars, earlier revealed in bright swarms, had begun to become slightly obscured by the usual blanket of fine dust which hung forever suspended in the air. Time passed. The silence, which had followed Arnold's verbal speculation about the corpse whose burial ground they shared for the night, had deepened, and now was unbroken, except for the soft sounds of their breathing. After some time, both men, off on different planes of sleepy, ruminative reflection in this expanse of empty desert, drifted towards a neutral sleep.

The hard sand, now quite cold and belying the fierce daytime capability of the sun's heat to mold both a crucible or a coffin from its silicate particles, paid no more attention to them than it did the blackened corpse sleeping eternally nearby, as another dreamless, totally indifferent Arabian night descended upon all three figures, bathed by the coldly unconcerned light of the far-off cosmic emptiness.

SADDAM'S TOILET-1

Curiously enough, it seems to have started in Riyadh...not the incident, but the diarrhea, although the origin of both could probably have been shown to be associated with boring afternoon bouts spent squatting over the quaint hole in the tile which comprised the villa's bathroom convenience fixture. The salient point, certainly, was that all things in life--no matter their position on the food chain or the physical context of their existence--end up being flushed down the figurative toilet of life.

It had been quite a while since I had been on leave from the Kingdom. The tell-tale signs that limits of tolerance for Arab cultural variation had near been reached were becoming obvious. Among these, one was particular telling, based upon familiarity with my own tendencies: I was once again catching myself lounging fitfully in front of what the Brits call the *'chube'*, making snide and ironic remarks about the quality of English programming in my off-time, the irksome personal quirks of the BBC World Service television broadcasters themselves (cue: visions of horsey-faced, homely Saxon female introducing the weather forecast) *"...'ello a-gaine."* starting to get under my skin. Also damning was the increasing frequency of moments spent fuming over having to take a trip to the WC, only to find that some *True Believer* has just moments before preceded me into the enclosure to prepare himself for prayer-call at the bidet, managing to saturate the whole enclosure--toilet seat, floor and walls--with water, like some duck gone insane in a 12-inch diameter lake.

For a westerner--whether from Australia or Canada, or just about anywhere else in the "western" world--one of the worst possible crimes a person (always male) can commit against his fellows is to take a whiz without lifting the toilet seat. For those who follow, and who must seat themselves uncomfortably on that wet appliance of necessity, there are few things which bring more surely an urge to strangle someone than having to sit down on a freshly sprayed toilet seat. Thus, when a local believer has importuned all of us infidels with the requisite indulgence of his faith's requirements for ritual cleansing prior to prayer (5 times a day, I might add, and facilitated in this heinous act by the French Company which manufactured the bidet and sprayer nestled alongside every toilet in the Kingdom...*sacre bleu!*), the discovery of said sabotage in the face of dire urgency is essentially grounds for justifiable homicide.

This is, of course, not a feasible recourse in the Kingdom due to the fondness one generates for one's head after spending most of one's life attached to it.

As if that weren't bad enough, having to live in an old-fashioned villa with its Arab version of the Japanese-style benjo orifice in the floor is a still further source of delight that awaits the typical expatriate at home.

The ‘hole-in-the-floor’ approach has its hearty proponents, certainly (mostly idiots), although any medical doctor will tell you that squatting over such a fixture is an unhealthy strain on the average bladder (assumedly for the male, although nothing is mentioned about the difficulty the ladies might have aiming a stream into the target, being by nature ‘setters’ and not ‘pointers’). My own experience with the abominable hole has never been a happy one, certainly, and even the momentary demonstration of pedal dexterity demanded by having to line one's feet up in the small concrete footprints which straddle the hole fails to amuse after a certain term of intimacy with the device has developed.

Our particular residence villa, similar to that provided to all the American instructor pilots working with the Royal Saudi Air Force students, had a particularly horrible squatter in it. The room itself, crowded by the pipes of the suspended Italian hot water heater that always looked as if it would tear off the wall, was small and stuffy. The one window's sliding frame had long since given up the ghost and the result was that the first step into said room produced an immediate and simultaneous urge to gag, don some sort of gas respirator and indulge in a whimsical wish that a quick blink of the eyes would somehow magically transform the wretched place into a sumptuous *'place de bain'* from a five-star European hotel.

Further, the hole itself, inevitably centered in the worst possible spot in the small room, had all the attractive appeal of a century-old conduit of the central Parisian sewage system in the *Mont Parnasse* district. Encrusted with the calciferous slime of years without cleansing, and evidencing a vile unfamiliarity with any sort of disinfecting solution, the hole gave one the willies just positioning one's self over it. And, as an Air Force *fighter* pilot, the subsequent "bomb release" action unloading onto the target, as it were, gave the child in me absolutely no pleasure at all. In short, it was a most unpleasant way to indulge in what Ernst Mach did at no time ever sublimely refer to as *"...one of the three great natural pleasures of life"* (he also did not remark about the other two except not to say that one of them was an excellent cup of dark roasted *kafe mit Schlag*).

And so, given the inevitable decline of a pilot's patience for the quaint cultural resources for aiding intestinal evacuation in the face of these daily challenges, in combination with all the other daily aggravations of local life, the warning signal that the limits of patience were being neared was more than simply a primary indicator of an impending requirement for some leave. My own personal limit had just about been reached earlier in the day, on a training exercise out over the desert...

I had been flying IP for a student in the lead aircraft of a flight of two of the Saudi F-15D trainer birds and came the time, when in our mock aerial interception maneuvering, the trailing aircraft was due to practice weapons release procedures (using our A/C as a target). We were carrying heat-seekers among our several other types of ordinance, and the simulation procedure was simple enough. It called for a straightforward intercept, lock-on, and 'dry' practice (simulated) firing, for which the cockpit weapons arming system selectors would be left in the safe or 'unarmed' position. Our own aircraft was finally acquired by the trailer Eagle (flown by another IP and a student) after some difficulty, and the unmistakable warning alarm of a missile lock tone finally came over my headphones. Nothing startling, of course...routine target acquisition by the interception A/C's fire-control. My bird was simply telling me that I was about to be creamed up the ass by 500 kg of virtual high explosive.

I was sitting passively in the back seat, letting the student fly our bird, and momentarily glanced behind in an effort to try to see the 'hostile.' Suddenly and unexpectedly the lock-on buzz changed from the familiar buzz tone to a very unfamiliar and definitely unpleasant one: the no-nonsense, business-like standard alarm tone of an actual launch! The student hot on our tail had somehow or other loosed a *live* heat-seeker at us!

Thinking back on this at the moment, a poor joke about brown ejection seat cushions comes to mind, but if my own pucker quotient hadn't already been appexed when the launch tone sounded I doubt whether there would have been any aggravation later over something as inconsequential as a wet toilet seat in the life support room, back on base. Fortunately, we had managed to disengage and squirt away from the heat-seeker just in time, the old *Red Flag* air-combat lessons not entirely forgotten and showing admirable self-restraint, I managed to save up most of my resulting choice comments on the student's proficiency with air-to-air practice launches until we hit the deck back at the field. Still, it had been somewhat of a scare--coming as it did so unexpectedly--and it was simply another force pushing me towards an understanding that it was time to get on the Saudia bus and get the hell out of Dodge, for a breather...the proverbial *straw*.

Suki was back from the embassy when I arrived at home and I brought up the suggestion of taking a leave. She responded as I knew she would--with animated interest. It was time to visit Austria, as we had discussed it all beforehand in selecting a destination and laying out an itinerary in advance.

Now Suki is a brownish-yellow little female critter of awfully pleasing configuration. With her long, black Japanese hair, her wonderful, dark almond eyes and just the vestige of a nose that manages to balance the rest of her pretty face just right, she is a considerable comfort to have enhancing the life of an old lifer like myself. With curves to match her handsome features and a lithe, willow-like figure of artful grace, Sukiko was a prize by my own reckoning, no matter how you looked at it. Although we were no longer kids, both of us being in our 40s, she was handling the aging process beautifully. For my part, air-to-air missiles were not!

She had a beautiful way of coming softly into the room, radiating harmony and wonderfully feminine, womanly charm that would undoubtedly have brought satisfaction to some warrior-daimyo of feudal Japan in centuries past. What a sweet gift from whatever gods there were! Somehow, I just couldn't even imagine her coping with that blasted squat-hole in the bathroom, even though it had some hereditary relationship to the Japanese *benjo* appurtenance already alluded to. I guess I had the same problem when I was a child, imagining that my parents could ever have done something as exotic (to a child) as screwing, like the sex manuals suggested.

At any rate, Suki didn't share any of my bizarre reflections on Arab toilets, and the day's frustrations with wet toilet seats, married quarter 'squatters,' and idiot student pilots were shortly put on hold as she charmed me out of my vituprous mood with her usual soft, sensual massage of the aching neck muscles which the aircraft seat harnesses had managed to mangle under extreme G-loads. Even the indelible impressions of horror over the state of toilet seats in the restrooms of King Khalid International Airport during the month of Haj couldn't surface through the soothing screen of Suki's amazingly strong fingers, as she continued to knead my shoulders.

But like a submerged log hidden dangerously below the surface of my sensory threshhold, that particular memory put up a brief struggle before succumbing to the lower depths of blissful relaxation.

It had been my luck to have to return to the Kingdom from leave precisely at the peak of the Islamic pilgrim influx, that time of the Al Heigran year when the devout Muslims of the world attempt to fulfill one of the five 'Pillars of the Faith.' Accordingly, the airport at Jeddah was jammed with a seething knot of raw humanity that confounded and dismayed even the most experienced expat traveler. So vast was the crowd, packed into the substantial terminal space, that there was literally no room to walk more than a foot before being faced with the decision to walk over a sprawled body or *on* it. The sight that had greeted me upon stepping off the Lufthansa Airbus 320 had been bad enough--thousands of dark-skinned, poorly or incompletely clad, unwashed and unhealthy pilgrims, lying, squatting, sitting, perching, leaning and sleeping, generally filling every square centimeter of empty floor space to the point where there had been no floor tiles visible through the uniform brown tones of the bodies covering it. But when the inevitable moment came, and the urge to locate a men's room settled over me, I had been in for another, more appalling surprise.

The seats of the toilets were all--every last one of them--covered with revolting smears of *human excrement*. It was impossible to sit on the seats in the conventional manner, without depositing your butt on half a dozen clots of horrible, half-dried human shit. And worse yet, there was no paper to be found anywhere--not even paper towels.

Over each western style porcelain commode was affixed a worn decal showing a stick figure squatting on top of a toilet, with a circle and diagonal red line through the drawing. It dawned on me that, despite the installation of the western shitters, the many desert *boogey-men* of the 4th world (those unfortunates even further removed from civilisation that those of the 3rd world) who were accustomed to squatting over the ubiquitous hole in the floor that served as a toilet, were not capable of placing themselves on a toilet seat but insisted instead on *standing* on the seat and squatting over *it!*

The result was predictable--poor marksmanship that resulted in the clotted shit which festooned the seat components. And it was not until some months later, after complaining to a Muslim friend about this, that he explained that the more ignorant people felt that western toilet seats were 'unclean' from a religious standpoint, and labored under the delusion that putting their body in direct contact with part of a toilet fixture intimately associated with the defecative act was *harram* (unclean). The irony of this explanation gave me a brief bit of ironic amusement as I reflected on the symbolic nature of uncleanliness--as contrasted to the overt and shit-smeared result of this religiously archaic attitude.

I had had to ignore the wall-to-wall feces which decorated the Jeddah airport terminal's toilet facilities, and stepping carefully to avoid stepping in gobs which had missed the toilet entirely, was forced to straddle the bowl and let fly in the native manner. It was one of the most unpleasant experiences of my life and I have seen some pretty horrible sights in my 25 years of combat flying.

At any rate, I was melting under Suki's touch and soon I was as calm and cool as a bowl of almond bean curd fresh out of the freezer. After what seemed like a small eternity of these healing ministrations, I begged off further pleasure of this sort and followed my graceful wife into the bedroom like a sleepy puppy seeking a warm rug to curl up on, after a full meal.

Suki, however, was not sleepy. Once in bed, and lying next to her smooth tawny body, I felt those same skillful fingers touching other parts of me with the delicate lightness of a spider's touch. I opened my eyes to look at her, and saw the sparkle in those deep black pools of light which her eyes admitted only special people into. Suki was very much awake, and it was time for the some 'payback.'

Later, with both of us drowsily sated, and in that half-way state that precedes sleep, I glanced over at her partly profiled, willowy body. Her eyes were closed, and the gentle curves of her woman's figure somehow filled me with a great satisfaction. She was the most beautiful, exquisite creature in the whole world to me, and even when I closed my own eyes her beauty did not vanish as the philosophers admonished it ought.

Her hair, long and straight and as dark as the mysteries which she contained secretly within herself, flowed over the pillow in an orderly cascade of luxurious threads of ebony silk. The hands, delicate and long, yet as strong as the titanium ribs of a fighter aircraft, rested on the sheet, the slight, involuntary muscular twitch of encroaching sleep giving her slide into nighttime oblivion away.

A single magnificent rounded breast had somehow immodestly escaped the covering sheet, and the sight of it generated one last surge of savage sexual lust deep in the guts of my *Ki* until finally, I too began the slide from this conscious world into the bottomless folds of darkness, where Suki already waited for me.

I think I dreamed that night. Something involving an in-flight emergency...having to punch out...the seat smashing through the canopy, which had jammed...hitting the 600-knot air stream....and feeling pain in my lower spine as the roman candle I was riding speared upwards, in a rush that knocked the wind from me. Fragments of the dream are all that remained the next morning, as the mental cockpit recorder automatically rewound and played through in fast forward, spilling the guts of the dream out beyond my more pedestrian ability to capture and fully retain it. The only distinct part I can seize upon in any detail was me, separating from the seat with a kick in the pants and coming down under the chute to land in a huge, stinking hole in the floor of the desert that stretched a good fifty meters across. As the murky brown, turgid waters closed over me, the nylon folds of the chute collapsed on the surface of the abyss like a surreal, giant white sheet of toilet paper...

I must have cried out, or flung out my arms to get out of the imprisoning parachute harness in my sleep, for the next thing I recall, Suki was gazing at me from her side of the bed, propped up on one elbow and regarding me with an unreadable look that could have been expressive of anything from curiosity to concern. *"Hey Tiger, bad dream?"* The gaze turned into one of faintly disguised humor, as I swam up to full consciousness.

Remembering the foul, brown texture of the sinkhole, and recalling the stink of the greasy green waters that had threatened to choke me, my still sleepy mind groped for an explanation: *"I think I just bailed out into the asshole of the Universe."*

Suki simply smiled at my rudeness and rolled off the bed, slipping a T-shirt on that left her backside bare, before padding off in those horrible bunny-slippers I hate, to get the water started in the kitchen.

I regarded her beautiful, heart-shaped ass fondly as it wiggled deliciously off and out of sight, my regard for her attributes undimmed by the slowly fading detritus of sleep. After a bit, I finally got up.

"Coffee," came the melodious voice which was attached, although most circumspectly, to that delightful part of her anatomy which I had admired. The luxurious aroma of real coffee, French-pressed, got a lock and vectored in to my nose, as a new day began.

SADDAM'S TOILET-2 *('Merde in the first degree')*

t was another lovely summer day in the Kingdom. I had wakened with a head that felt as if there was nothing between my ears except inflamed sinuses. Outside, the heat was already rising in the dry flat confines of the compound. Through the bedroom's window I could see, squatting in the shade of a ragged piece of canvas near the entrance, the venerable old *Baba* (old man) who served as a nominal gate-guard; he was thoughtfully scratching his venerable balls with his left hand as his right one worked the tooth cleaning twig through his mouth. With his old rheumy eyes glazed and staring off into the heat-haze of the horizon, it was impossible to imagine what ancient, ancestral thoughts were making their daily rounds in his brain...not that I really cared, of course.

As the coffee's tantalizing smell sank tendrils into my brain, wooing it with the promise of a jump-start, I reflected that this was probably the right time to take a break, after all. Yesterday, after the flight, the flight surgeon had had me taken off flying status for a week to allow some time for a head cold to shake itself free. Somehow, the bug also had my gut in its grip, for I had had to navigate to and from the W/C throughout most of the night. It isn't easy having a serious case of the loose runs standing up over an archaic Arab shitter. Not easy, and definitely an act requisite of no small amount of skill and pretty disgusting as well. Fortunately, although I wasn't a close air-support pilot, my targeting skills were up to the task...even late at night.

Out in the kitchen, Suki, finally moved to abject curiosity over why the usual coffee aroma snare had failed to rope me out of bed and draw me into the dining room, poked her silky black mane around the corner and gazed at me with what I call her *'Bambi in the forest look.'* The dark pools under her eyebrows totally suckered me out of my ruminations on old Arab men, nasty head colds and archaic plumbing fixtures, framed as they were by the artfully disarrayed strands of blackest Shanghai silk. At such moments, one could almost palpably sense the Chinese essence of her mother's ancestry in her appearance. Suddenly, my whole attention was riveted on her substantial comeliness.

"Grab my coffee and come in here, Sooks. We Need to talk over the leave." Arching her eyebrows with the hint of an amused smile, she padded off quietly to get the coffee and reappeared with the cup of steaming black fluid that had teased my nose so alluringly upon awakening.

Suki was wearing nothing but a gauzey white slipover, a powerful incentive which would have even wakened the recently dead if it hadn't have been for the contrapuntal, slightly disconcerting effect of the fluffy pink cotton rabbits she wore on both feet. Still, the sight of her, standing in the doorway like that, tended to make me forget my ear-to-ear sinuses, and everything else for that matter...everything except the perfectly beautiful outlines of her body protruding softly through the thin fabric and outlined by the still weak rays of the morning sun.

Putting the coffee down on the bedside stand, Suki came over to me and stood just out of arms' reach, her hands akimbo on her hips, legs spread in that ‘so what's next?’ attitude.

"I may feel like shit, my dear, but you are the best medicine known to mankind." So saying, I grabbed out, timing the distance and the response needed, and snagged her wrist, pulling her off balance and towards me in a tumble. Her graceful 90 pounds collapsed neatly on top of me and immediately she sat astride my hips with her lush thighs pinioning my legs.

At such moments, I swear that any man would have to be a eunuch not to respond fully and automatically to her charms with a certain portion of one's anatomy and I was certainly not of *that* disposition. Suki still hadn't said a word, but let her eyes do all of her communicating, another of her peculiar but exotic special talents. Lying there on my back, I was oblivious of all the previous thoughts I had been batting around in my head. Forgotten was awareness of Baba's old man thoughts of lost youth at the compound gate, and even my uncomfortable night in a holding pattern over the shit-hole. The clean, natural essence of her lovely body flooded my senses like a rush of floral incense. By comparison, I suddenly flashed on the overweight, smelly Indian woman one of the British pilots had married...ugh. There was absolutely no comparison to be made...none at all. It struck me as immensely ironic that the race which had produced the amorously essential 'how-to' of the erotic arts, the *Kama Sutra*, still hadn't managed to invent the ordinary shower!

Suki arched her back like a lazy cat, stretching her long, slender arms up and out as I pulled the shift over her head to uncover her splendid physical gifts. Her eyes regarded me with that humorous curiosity that is so characteristic of her. I could imagine her saying, *"All right, let's see what this Gaijin can do...vaunted TopGun Romeo that he fancies himself to be. You've done the preflight...now let's get airborne!"*

Then, moving her thighs upwards with a luxurious delicacy, she moved forward over my hips so that the tip of my swollen eagerness was lightly touching the navel in her firm belly. The sensitive tissue at the end of my engorged penis could feel something like the feathery touch of a butterfly's wings quivering against it. I looked up at Suki's chest. Her smooth, medium-sized breasts, so perfectly rounded and gorgeous to behold once freed from any constraints, framed her face, as she slyly gazed down at me between their pouting, pink nipples.

And suddenly she was *gone*, briefly disappearing somewhere into another universe inside herself, a light sheen of sweat making her skin glow. There was a slight illumination to her face, as if, from inside, she was concentrating on mysteries I couldn't even begin to imagine and invoking old and long-forgotten powers to her bidding.

It was all the work of an instant, and in less than a few seconds she shuddered, eyes rolled upwards and tongue poised wetly on the verge of her parted lips. Then, once more in control of herself completely and back from whatever voyage she had embarked upon within, she moved her firm, lithe thighs upwards once more and placed her cleft woman's part, hidden by the coal black fur between her legs, directly over my shaft.

Bowing forward so that the tips of those perfect breasts kissed my nose with their unique scent, she sat back down upon me, taking me fully into her recesses with a decisive, moist suction, the strength of which always surprised me.

And now the rhythmic squeezing began, the superbly controlled muscles of her thighs pulsating, undulating around my erection, milking it like a cow's teat. It was, no matter how many times we had done it, always a new experience, the strength of her love making muscles impressive and awesome.

The powerful sucking sensations continued pleasingly, but I was already far too aroused to need much further inducement. Reaching out and gripping her smooth, slender upper arms, I pressed the sinews in them with a suggestion of my hunger, to communicate the deep need of her creation within me to her. Back arched, already riding the massive mountain wave of an initial orgasm, her eyes flickered open for an instant and I read in them what there was to read.

"Hank," she murmured, *"Take me in the ass. Do it now. Make it hurt a little."*

It had amazed me when I first learned that my sensual cat-woman liked to be forcefully taken in that manner. I had forgotten the ancient traditions and complexities of the ageless Japanese erotic arts, and had been stunned...yet secretly delighted...when she had first suggested a preference for sodomy. The ludicrousness of the taboo against this act in the west, considering the ironic role it had forever played in being considered an acceptable substitute for normal sex between unmarried men and women in this part of world, struck me as I contemplated what she had once told me when first revealing this preference. When I had asked her, somewhat shocked like the good Christian choir boy I had been brought up to be, if she didn't consider that to be degrading, she had responded, darkly: *"Abuse and degrade me when I ask you to...but never unless..."*

There is, after all, some latent perversity in even the most-saintly among us...and usually much more in that sublimated reservoir than is ever suspected, until the dam is cracked and the flood of forbidden urges and sensations are released forever, like all the demons in Pandora's trunk. It is usually then, after the demons have all flown, that we see our own faces reflected on the mirrored inner surface of that fabled chest....

Her eyes were squeezed tightly shut, again. It was time for some requested *'tough love.'* Gripping her shoulders firmly, so as to not fall out of her in the transition, we both performed an amazing gymnastic maneuver she had taught me, which enabled us to stay enmeshed in each other until she was on her knees, bent forwards, back swayed, and ass up-thrust, with me on my own knees directly behind her. Then, her hands squeezing the pillow in front of her, she released her fearsome grip on my male part and I withdrew it from her, dripping with the female dew of our initial love-making.

Placing the tip of my spear against the small, tan wink of her perfectly clean sphincter, I smeared it with some of her own moisture and then...like a snake stealing out onto a limb of a tree to strike a bird...I slid my firm flesh into her ass with a smooth, deep thrust. Every muscle in her body bunched, quivering as if stung with an electric lash, knotting for a split second and then yielding as I entered her in this private vulnerable part of her body. Her hands gripped the pillow under her like claws then, her teeth clenched upon the sheet; I felt an even greater suction extend its grip on my penis as she used the powerful muscles of her anus to imprison me deeply within that forbidden part of her. I could sense the strange passion growing within her, her gasps growing louder with each frenzied thrust into her ass, then more shudders, as I continued to thrust more forcefully, impaling her on my erection with the insane madness of a spearman cleaving an enemy through on his halberd.

Feeling the savage, sadistic pleasure build within me, she began to join my thrusting with her own responsive spasms. The sound of thigh against soft buttock cheek rent the air with loud slapping whacks as we came closer to mutual oblivion, riding each successive wave of spasmodic lust higher and higher. Her own little indecipherable grunts and exclamations of orgasmic sensation growing with each brutal penetration of her cavity until finally she screamed out into the pillow, *"Aiyyyyeeee!"* The sound came from somewhere deep within her as I felt myself about to explode, as well. She had my shaft locked into her with a greediness that made me deliriously lustful. My sense of her absolute power over me was stupefying...I felt drunk with bestial savage frenzy...and then I lost what little control I actually had and she felt all the hot, molten fluid of my frenzy flood into her gut as I rode her beautiful ass like a stallion would a mare.

Slamming into her time and time again, I lost any sense of contact with reality. It was like nothing ever experienced before, and then it was over. She went limp and sagged forward, pulling my member out of her ass, dripping, in the doing. Part of her always seemed to die in this process, such were the forces released each time we coupled perversely like this.

It took some time before either of us could move, or even breathe deeply. Finally, looking slyly around at my bloodshot eyes, she murmured with a husky voice cut from raw silk, *"Was it good, Tiger? Did you enjoy degrading me?"*

For an answer, I slipped both hands around her perfect moist breasts and marveled at how firm and light they felt, how little I actually knew about this sliver of steel sheathed in velvet who toyed with me in ways that reached far beyond even my not-impoverished imagination.

I could only manage a bemused, blank stare of disbelief at her, still reflecting upon what I had discovered within myself at such moments as this. *"Words are futile, dear heart."*

Sweating myself, from all this spontaneous eroticism, I shrugged. More to myself than to her, I muttered, *"Somehow or other, we have got to get this trip planned. If you keep this up, we'll never get out the door and I'll probably die of my head-cold before the next opportunity presents. Either that or one of my students will finally launch something that DOES hit me... that is, if there's anything left to hit after this sortie...."*

Finally taking the coffee-cup up, I took a gulp and regarded Suki, who had by now gotten up out of that provocative--if exciting--posture on the bed, and was arranging her hair perched on the edge of the bed. A small puddle of moisture formed on the sheet beneath her,

She was looking at me with her 'Guess who just ate the mouse look?,' the faintly ironic look of amusement shining there in her eyes more brightly than ever. And then, as I regarded her beautiful profile, she moved off the bed and toward the bathroom, pausing just for a fragment of a second to flash a final flicker of unreadable bemusement at me--an exhausted heap on the bed--before vanishing around the corner.

"Join me for a shower, Tiger?"

You would have thought that *she* had violated *me*.

SADDAM'S TOILET-3 ('Bowl movement in E-flat')

The Middle East--or *Southwest Asia*, as the milspec stooges are fond of referring to it--is a land of extremes. Extremes in temperament, attitude, opinion, religion...especially religion. I recall extracting this particular shred of thought out of my head one afternoon, while pulling some high G at altitude with a student Eagle driver aboard. The son of some prince or another (Saudi Air Force officers are usually all from royal families), my student was practicing some intercept vectoring, operating off the ground radar complex at Taif.

Keeping us company were two F16s from a TDY American squadron, and as usual, the Viper jockeys were trying to impress us Eagle driver types with their sharp maneuvering, tight-turning aerial combat capabilities. My student, eagerly trying to keep up with the lighter one-seaters, was clearly enthused over having such fancy company along for the ride.

As we slashed out and up, over the edge of the Western escarpment of the Hijaz, everyone else was caught up in the momentary visual theatrics of seeing the 'ground' suddenly fall away beneath the fighters as the terrain profile below us suddenly dropped some two thousand meters in the span of a heartbeat--even the staid American jocks were stimulated to make laconic fighter-jock type comments as the brown plateau instantly became 7000 feet of blue void...

"Oh, Mama....are those ants below us, or camels?"

"If they're ants, we're in deep shit, bub...vectoring off on heading one-two-zero."

"Rog."

Two additional clicks on the headphones indicated that the second Viper had acknowledged and was taking up station off the starboard wing.

"You've got it, Hamed. I'm just along for the ride," I advised my student, and released the stick when I felt him take control.

Extremes. We had been at the villa several weeks ago, returned after a long training flight and happy to pop the few beers we had managed to shag from the Lockheed boys. After a bit of hanger flying, and some reminiscences about the delivery of the first Saudi F15Cs to Taif's RSAF Fifth Fighter squadron (the commander had flown the first bird in, nosed up too high on the flare and ground a good 6 feet of the proud bird's thrust-cones into metal hamburger), the other IPs had finally adjusted their shades, prosaically allowing that it was probably time to 'turn and burn back to families.'

Squinting against the intrusion of the mid-day glare into the darkness of the living room, after rolling into the hanger, all had trundled off into the Mitsubishi 4-wheeler, and driven back to their own quarters. Overhead, the solar furnace of a sun was at zenith. It was hot, *extremely* hot...

Having the usual pasty white hide that most Riyadh based Americans usually sported, I was determined to catch a few rays up on the roof of the villa despite the insane heat of the mid-day sun. Throwing the last of the beer down, I had shucked the sweat-stained flight suit and hiked up the stairs to the flat, walled-in roof which each villa featured.

On cool winter evenings, such private roof areas were a favorite refuge for Saudi families, who enjoyed the opportunity to savor the open sky and mild temperatures. In the middle of summer, however, no one--not even the Arabs--came out onto these flattened residential frying-pans.

Opening the roof door, a blast of super-heated air swept into the entrance and I entered into a white cauldron of shimmering sunlight. It was like leaving a refrigerator to enter an active volcano lava tube.

I had brought a book with me, and my sunglasses, along with an old tan camo-fatigue cap I had become used to wearing for an eye-shade. The taste of the beer lingered pleasantly as I settled down on some old sun-bleached cushions we kept for lounging around up there. My God, but it was *hot* up there.

I had been baking for less than 15 minutes, determined to do a flip-side thing--exposing each half of me for about that long--and was lying on my back, book grasped in hand, head propped up against a foam pillow. I was finding it hard to read, so intense was the heat, and every so many minutes little fragments of our conversations about the early Eagle deliveries to Taif kept filtering back into my thoughts like little phantoms of recollection.

Suddenly, the roof-top door opened. *"Hank?"* came the soft, cat-like voice I am so fond of.

"Out here, Sooks." I moved the book aside, turned my head and squinted towards the dark slit of the door, being held open and ajar by several inches.

"How was the flight, Tiger?" The door was still only slightly cracked, and I couldn't see anything through the narrow opening. *"Nothing special, sweet thang, just a routine flight out west to Taif."*

"Tired?"

"Nah, just trying to catch a dose of Vitamin D. What's up?" The narrow darkness of the doorway suddenly expanded

widely and I could see Suki outlined in its ebony shadows...a golden figure with a solar aura. She was standing there, lounging in the dark of the entrance structure with nothing on but an exceptionally wicked and high-cut black nylon tank suit. *"Mind if I join you?"* she purred.

"Come on, but I'm just spending a few minutes up here--you could roast yourself with anything more than a quickie in this heat."

She lowered her sunglasses just a fraction and gazed at me under those wispy eyebrows for a second, before stepping across the two meters of space to join me on the cushions. I could smell the scent of clean skin waft over me as she settled demurely down next to me. My skin was already so overheated in just the few minutes I had been out under the sun that her smooth, cool flanks felt like fiery ice on my own, as she slid her hand over my chest.

"You're sweating already," she observed, bending her head to dart her small, moist tongue over my salty pecs. *"Mmmmmmm, salty!"*

Clearly, Suki was hungry. Sometimes I felt she resented my being able to fly off into the depths of the cool skies while she had to endure the insufferable heat of this parched land; and there were times when the strength of her resentment came through in the roughness of her playfulness at such moments as this. She had taken my left nipple into her mouth and using her small, even teeth, nipped the tip of it with something less than a gentle touch. I started, dropped the book and looked full at her.

The mischievous irony was there in her glance. Even hidden behind the dark Foster-Grants with their thick, black frames, I fancied I could see it playing in the pools of her eyes. I glanced down at her slim, elegant body, taking it fully in as I guessed at her thoughts.

The black tank suit was one of those tight, high-cut things that cleaved the thighs on both sides of her mons, leaving a silky mound prominent between her legs as it rose up and then fell back to rise again at the apex of her perfect belly. The suit clung to her curves with a grip that always produced an erotic thrill in every single molecule of my maleness and it further rose from the swell of her belly to caress the two, firm mounds of her separate, lovely breasts before clustering in a few ripples of the stretchy fabric at her neck. Already perspiration was starting to dampen the Lycra, and the darker, moist patches under her breasts shown out against the dryer fabric which adhered to her.

It was always like this whenever she deliberately opened the floodgates of her powerful sensuality and let it flow over me. It was like some overwhelming tidal wave of sexual lava, smothering me inexorably in its irresistible wake. I reached out to cup one of those soft, yet firm breasts in my hand and tried to peer through the glasses at her hidden eyes.

"Are you trying get me aroused, Sooks? If you are, it won't work, because I've been in flight for hours."

I leaned towards her, folding over the right side of her body and fitting one knee between her sinewy, slender legs. Automatically, she applied gentle squeezing to my leg, bringing her thighs together, tantalizing, forcing me to work for the foothold. Lowering myself upon her I felt the firm swells of her breasts pushing up on my chest, the tight nylon fabric straining to contain them within. And then, pushing her head back, I mouthed her neck, the silken black hair of her lovely head falling back down her shoulders as I entered her mouth with my thirsty tongue.

The cavern of her mouth felt like a wet maelstrom, as she sucked with hot passion upon my probing tongue. Her eyes were flickering with animated delight behind the sunglasses as I pulled them away...resistance was futile, and I knew it! Above my back I could feel the fires of hell burning down upon us both, but I lost interest in everything except this surging, liquid life-force that was struggling to capture me within it. I was probably already burned, but what the hell! The burning sensations beneath me were far hotter than those above, at the moment...

Inchoate gurgles were coming from her throat as I gripped her tight little butt in my hands and squeezed the taunt cheeks under the flimsy nylon which restrained them. One hand slipped between her legs, and as I forced her own legs apart she languidly drew a finger between the nylon edge of the suit and the right cleft of her thigh, exposing a few wispy curls of jet-black pubic hair. Drawing the fabric back, her whole mons was now exposed and she thrust it up towards my face like an ocean wave eager to break upon my mouth.

I lowered my mouth to the inviting mound and slipped my tongue deep into her heated cleft. A surge of vibration shook her as my tongue massaged the small protruding swell of her clit.

"UnnnnghGH!" Her back was arched now, and her hands were up above her head, as if seeking some sort of surrender.

Truly excited myself by now, I pushed her knees up and apart, and grasped her butt in both hands, twisting her litheness and turning her over so that she came around and into a lordotic stance. She could feel from the strength in my grip of her female body that I was powerfully up now, and very much ready for her. She shook her black mane to the side and, nearly grunting the words from her lowered head, snarled *"Now, Tiger, now!"*

Mounting her from behind was always a supreme turn-on for her. It was one of her favorite positions, to take it from behind. I would straddle her beautiful firm ass, spreading her knees with my own, and with one hand reach out and grip her neck to shove it down so that her back bowed and her proud, heart-shaped butt reared skyward. Thus splayed, her beautiful breasts, despite the restraint of the tight nylon, would sag down and move liquidly with every small movement of her small chest. They were lovely love objects, thus displayed, and I felt the surge of raw lust build higher within me.

Then, I would grasp the nylon edge of the suit, pulling it over her ass and to the side with one hand, exposing her entire rump with its small, brown sphincter and moist slit, with the other hand grasping the fabric of the suit in the small of her back, using it like a harness to keep her in position as I prepared to sheath my throbbing shaft deep inside her moist recesses.

Her head shook from side to side, freeing the mass of coal-black hair, as I placed my penis against her cleft. Feeling the dribbling moist drool of her passion at its tip, I suddenly reared up into her, filling all of her smallness in the searing flash of an instant. The fullness of my attack was electric and she shook as if impaled on me from end to end. At the same instant, letting out a growl from deep, buried parts of her femaleness, she ground her muscles tightly in to grip my shaft and started a rhythmic squeezing that milked it with surprising power. It was as if she were trying to suck all of me up into her compact body, gyrating and rocking as I began to thrust in and out of her slippery recess.

I found myself pounding into her faster and faster, harder and harder, the sun stunning me as I felt the blood rise within my veins to the bursting point. I was engorged with power, enraged with a lustful savagery which only she could create and bring into full being with the magic of her magnificent womanly chemistry.

We were both nearing a climax, nearly spent on each other, and as I slammed into her harder with each thrust, she bucked and reared back to receive each intrusion as if she were dying to take more even than I had to give.

Her whole body was wet with perspiration, and we were both animals rutting like beasts under the ferocious Saudi sun, as we soared higher and higher towards total fusion. I gripped her small waist and pulled her back upon my spear with renewed force. She quivered then, and I exploded fully into her with the hot love juice of our passion. She gasped as she felt the flood come into her and fill her with stickiness as I spewed the ancient seed of life. As the final spasm shook us, I grasped her butt in both hands and gripped her in an embrace of steely passion, and we were both at once entirely spent, consumed, and exhausted.

After a few seconds, I once again became aware of the sun overhead, the extreme heat of something which could no more be denied in the desert wastes than the need for food and water.

We were both exhausted, and Suki pulled away from me, drawing the tight black nylon back over her rear once more. *"Ahhhhh, Tiger. You were an animal just now."*

I looked over at her eyes, now hidden again by the sunglasses. *"I think I married not a pilot, but a savage!"*

Indeed, I felt very much like some sort of sated primitive savage. As I sat admiring her damp, passionate beauty, stretched out and spent under the savage glare of the merciless sun, the intrusively loud, bellowed strains of an amplified prayer call came blaring out over us.

It was the Islamic Sunday and in the background we could both hear the muttered imprecations of some Imam reciting the Holy Koran into the electromagnetic reaches of inner space. What madness!

The absurdity of the moment seized us both, and simultaneously we had found each other grinning from ear to ear over the splendid irony of having been caught mating like raw, rutting beasts in some burning forest at the precise moment of high prayers on the Kingdom's holy day. The laughter brought both of us back to earth and mindful now of the exposure each of us had had to the unforgiving sun, we hastened to gather up the few small articles there and darted back into the roof entrance's doorway. It would undoubtedly be a fine sunburn and I was badly in need of some water right away!

The thoughts of that moment on the roof, suffering extreme pleasure in the midst of a moment of extremely religious piety, under an extremely merciless sun, filled my thoughts as the student climbed up to our pre-planned cruise altitude, the next morning. Taif ground early warning radar had guided us over on a tight, high and fast vector towards Jeddah--one which, as I recalled it, would take us very close to Mecca. Not quite over it, for such things were forbidden, but pretty damn near. Near enough to gaze down and spot the small disruption of habitation in the sere, hilly desolation of summer heat that marked Mecca out in the otherwise drab uniformity of a Hijhazi landscape, and muse pleasantly on the delights of being able to do *'other'* things while the brothers were all clustered in the mosques thanking God for imagined blessings. The thought that Suki had been in the same basic posture of "supplication" as the brothers, while they were prostrating themselves, was momentarily a delightful flash of mildly sardonic awareness, as the Eagle continued to slash silently through the cold upper reaches of the deep blue stratosphere.

The flight continued. Our twin Viper escorts maintained station until we were released to head back to Dahran. At the juncture, they veered off to dash back on reheat to the new coordinates, while we set our own course homeward. My student, Hamed, was eager to get back to base to attend some sort of gathering one of his Sidiyks had going that night, and I..well, I was still taking my time going over the lovely curves and the spirited passion of my beautiful she-wolf, who waited for me back home. That moment on the roof had been unique, dazed by the sun as we were. It had been the mating of the sun-crazed and completely uncaring, a primitive merging with the ultimate powers of the undeniable universal instincts, and it had been a frightfully powerful fusion of our two physical bodies and souls that would linger in my thoughts long afterwards.

Late in the day, with the sun tentatively hovering like a red ball on the horizon, we set up our final approach to King Khalid Military Air Base, landing checklist run through, all systems in the green and on the beam for a set-down after chasing streams of electronic energy across the skies of the Kingdom for hours on end. I let Hamed do the approach and was amazed and pleased when he set the bird down as light as a feather on the two main gears, gradually letting the nose drop as the craft braked aerosynamically.

It was no 'Chinese landing,' as they used to say in the bad old glory days, but a perfectly mild, moderate, balanced ending to an otherwise balls-to-the-wall flight in this land of extreme contrasts.

When the bird had rolled to a stop, I popped the canopy and Hamed and I handed our helmets to the ground crew and ambled stiffly down the ladder. Both of us streamed with perspiration once the aircraft AC was cut off, and the dry heat of the desert flooded into the cockpit.

Hamed was a good student, and now he was off to join his friends for a bachelor's party in town...not much excitement for a western boy, as I well knew. As for myself, I stopped by the life support room, dropped off all my other personal equipment, filled out the flight profile forms and then grabbed a cup of coffee--extremely bad battery acid, but with caffeine none-the-less--to guzzle on the way to my car.

As I opened the car door, damp with sweat, the bellow of evening prayer call sounded out across the dusky flightline, and my thoughts were once again straying back to quarters, to the beautiful tigress whose powerful passions so amazed and stimulated me. Extremes....the thought lingered...I was extremely glad to be on my way back to quarters, where Suki would doubtless be waiting to spring upon me once more...

Maybe there was even an overlooked stray beer left...and then, I thought whimsically, a healthy bowl movement in E flat. It wasn't a perfect life, perhaps, but then, what was perfect in an imperfect universe? Except the moments of lust, passion, amusement and raw life, and the occasional blasting of your own ass across the skies at twice the speed of sound?

It recalled to mind an old saw that some young jock had repeated in the briefing room, one time, about piloting a hot plane being *better than sex*. That poor kid had obviously never met a Suki of his own!

THE FIRST (NEAR) ASCENT OF HEARTBREAK HILL (Chapter 1)

Just recently, in acknowledgement of our having survived 10 years of marital co-existence (note: this tale was written in 1996), my wife and I returned to the Santa Cruz area for several days of rest and recollection amidst the recurrent storms which have been a feature of this winter's *El Niño* onslaught. Following a miraculous and enjoyable day of calm sunshine along Capitola's shores, we looped back up to check out the old familiar watering holes on Pacific Garden Mall (after the quake, renamed 'Pacific Avenue'), as the rain once again descended upon the coastline. Following the short drive up from Capitola, my old Porsche was starting to founder in the deluge like one of the Titanic's lifeboats (there's a reason why they call 356s 'bath-tub Porsches', you know...but you knew that, didn't you?) by the time I found a parking space, but we were soon walking the short block or so up to the Mall under Ming's battered Boxer Rebellion relic of a bamboo umbrella.

Everywhere, people in shorts and T-shirts were scurrying for shelter—whether simply amazingly casual about the chill air's bite or evidencing the usual effects of *Tourist Brain Fade Syndrome* (after all, it's never cold in Santa Cruz, right? Just perpetual summer, year 'round, right?), I wasn't certain. Still, it was great fun watching all the exposed blue flesh about us as we, bundled snugly into fleece and *Chi Pants* and Gore-Tex, rounded the corner and came upon a Starbuck's patio courtyard (perhaps the blue people were all part of a Celtic 'Braveheart' tour group...?).

The shock of seeing the sinister bland and aluminum whiteness of the Starbuck's facade caught me somewhat off guard, for in the depths of my mind I had been half-expecting to encounter the familiar log-timbered, Germanic Black Forest kitsch style that characterised what used to be *Heinz's Biergarten Delicatessen*. However, lost in ruminative anticipation as I might have been, I was completely unprepared for the sterile, dull and remarkably unimaginative decor that now existed where the landmark biergarten used to be. It was, to my way of seeing things a sacrilege, almost as if a Santa Cruz landmark adobe had been razed and a MacDonald's put in its place. Think of the Taj Mahal with a big, grotesque Mermaid sign hung over the entrance with the word STARBUCKS broadly emblazoned below and you have a small glimmer of what it was like.

Nevertheless, as I stood there stunned into immobile stupefaction at this blasphemy, Ming walked determinately in for coffee (however I fervently hate the monopolistic aesthetics of Starbuck's megacorporate world view, I will admit their coffee is very good and you can't imagine how it kills me to say that: sort of like saying that great sex is worth getting AIDS) and I followed obediently, more like a lamb to the shearer than the haughty alpha wolf of my family pack out for a howl with the buds.

She ordered the Quintrupio Espresso American, while I settled for the obligatory *Espresso Antoine de Saint-Exupéry* (another Santa Cruz institution nearly forgotten in the modern post-quake crush) and I planted the seat of one of my last pair of remaining Chi Pants (note: a singularly unique article of clothing originated in Santa Cruz of the late 80s that featured a comfortably gusseted crotch that allowed *'the boys'* some breathing space) firmly on a bench and began gazing at all the edificial changes that had taken place in this street's familiar old sanctum sanctorum of the *Knowing Literati*.

As Ming delicately sipped her lethal brew (Sumatran Giant Rat urine? The darkly evil liquid was probably at least as strong in terms of its pH), it wasn't long before I was slipping into a 10 year old Pacific Garden Mall fogbank (more like a recollective black hole) of recollections.

I suppose you might say it had all started after work one day, as we--the stalwart crew of the cardiac cath lab at Santa Cruz Memorial Hospital--sat in desultory array around the tables in Heinz's Biergarten Delicatessen. It had been a rough day at the Santa Cruz Heart Institute and everyone knew that when the going got tough at the institute, the tough usually got going to Heinz's when the day's schedule was finished. *Studley*, our archetypal New Age transplant from Missoula Montana had been well into his 5th Spatenbrau and the rest of us had been working on our table beer rings at Heinz's *Stammtisch* when Nastie, our radiographer, suddenly surprised us all with a unique proposal. He must have been truly inspired (or really wasted, since they both amount to the same thing), for he put his beer down, rose unsteadily to his feet and turning a flinty grin towards us all, uttered the fated words: *"Let's climb Heartbreak Hill..."*

In a heart-beat I was once more seated in Heinz's, and it was a Santa Cruz Fall, in the year 1988...

Heart Break Hill...the highest and toughest ridge on Mt. Cardiac! Just the echo of that dreaded name, hanging like a precarious snow cornice in the Autumn air of the Pacific Garden Mall, brought on a cold chill that crisply walked down my back like the tumescent memory of Betty-Jo Bioloskie's nakedly wet dancer's toes. Facing Nastie after absently downing the remainder of my beer, I tried to appear sneeringly calm as I carefully imagined righteous disdain dripping from my mustache like the drops of beer that routinely rappel off my upper lip when I drink beer.

"You, sir, are drunk," I said. *"Besides that, it's never been done before-at least no one has ever been up there before and returned to tell about it--and you think we ought to go climb that wicked mother?!*

I could tell from Nastie's somewhat glazed look beneath his beer goggles that this was *egg-zactly* what he was suggesting, in all seriousness and no thanks to the best Bavarian beer this side of Emperor Franz Ferdinand's august crypt.

"Hey, we've done some crazy things before, haven't we? Why not one more demonstration of our collective disregard for the objective hazards of stoopidfoolishness (he said the last two words together, as if they were one) before we're too old to get ourselves into any more trouble, eh?"

This last rejoinder had hit its intended target, I could see, as each of us--kicked casually back under the patio's Spatenbrau umbrellas--stiffened slightly upon hearing the words 'too old.' We were indeed growing slightly beyond the pale—all of us--and even last week Lennie had glanced at an inspiring poster of some ancestral Lynn Hill precursor doing some suggestive mantling maneuvers on a redline 5.34 route, clad only in Lycra, without even lifting a tufty eye-brow. Not even a quiver of interest in the sweaty little nipple-points under her sports bra top that stood enthusiastically out, in what was obviously a *VERY* chilly breeze on that wall of rock.

Shocked at the time, I had made a mental note to test Lennie's reflexes shortly thereafter but had rather quickly forgotten about my intention when Studley, sitting next to me, had dropped the 5-pound piton hammer he was playing with on my big toe. Ignoring the painful toe and quaffing another gulp of the lovely amber brew Heinz coyly refers to as 'maiden dew,' I looked quickly around the room. Studley, ace womanizer and sometime former cragsman turned golf pro, was now 41 and showing as much topside turf as a billiard ball. Next to him, Nastie, possessor of the distinctive cachet of being the only American rock-climber who could pass for OJ Simpson's twin-brother and as sturdy an FIAA weight test standard for severely stressing climbing ropes as ever existed, was also no mere child at the hoary old age of 45.

Lennie....*where had Lennie gone?* I looked around before spotting him sitting on the floor, beside the tattered potted Adder's Tongue Heinz kept by the door, shoes off and picking the toe jam from between his pedal digits. Lennie was still in fine shape for a 48-year-old, his gnarled hands covered by a score of old, healed scars from radical jam-cracking days of yore. Too bad Lennie's brain had never fully recovered from the blow to the head he had taken from Audrey Farber's pelvic bone one wild and crazy evening, some years back at a high base camp, trying--as he explained it to us--to bring her out of some claimed hypothermic condition she had contracted on the descent from the peak they had both summited earlier.

Now there was a man who knew just about everything one could about the various techniques of warming another climber's body with his own in an emergency involving lowered core temperature....except I had long suspected that the victim, who was invariably female, had been suffering from *increased* core temperature rather than the other way around, judging from the steam clouds that had vented from their tent. Ah well.

And then there was Doc Hector, our resident pulmonologist *cum* climber, who had been the only drop-out from the famous University of Colorado Mt. Logan High Altitude Experiments of the winter of 1969. He had once managed to hook himself up to an oxygen/nitrous oxide mix of 15% 02/ balance NO2 in one of the studies and was suspected also of sneaking out for a joint every now and again (interesting effects at 15,000 feet, too--especially the spectacular visit by a winged and psychedelically aura'd

Tim O'Leary, while Doc was sitting on an outcropping once, high up on Denali) during the hypoxia tests. Permanent brain damage or merely a gentle soul of the 60s with a wireless direct hot-line to God? At any rate, Doc Hector was our official climbing physician, as well as keeper of the Holy Tablets (Chloral Hydrate, Dexedrine and Furosemide), for use whenever they were needed. No youngster he, either, and known to slip into a semi-hypoxemic state even at sea-level, on occasion. Especially when well into his cups.

And finally, there was myself, Errol Embolism, one-time Weird Science Fair door prize winner and the guy voted most likely to be avoided by any half-way decent woman within visual recognition range in his graduating class of post-docs...rock climber, abysmal poet, perspiring writer of tepid mountain prose and Denali drop-out.

Yeah. We were quite a crew of reprobates, as anyone could see, had they but dared to set foot in Heinz's while the crew were unwinding after a hard day at Aorta Central.

Tried, true and tested, all of us, we had pulled many a patient's shit out of the prospective cardiac bypass surgical list's toilet. And now Nastie was suggesting one last crazy adventure on the *Mountain of Doom* before we all became candidates for the Ronald Reagan Memorial Old-timer's Disease Home for Forgetful Climbers.

Climb Mt. Cardiac, ascend Heartbreak Hill?! It was a sobering thought, unfortunately, and that's just exactly what no one wanted at that particular moment. As if in unison, we all glared *en-mass* (most of us who could still glare, that is--a few of the crew simply drooled in a disconcerting manner) at Nastie and settled back into exercising our biceps with lifting reps of Heinz's cast pig-iron, one-liter steinkrugs. No more was said that day about this disturbing thought. For my part, after the startling thought had passed (and a few of us had passed *out*), I remember only having stuporously straddled my Yamaha 550 Seca crotch rocket (after about 6 Spatenbraus) and making it safely home, via Highway 1, to my beach house at Sunset State Beach (*alive*, thank you God!)...

Several days later, however, Linda Loma, the devastatingly fit, culturally chilled-out and ultra-social darling of the Santa Cruz older-than-40-but-you'd-never-know-it-club, happened to stop by the hospital. Linda was a medical journalist—a *'staph writer'*, as we snickeringly referred to such journalist types who specialised in health news topics--for the *Santa Cruz Senile*, the city's oldest newspaper. She was also a climber (aside from the fact that she had a GREAT set of *personal* peaks), and as a newspaper person, no stranger to the roaring controversy that the battle between Santa Cruz Community Hospital's Heart Institute and The Dominican Medical Center's counterpart had grown into.

Today, Linda was at the hospital on business, searching for old wounds to reopen in her never-ending efforts to titillate the public by revealing the latest excesses of modern high-tech medical flim-flam. I was, at that particular moment, in no mood for Linda, or even for feeding her medical flim-flam gathering apparatus, having just heard from my surfing bud that he had smashed up my classic vintage Hobie longboard on the rocks at the foot of Steamer Lane, and suggested a bit bluntly that she take her perky pulchritude off to the halls of Dominican Med Center. Linda, however, would not be put off so easily and soon her true purpose in dropping by became known.

"Errol" she began, unctuously thrusting those gorgeous twin globes of hemispherical flesh in my direction, *"I heard you guys are planning to climb Mt. Cardiac. Is this for real? Is it true? What's up?"*

I could see it was going to do no good at all to try to put Linda off, ace reporter and sensual little news-ferret that she was, so I leveled with her.

"Where'd you hear that, Linda? Yeah, it's true, I guess. Lemme see, umm, I guess the Eastern Wall of the Southeast West Ridge of the Northwest Face that's still unclimbed…Heartbreak Hill, so…ummm...that would be where we're headed."

Suddenly Pandora's box was yawning open again, after having only widened a tiny crack at Heinz's earlier in the week. Damn. There would soon be hell to pay and doubtless another prospective hypothermia victim for Lennie to 'revive'. What a selfless and heroic letch Lennie was! I could already hear, in my mind, the small gasps and throaty groans of yet another gorgeous 'victim' reviving under his courageous efforts to warm her frozen body with his own hot flesh. What a guy!

"Errol....I want to go. You know I can do it. I can climb A9 5.13 VII with my eyes shut. Lynn Hill's a member of MY fan club. Errol...I need this to complete my '20 Mediocre Summits and 1 Sub-oceanic Seamount' list. This is an opportunity to finally culminate my years of climbing work, plus it's something unique to talk about at margarita parties at the 'Crow's Nest.'"

Linda definitely had the bit between her needle-like teeth on this idea and there were enough of them revealed by her dazzlingly hygienic smile to make any fully grown potential paramour (and that likely included fully half of the Santa Cruz male population) anxious when she was in fully ardent cry.

I finally managed to get rid of Linda, when the geyser-like spurt of a post-cath patient's femoral artery puncture site suddenly indicated a need for further pressure, but later on

I scared up Nastie and vented on him for having spread his great idea around beyond the protective limits of our Heinz's faithful crew cohort. The cat, as it were, was now out of the bag and we now faced the necessity of actually having to carry through on this wild idea to scale Mt. Cardiac and ascend Heartbreak Hill. As Linda Loma herself had once memorably uttered after a particularly *proteinaceous* encounter with Nastie's legendary reproductive apparatus: *"G*U*L*P!"*

Reluctantly enough, it seemed, everyone pulled together and planning began for this last great *hoo-hah* adventure before Dominican Medical Center finally managed to throttle the regulatory pahootie out of our SCHI operations. After all, who knew where the present battle would end up? Although Santa Cruz Memorial Hospital had its parent organisation in Los Angeles behind it, Dominican had the full support of the whole damn Roman Catholic Church behind it, and worse yet, that unholy dominatrix of ritual dogma, *Sister Lulu Overunder* was their CEO!

We might all find ourselves out of work shortly, as the winds of the medical war being waged for market share heated up the whole community. Life in Santa Cruz, after all, had become near paradisiacal for most of us at the Santa Cruz Heart Institute and we were loath to relinquish our firm grip on the hedonistic pleasures of languid Santa Cruz living.

Each of us had a lovely little picturesquely scenic hideaway to retreat to at the end of each day. My own was a four-room cabin out at *Sunset State Beach*, perched up on a sand dune within the Park's confines and one of about only two dozen such homes thus privileged to have been built there before the State declared that spectacular ocean-side setting a park.

The others of us who had been brought in to staff the

heart institute had also found similar great digs. And then, we all had Heinz's Biergarten to retire to, regularly seeking the great and all-consoling mental miasma that good German beer produces when the day's OR stress level required post-op respite.

Heinz's was certainly a unique, if controversial, part of the Pacific Garden Mall. With its quaint little pseudo-Bavarian decorations and cement wall-enclosed patio, wrought-iron fence, three-week-old and petrified *'Fresh Deviled Eggs'* (fresh only at the beginning of each week), and its daily crowd of assorted street people squatting on the patio, it was both the scourge of proper Santa Cruz society and the soulful refuge of preference for homeless people, as well as a small group of us more conventionally propertied, post-Bohemian groupies who loved the sheer anachronistic ambience of the place.

At Heinz's we could all come together, hoist our steinkrugs filled to the brim with golden Spatenbrau and sit back after work each day, observing the unending, fascinating parade of visual delights that never failed to throng the Mall. When closing time came, us regular *Stammgasts* ('regular customers', after the German term) would sit at the *Stammtisch* (literally 'regular customers table'), by this time quite well lubricated with Heinz's Maiden Dew, and hold forth for another hour or two at least before departing for home.

Thinking back on my own daily departure for Sunset State Beach from Heinz's, part of the route of which was via Highway 101, today gives me a cold chill, for I was in the habit of daily riding my Yamaha *Seca 550* motorcycle near the speed of sound while thus pickled. I recall numerous occasions, while speeding along on that highway in the growing dusk, of being near-fixated by the *blurr* of the passing strips of yellow lane-divider I kept crossing over. Not a healthy habit to indulge in for those who plan on avoiding organ-donor status! Of course, that was 10 years ago and today I am a bit more careful in observing the legal proprieties--as well as the safety ones (I keep the speed down a shade *below* Mach 0.85).

At any rate, we had decided to climb Mt. Cardiac and climb we would. For all we knew, it would be the first and last ascent of this landmark ridge made by anyone, the crowning achievement of a lifetime of slovenly, half-assed mountaineering, interspersed by moments of truly sublime climbing mediocrity. Things at that point, after all, had been starting to look a bit grim for the Santa Cruz Heart Institute in its battle against Sister Lulu Overunder and her henchmen at the Dominican Medical Center.

It was probably just as well that we have one great last, collective, orgasmic fling on the rocks before the asshole of our bucolic Santa Cruz lifestyle slammed shut! Additionally, there was probably no time to spare if the climb were to be made before winter set in.

* * *

[Note: This tale was begun on a beer coaster, one afternoon after Steamer Lane had closed out and the Santa Cruz Heart Institute Irregulars had all gathered at Heinz's Biergarten in Pacific Garden Mall. This is also where it ended, thanks to half a dozen Spatenbraus. Perhaps it will continue afresh, one of these days, although shortly after this first chapter was scribbled, Dominican Santa Cruz Medical Center did indeed succeed in closing out the Santa Cruz Heart Institute. It's now all part of the fabulous history of that Golden Era in California's original 'Surf City'! *Here's to you, Sister Lulu Overunder!*]

PS: Dominican Santa Cruz Medical Center's infamous Dominatrix of Severe Mercy (Sister Lulu Overunder) recently retired (2004), having had what to her was probably the infinitely satisfying fulfillment of having successfully ended our halcyonic Santa Cruz idylls.]

.

RABBIT MOON, TIGER MOON

"We had much to do
and quickly.
The sky-earth spins
and time is short.
Ten thousand years is long
and so, a morning and an evening count.
The four oceans boil and clouds fume with rain.
The five continents shake in the wind of lightning.
We wash away insects
and are strong."

-Mao Zhedong, 9 Jan 63

Old Yao waded into the lapping froth of spent surf. It was not yet fully dark as the faded imperial ochre of the dying sun flared out upon the rocky sand. Yao did not notice the futile explosion of color, for his thoughts were racing ahead to more practical things. Soon it would become very cold without the brittle rays of the slanted sun for warmth. Yao did not have to remind himself of this obvious fact as the dark and frigid waters of the Pacific Ocean penetrated his tattered old boots. Thinking vividly of the cold expanse of unfriendly water stretching out before him, he glanced back at the beach before nimbly pulling himself up and over the side of the small fishing boat.

On the shore, standing mutely in a quiet row just beyond the water's reach, Lee's three remaining children watched their father intently. He smiled a brief, inner smile to himself. It was always thus, he thought as he turned his attention to the matter of getting the small craft underway. Each night the children saw him on his way as he set forth on the lonely emptiness of the big Monterey Bay. Soon they would grow up and be forced to deal with the same problems of living that he and his wife faced. It was not a happy, fulfilled life, he reflected, but it was as good as any. The squid were still plentiful, and the decision to fish at night had for the moment resolved the bitter unpleasantness with the dark-skinned *Guai-Loh* (a Cantonese term that literally means 'foreign devil') who resented Chinese fishing boats competing with them during daylight hours.

Fishing at night, in the frigid waters of the winter ocean, was hard enough on the younger men of the village, Lee knew, but on the older men such as himself and his cousin it was a continuing ordeal that tested the most-hearty to their limits of endurance. Still, what must be done…the reflective fragment ended itself as he allowed himself another brief, ironic thought: there was always a way if one searched diligently enough and when that diligence was encouraged by the need to provide for a family of ten hungry people—three of them young, growing and unable to help provide much toward the family's upkeep—it was strong motivation to come up with solutions.

He lingered a moment over this, realizing that he was not being entirely fair in this assessment of his children, for they were not yet adults and they did contribute considerably toward the overall maintenance of the family in their inconsistent, childish ways. He paused. They did not have much time to play, for all the small tasks mother had them busy doing. Perhaps in a better life such things such as play might be understood and relished. Under the circumstances, however, childhood was brief and maturity came rapidly, out of necessity.

He glanced back quickly at the shore. The rough-planked shack which the Lee family considered their fortunate abode sat among the others, crowded onto the higher plateau of the beach. From the flimsy tin stack protruding from the roof a wispy tendril of smoke issued, proclaiming the fact that his family was about to sit down to the evening meal of fish *juk* (also known as *'Congee'* or rice gruel) which was the regular fare.

He had had some already, of course, to prepare for the coming cold of the night. Overhead he noted the moon, looming largely on the horizon like a pale, luminous specter. He shivered involuntarily. In a few more days the new lunar year would begin. Almost unconsciously, he found himself thinking about the family debts, some of which would have to go unpaid. A sharp pang of unhappy thought speared him for a second. His wife...so smart, *too smart!*

Even her resourceful, clever intelligence with money could not solve that one. If there was no money, there was no money, and the family's needs battled in his mind with the prospective shame he faced. The family had to have first priority, he finally decided, as the brutally cold of winter in this new land bullied them. If there were no family, the debts could not be paid anyway, therefore the family had to come first. The very strong sense of shame which accompanied this last thought made him grip the oars of the boat more firmly and set his back into rowing out onto the yawning waters that stretched out from the stony beach. The small boat's wake caught up the moonlight and dispersed it like quicksilver as each oar gouged the seaweed-choked spume.

Yao reflected a bit more on this unfortunate situation as his sinewy arms stroked the boat beyond the small surf line. He could see a few lights now among the scattered shacks on shore. The sun had finally given up its struggle to stay afloat and was now nothing more than a dull red memory in the thin black line of clouds hugging the distant horizon. Already the moon, pale and swollen as a winter melon, rose into the sky to oversee all as ruler of the night. It was a weary moon, Lee Yao thought. There was no moon bright and promising enough to erase the shame he felt over being unable to pay off the family debt prior to the imminent journey of the kitchen god to make his heavenly report on their household.

The depressing thoughts were no good, he decided. It would serve no practical purpose to sit and mope about over misfortunes like old grandmother. He was out here to fish, to catch food for the family, and that is what he would dedicate his energy toward this evening.

Glancing forward into the shadowed prow of the small boat, he sought the shape of the small padded clay bottle which held precious hot tea. His wife had filled it from their rapidly diminishing supply, knowing how vital it would be to help preserve his warmth on the chill, dark ocean waters of the bay. She had thoughtfully included several small, home-made *chau-siu-bao* (pork-filled buns), amazingly, although where she had managed to find the pork he had not the slightest clue.

Lee Su-Ling, his wife, the mother of his children, and his companion in this life's struggle to make ends meet—how strong, how uncomplaining and how important she was to him! Despite the stoic hardness of many years of unceasing labor and effort, he permitted himself the briefest of tender feelings for the part she had played, as always, in his life.

She had been one of those rarest of creatures in the life of young Chinese men sojourning in this new land: a Chinese woman, young herself, almost too good-looking to be lucky, and as time had proven again and again, an abnormally intelligent woman as well. Of this last qualification, Yao had decidedly mixed feelings. It was not, in his opinion, good for a woman to be too smart, for smart women often had too many strange, untraditional ideas. Not good for the family, as *Lao Gung's* (the Master of the

House) ascendant status in such a family was not as exalted or as assured as traditional values required that it be. It had caused many small, awkward moments of minor irritation in past years; but to be fair, her native intelligence had proven to be a resource and asset of great value in circumstances which might have otherwise proven severely trying.

Her ample mettle had risen to the challenge of trying to bring up a family on this rugged but strangely beautiful coast. Through the worst of it, through the times when there was little food to be had, when the racist prejudice of the *guai-loh* had damaged their pride just as thoroughly as their property, when they had lost their second-eldest son, she had not just remained steadfast and calmly impervious to the insults and pain, she had actually managed at times to be cheerful!

What inner reserves did she draw upon at such moments to meet the bitterness with renewed energy and resolve, he wondered? He knew she had felt the sharp, stabbing prick of pain just as keenly as had he, for he had found her privately convulsed with silent tears not long after their son had been lost overboard, the innocent victim of a collision with a boat full of drunken Portuguese fishermen who had run his small boat down with deliberate intent. He had seen the tearless tears of heated anguish, and had wondered at the shame in her face to have been thus caught by her husband in a rare moment of visible personal pain. He had glared at her flushed face in the surprise of the encounter, some distance from their house, and hardly breaking stride had continued walking along the shore in embarrassed silence. Oh yes, she could keenly feel and share his pain.

The moon, ever rising higher, was now full up in the night sky. The water around the boat shimmered, catching the reflected light and breaking it up into so many dancing star-points of brilliance. Yao lit the punk of the stern lantern and hung it up so that it stood above the water, casting light and shadow to chase the moon's rays in a race across the misted wavelets.

Su-Ling had turned his head the first day they had met, for she was a rare jewel of a woman among many ordinary stones. He couldn't at first believe that she appeared to be attracted to him as well. For all intents, the marriage had been arranged by the families, as all were, according to ancient custom. Before the actual ceremony, Yao found himself marveling at the fact of her beauty and how rare it was to be doubly blessed with a wife whose beauty was as obvious as her ability to bear strong sons and provide a good home for husband and family.

Intoxicated by her fairness, he had only later discovered, to his mild discomfort, that she was a literate, somewhat educated woman, with a keen and penetrating intelligence of her own. He himself had taken the civil service examinations and had held some small post in China before coming to *Gum Shan* ('Gold Mountain', the Cantonese term for America)—a testament to his own literacy. But to find himself with a woman who was clearly his equal in many things--*that* took a bit of getting used to. Still, she had fulfilled her wifely duties with aplomb and clearly was a valued asset to the welfare of the family in so many ways which could be neither counted nor enumerated.

Floating in the lapping swells off shore Lee looked across the dark waters to the distant beacon of light which their fishing village had become. As his rough hands automatically manipulated the nets which they had become so accustomed to casting in these familiar waters, his thoughts remained focused upon Su-Ling. The peaceful expressiveness of her face manifested itself out of the darkness in his mind's gaze. It was her eyes which were so out of place in that positive, resolute and confident look she wore most of the time. The deep sadness in them was skillfully hidden, but still discernable to a husband's privileged contemplation. It was her eyes which spoke all the untellable stories, which gave mute testimony to the experiences which could never be admitted to anyone—not even to himself. Those deep brown eyes had shadows which no man would ever penetrate, depths which would never be plumbed and which contained whispered things never to be brought into the open truth of daylight.

There was so much about her which she would not share with him, but this was perhaps fitting, for he knew the wisdom of the old saying which went *"...that which may be easily spoken cannot truly come from the heart."* Of one thing alone, he was dead certain: she was the stronger of the two of them. Hers was the strength of the willow when the storms of life threatened to snap his oaken resolve.

Su-Ling refused to vanish from his mind as he patiently ran the nets out over the worn gunnels of the wooden skiff. The knotted strands of hemp slipped smoothly from his hands into the liquid coal of the ocean's surface. The memory of a rare night they had had alone together, when Cousin Li had taken the family with him to San Francisco, returned to him from some obscure recess of his mind. It had been so strange at first, to find himself with no other noisy presences in the small shack except Su-Ling and himself. He had found the sudden intimacy uncomfortable and unusual, at first.

After he had returned from his fishing that fair summer night he had quietly cleansed himself of the fish grime and stench. Entering the two-room shack on piles—normally congested with the family's ten members—he found her awake and waiting for him in the silent darkness of the pre-dawn hour. He stood there briefly, allowing his eyes a moment to become accustomed to the indoor darkness. He could remember feeling, rather than actually seeing, her deep brown eyes upon him as he removed his worn garments and hung them by the bed, as she had long insisted he do.

The house had been somewhat muggy within, despite a mild fog which had just started to drift lazily in from the bay. He left the window ajar, welcoming the soft coolness which filtered obediently through the opening like small wraiths of chill sea mist shadow.

Wordlessly, he had gotten under the covers and found her slim body strangely cold and warm at the same time. *"You stink like fish,"* she joked, and stifled a quick gasp as his cold leg touched her warmth.

"You feel like one," he had joked in return.

After that, neither said more until much later, for the unusual and wonderful gift of such luxurious, private intimacy was far too precious to waste further words upon. His hands had closed upon her smooth, supple body with a hunger that had not be easily sated for some time. And she, in turn, had taken him into her with such a furious, consuming desire that together they had immolated themselves into spent, empty husks long before the North Star had risen above the horizon.

Much later they had lain utterly drained of energy, enjoying the peace-filled quietude of the early dawn, interrupted only by the muted thrashing of the light surf upon the rocky shore below the cabin. The smell of salt air mingled deliciously with the scent of her body and the not unpleasant odors of their joining.

And now he sat, rocking gently on the waves, face outlined by the harsh glare of the stern lantern as he worked the nets. What a night that had been, and how much her woman's heart had spoken wordlessly to him in those few hours of the single night.

In amazed recollection, he marveled at the soft, yet strong sinews of her thighs and how she had wrapped her legs about his waist, pressing him into her so hard that it had surprised him. He had supposed that his wild passion would have hurt her, and yet her tearful gasps were not from the pain of his passion alone, but from the storehouse of repressed emotions which added such forceful impetus to her lovemaking, or at least so had he surmised.

He had been spared the sight of her sad, ageless eyes as they melted into one another that night; but he remained certain that had he been able to catch a glimpse, it would have been the glowing eyes of the tiger into which he looked rather than the deep, brown pools of feeling which he thought he had come to know so well.

There was in fact the tiger in her, for that was her birth year, and that night she had coupled with the wild strength of such a beast in the clutch of her slender wrists and the grip of her animated loins. Yes, the tiger was within her, mostly well concealed, as was the tiger's natural habit, but lurking there, waiting to spring forth when the moment turned to favor, it could be felt.

Lee Yao thought again of the new lunar year, and of the four offspring of his female tiger. Of the four, two had been boys, one of whom—the second eldest—was now gone. The two youngest were both girls. And although they were not as useful as good, sturdy sons, they both had their mother's look in their eyes, strong young she-tigers, he thought. That will be good for them in this strange new world, as the unknown future awaits them in perplexing *Gum Shan*. They would need their mother's strength to survive the hostility and hatred which would befall them as a consequence of their sex and birthright.

Poor little tigers, thought Lee Yao once again, as he gathered up his nets under the glare of the stern lamp. It had been some hours now since he had ventured forth from the warm harbor of his home, and the chill of the wintry night pierced him through as it prickled the wave-tops like small spikes of wind-borne bamboo. He could see some of the other lamp-lit boats from his village slowly turning shoreward—apparently, they had caught their fill of the small squid for the night. Good. There would be much to do in the morning, after a few brief hours of sleep.

Hauling his own nets back into the small craft, the smell of the squid rose about him as their small, slippery and ghostly bodies cascaded over the sides of the boat in a shower of slimy luminescence. The dank aroma of the deep and ancient ocean canyons beneath the boat welled up with them to spill into the crisp dawn air. In the watery wash of the boat's bottom, the thousands of tiny ghost-squid caught the shimmering pallor of the magnificent full moon fixed overhead.

Mindful of the arrival of the lunar new year, and of the complex, never-ending demands of his life, Yao carefully made the nets secure. Waist-deep in the load of squid, he took another swallow or two of the tea—now grown cool but still curiously refreshing even on such a cold night—and stretching out his weathered arms, pulled for shore. Perhaps with the meager return from the night's catch, and the combined savings from the past month's work, they could still honor their liabilities before the new year's celebration was ended.

With this thought, a strong spirit of hope swelled up within him, like a fresh sea breeze might sweep across a breathless summer beach. With his tiger-woman's strength and perseverance, and with the help of the celestial ancestors' intercessions to influence the deities, the Lee family would persist and strive, and perhaps ultimately succeed in this daunting new land. Perhaps they might even stay here, instead of returning to China with their *Gum Shan* wealth! Who really could tell what the future would bring? And moreover, why worry about all that right now? The future would take care of itself if they continued to take care of the present to the best of their ability.

As he reached the shore, he jumped out of the boat and waded the remaining few yards to the sandy bar below the rock promontory. The bright moon no longer looked as weary as he had thought earlier, Lee Yao mused suddenly. Above him the cold, radiant light of the full moon flooded the coastal landscape of winter night, illuminating in shadowed relief the clustered shacks of the village above him. Tying up the boat to the iron rings he had pounded so painstakingly into the rock of the small cove, he moved up the path to obtain help in bringing the squid up to the drying racks.

Su-Ling would be awake and waiting to help warm him when he finally finished and was ready to sleep the few remaining hours left until morning light. The children would be asleep, or pretending to be. Uncle and Cousin would be politely unconscious of his arrival. Ancient Grandmother would likely be snoring, as always. And in a few days, the celebrations of the new year would sweep them all up in the many year-end rituals.

He paused to gaze one last time at the brilliant February moon overhead. A rabbit, moon-gazing, he found himself thinking, as he thrust his head up in a supposed mimicry of the old legend of *Chang'e*. A rabbit and a tiger, together facing this new world. The cold beauty of the opal moon made him shiver as he paused briefly to ruminate before his weathered door. Pulling out his prized old pocket-watch, he noted it was several minutes after midnight.

The Year of the Rabbit had begun *two weeks early*.

* * *

[Note: It has always struck me as the greatest irony that the actual coastal location of the historic Chinese fishing village which inspired this story is now occupied by the elite and exclusive *Pebble Beach Golf and Tennis Club* facility near Carmel, California.

The original *Pescadero Chinese Fishing Village of the mid-1800s* was located on the point protruding between Pebble Beach Cove and Stillwater Cove, and the old fishery itself today literally lies under the Seventeenth Green of that exclusively high-status golf resort.

Despite the rich cultural history of this contemporary playground for the powerful and wealthy, there exists not a single marker or monument testifying to the early inhabitants' lives on the grounds of the Pebble Beach resort. From my perspective, this remains a shameful indictment of a lingering tradition of racist white disregard for the pioneering of these early Asian inhabitants of this most beautiful, serenely sited locale.]

A STORY OF KAUHUHU, THE SHARK GOD OF MOLO-KAI

Kamalo was one of the kahunas (priests) of the Ali'I High Chief Kupa, on the island of *Molokai nui a Hina* (*Moloka'i sacred to Hina*). Kupa had a house built within temple walls in the valley called Mapulehu, which ended in the harbor, now called Aikanaka. Kamalo's temple was a short distance away in the village of Kalua'aha, which faced the channel between Molokai and Maui.

Kamalo had two sons, *Kekipi* and *Keha*, and a beautiful daughter, Lanilani, who thrived in the village and delighted in the brilliant colors of the sunrise and sunset. The boys were handsome, strong young men and possessed the very courage of the spirits of sky and sea, often accomplishing great deeds of daring.

Lanilani, whose name means 'The sky', 'heavens', or 'heavenly', was known all across the island as the fairest, cleverest, and most beautiful of all the young maidens of Molokai, but Lanilani equaled the strength and spirit of the boys in most things and had always been a brave and spirited girl. The boys showed promise of growing into strong warriors and lovely Lanilani was renowned for her love of the ocean and *He'e Nalu* (surfing). Kamalo was very proud of them all and patiently taught them the ways of the Heiau (temple), so they knew that those things that were sacred to the gods must not be touched.

The High Chieftain Kupa came to his home in the valley during certain seasons and everyone knew he was there when they heard the beating of his Pahu drums (a drum carved from coconut palm wood). In his home, two very special Heiau Pahu drums were kept, carefully covered with sacred Tapa cloth. When he chose to, with his unique skill he could communicate his thoughts clearly to his priests through the beating rhythms of those special Pahu.

It was during a fishing trip to Maui when Kupa was away for an extended time, that Kamalo's adventurous sons decided to see the chief's great drums for themselves. Lanilani cautioned them to obey their father's wishes, but they laughed and quickly dismissed her sisterly concerns. Shortly thereafter they raced along the beach and climbed over the ridge to Kupa's Heiau (temple).

There they cautiously entered the chief's home and, lifting the folds of the sacred Tapa, marveled at the large, magnificent drums that had been carved from great coconut palm trunks. The heads of these Pahu were covered with the stretched skin of a *Mano* (Tiger Shark) and the decorations were of giant waves and figures of *Manoakua* (ancestral shark spirits).

Truly marvelous drums they were and the boys were amazed at the skill with which they had been cut from the native wood. They ran their hands over the craftsmanship and tapped ever so lightly with their fingertips, delighting to the powerful vibration given off by the stretched shark skin. However, temptation proved too great, and the boys soon began to beat upon the drums with enthusiasm. The loud echoes of their drumming reached many ears as they beat upon the great sharkskin drum heads.

Several of Kupa's followers who were nearby heard the drums, but dared not enter the chief's Heiau. Instead, they waited, listened and watched until the boys took their leave, noting the identity of the irreligious intruders. Upon Kupa's return, his followers told him of the boys' transgression. The chief became furious and immediately called upon his Mu (Heiau sacrifice seekers) to take the lives of the boys and present their bodies at the Heiau alter in sacrifice to the Great God Ku. And so was it soon done.

When Kamalo learned of the death of his sons, a heavy bitterness filled his heart and his will became bent on revenge. He realized that he was no match for Kupa, so he consulted with various kahunas and seers throughout Molokai. He prepared gifts and sacrifices to take with him, making his way from one kahuna to another. Despite the power of these kahunas, each one was fearful of Kupa and would not help Kamalo, instead sending him on to another kahuna further along the shore of the island.

Undaunted by this, Kamalo was determined and pressed onward. Eventually, he came to the high sea cliffs on the north of the island overlooking Kalaupapa and Kalawao. At the bottom stood a Sacred Heiau dedicated to the Great Shark God, *Kauhuhu*. With great care, Kamalo climbed slowly down the high precipice and approached the kahuna of the Heiau.

After hearing Kamalo, the kahuna told him, *"Go to the great cliffs below Kalawao, to the cave called Anapuhi, the Cave of the Eel. There you will find the great Shark God Kauhuhu himself, guarded by Waka and Mo-o, his dragon watchers. Gaining his favor is your only hope to avenge your sons."*

The kahuna could give him no further help, but hospitably fed him and slaked his thirst with the juice of the *Noni* fruit before he journeyed on. Once departed, Kamalo made his way to the cave of his last hope, a sacrificial black pig slung across his shoulders. These final miles took a toll on him and left him weary to the bone.

The shark god's watchers saw Kamalo approaching and gleefully told each other that a fish was coming to be eaten by their master. But as he drew nearer, something in Kamalo's expression won their sympathy and they called to him to go away from this place, lest he lose his life.

"I seek revenge for my sons," Kamalo said, *"I have no care for myself."*

Then he proceeded to tell them how the High Chieftain Kupa had had his sons slain for beating the sacred Pahu drums. He described his travels throughout Molokai in search of a force powerful enough to help him. He told them that Kauhuhu was his last hope and that if he was refused, he had no wish to further live.

Waka and *Mo-o* contemplated Kamalo's story and due to the eloquence of Kamalo's words and his great skill in expressing himself, their hearts were now heavy for him and his loss. To their great surprise, they suddenly found themselves inclined to help this poor mortal.

"We shall help you," Waka said, *"but in so doing, we forfeit our own lives if your cause does not please our master. You must be very careful to do just as we say."*

"Hide in that pile of seaweed and fish bones there," Instructed Mo-o. *"Watch for eight great waves to come in from the ocean. Kauhuhu will arrive on the last one. If he sees you, he will eat you before you have a chance to speak. So, you must be absolutely silent until an opportunity is made clear."*

Kamalo did not have to wait long, for soon huge surf began to roll in to shore. Waves crashed against the cliffs, each one climbing higher and higher until the eighth one rose up and was caught by the wind. In a great gust, spray and foam were carried into the cave and suddenly *Kauhuhu* the Shark God was there in all his awful presence. Before the wind even died down, however,

Kauhuhu took his human form.

"I smell a man!" His voice thundered against the cave walls. *"Where is he?"*

Waka and Mo-o assured him that no man was among them, but the Shark God searched the cave walls and peered into every shadow before he was satisfied. Just as he turned his attention away from the matter, the black pig squealed. Kauhuhu leaped into the pile of seaweed and fishbones and plucked up Kamalo. In an instant, Kamalo found himself halfway into the shark god's mouth.

"E!... Kauhuhu, listen to my prayer! Then you can eat me!" Kamalo cried.

Surprised and intrigued, Kauhuhu released Kamalo and agreed to listen to his story, which Kamalo told in detail. As he reached the conclusion, describing how he was turned away by all the kahunas of all the gods, even the mighty Kauhuhu was overcome with pity for Kamalo.

"Had you come here for any other purpose, you would have been killed." Kauhuhu said. *"But your cause is just and sacred and therefore you are the only man who has stood in my presence and kept his life. I will be your Kahu, your guardian, and I will punish those who have acted against your sons. But there is a dear price that must be paid, also..."*

Thereupon, Kauhuhu accepted Kamalo's offer of the black pig. Then Kamalo received his instructions. His first task was to go back to the Heiau of the Shark God. From there he had to carry the kahuna over the cliffs to his own Heiau at Kaluaaha. There they were to build a special fence of *Kukui* wood and put up the sacred white *Tapa Kapu* staffs. Then, when they had amassed four hundred black pigs, four hundred red fish and four hundred white chickens, they were to wait for the arrival of the shark god…but not before Kamalo had instructed his beautiful and clever daughter Lanilani, to go to the High Chieftain's Heiau, bearing fruit and fish as gifts for the Chief and to act as his concubine.

Finally, when all was done as Kauhuhu had commanded, they would see a white cloud over the island of Lanai, huge and billowing and unlike any they had seen before. When the cloud grew to cover the island, it would move against the wind until it reached the peaks above Mapulehu Valley. Then a great rainbow would reach across the valley and Kauhuhu would be there to mete out punishment and avenge Kamalo's sons.

Kamalo made his way to the Shark God's Heiau on swift feet. He carried the priest up the cliffs to his home in Kaluaaha. There, he took care of the priest as they together built the fence, put up the Tapa Kapu staffs and gathered the pigs, fish and chickens. Kamalo, leading his daughter fair Lanilani aside by the hand, then called all the rest of those who were close to him together to live within the enclosure to wait for the promised events. Beautiful Lanilani was given fruit and fresh fish and told to take them to the High Chief's Heiau and wait there upon the High Chief, tending to his every wish and whim. Finally, all was done as Kauhuhu had commanded, and the rest waited, with their eyes turned toward the island of Lanai.

Day grew into weeks, and weeks into months as Kamalo waited with the patience of one who honors the word of the ancient Ama'akua spirits. Then one day, a white cloud appeared, different than any he had seen before. It grew rapidly and then began to move. It came across the channel and rested in the highest peaks above the valley where Kupa lived. From the midst of it and descending to the lush greenery below it, a magnificent rainbow appeared that spanned the entire valley, and Kamalo knew that the Shark God Kuahuhu had arrived.

Suddenly the winds picked up until they became a howling gale. Black clouds rolled in, flashing with lightning and unleashing torrents of rain. The trees bent nearly in two with the force of the storm. It was a most terrible and chaotic explosion of natural fury. The most devastating storm the land had ever seen. The rain flooded down the mountain, destroying everything and sweeping objects from before its path. Kupa's Heiau and house were torn apart into small fragments of wood and palm frond, and he himself was swept into the ocean along with his entire family and all his followers.

Included in those who were swept into the sea was Kamalo's young and most exquisitely beautiful daughter, Lanilani. There the Shark God Kauhuhu's people waited in the bay, hundreds of black and gray shadows darting through the seething waters in anticipation of the feast to come. The water beneath the surface teemed with ravenous sharks that fed on Kupa and the villagers until the harbor turned as red as blood itself. Only beautiful Lanilani was spared by Kauhuhu, who changed her into a gray Tiger Shark and took her to be one of his mates under the deep blue ocean depths that lay at the foot of Molokai's northern sea cliffs. Thereafter, due to the shocking slaughter of the High Chieftain and all of his relatives, the harbor was called *Aikanaka*, or "man-eater."

Even as Kapu was killed, the storm raged on, destroying the surrounding area, yet turning from the Kapu staff and leaving everything inside of Kamalo's sacred fence untouched.

Thus, Kamalo and his people were spared the mad wrath of Kauhuhu's feeding frenzy. Of Lanilani, it is said that to this day she watches over the people of Kamalo as their *Manoakua* (protective shark spirit).

Today, whenever the great Hula Pahu (hula drums) are beat during celebrations and festivals on Molokai, it is said that she surfaces in the Kamalo Bay to secretly listen to the magic of those powerful, ancient vibrations, remembering her former human life.

It is also said that when great clouds gather in the high mountains on Molokai, and a rainbow spans from the Halawa Valley to the shores of Kamalo, one must keep a careful watch for the sudden storms, reminders of Kauhuhu's wrath that sweeps down the valley to the Bay, from high up in the clouds above the volcanic slopes.

Thus it is spoken.

DOWN IN THE VALLEY (Chapter 1)

There's only one thing worse than being a teacher's kid: being the son of a preacher. If having an elementary school teacher for a mother can create some serious problems for a boy among his friends, I ought to thank my lucky stars (wherever they are in this universe) that I wasn't the son of a Congregational minister named *Pastor Pueschal.* But let me explain.

Despite the awkward German surname and his legacy of being the progeny of moral rectitude's chief proponent in our small California agricultural town, the pastor's son (Kris) otherwise had it all going for him. He was everything I wasn't. Being a descendant of Swedish Congregationalists, Kris was blonde and had that chiseled Nordic look without the stereotyped goofiness that was often ascribed as being a Scandinavian immigrant characteristic. To his further credit, it didn't take Kris long to completely throw over his family's taint of churchy goody-goodness. He was soon inducted into the ranks of the most popular bad-boy clique at Washington Elementary School.

I, on the other hand, was a future *'orfink'* (though I didn't know it at the time, of course) who had a hard time cultivating friends. Thinking back on things, I guess that's partly because I never really knew my father very well. When you lose your dad early in life like that, you tend to be a bit insecure and unsure of yourself. Dad died (at the age of 72) when I was only 4, leaving me with no brothers and sisters, and my mother a widow who suddenly had to support both of us.

My father, who had been a drummer boy in the Spanish American War, had met my mother rather late in his life (after a first marriage failed) when a mutual friend had introduced them, back in the San Francisco area of the mid-

30s. My mother, a college graduate and recently credentialed grammar school teacher from Idaho, had taken to dad immediately. He was a likeable Irishman, originally from Trenton, New Jersey, who had risen up through the ranks to eventually become a Major in the Army. Austere and possessed of a naturally commanding air of authority, dad continued his military career in the California State National Guard while simultaneously working for the San Francisco Catholic Diocese as their parochial schools' athletics program director.

The youngest of 10 other, older siblings, Pop's sole personal skeleton in the closet was that he had never gone beyond the 8th grade in school; my mother frequently remarked that had he gotten a high school education, he would have reached 'flag rank' (Brigadier General), at least.

Although mom and dad had been together since 1936, I didn't become more than a gleam in dad's eye until almost 9 months had passed after VJ Day in 1945. Ma told me later that uncertainty over the outcome of the war put family planning on temporary hold for the duration. That gives me the dubious distinction of being on the leading edge of the so-called 'Baby Boom' generation (the *Depends*, *Geritol,* and *AARP* Generation?).

We lived on Divisidero Street in the city's Marina District, on the second floor of an apartment building situated directly over an Italian-American family named the DiMaggios. They had a son who had shown great promise as a baseball player and when I was 3 years old, Joe presented us with a signed baseball on which all of his Yankees team mates had signed their names. I was later told (although I don't remember it directly) that when I was playing on the small little beach at the foot of the Marina one day (aged 4), I suddenly lobbed that ball off the dock and out into the bay. I suppose you might view that as some sort of omen. Perhaps I had later career potential as a pitcher I wasn't then aware of. Or perhaps it was an indication of how impoverished my appreciation for the value of money would be in my later adult life. Either way you interpret it, that incredibly valuable regulation hardball signed by Joe DiMaggio and his fellow Yankee teammates plopped nicely into the bay's salty waters and *blub-blubbed* quickly out of sight.

When dad died unexpectedly in 1950, Ma was faced with the need to leave her part-time job as an Emporium sales clerk and go back to full-time employment as a teacher. Being a smart, college educated woman, she quickly determined that the best place to find a teaching job in California would be in the state's lower Central Valley, with its many thousands of *proto-Steinbeck* field laborers. Therefore, shortly after dad's funeral, we left the San Francisco marina, packing everything up in dad's shiny 1937 Oldsmobile, and headed off into the agricultural interior of the state. I don't remember much about that relocation at all, except that one day we stopped in a small San Joaquin County town named Reedley (just east of Fresno) and shortly thereafter moved into some convenient veteran's housing units that were situated behind the town's high school tennis courts.

It was not an easy transition for my mother, I am sure, going from being the well looked-after wife of a dignified and well respected military field grade officer to being an impoverished and poorly paid school teacher, trying to both earn a living and support a small child. Ma persevered, however, and it was a fortunate coincidence that there were a few other military widows with small children living in that same complex to help ease the process.

The Reedley Elementary School District therefore soon had a new 5th grade teacher named Mary and for the next several years we managed to settle in to the small community of 3000 without too much difficulty. Since dad had been Catholic, Ma first attended the local Catholic Church, but after a bit she found the local Anglican Church a bit more to her preference. Something about not liking all that graphic imagery of bloodied bodies of Christ hanging off the crucifix and hemorrhaging sacred hearts bound up in thorny puncture vines. She also didn't like the idea of having to pray to Jesus through the Virgin Mary, when what she really wanted most was a direct (non-party) line to God.

We spent a few more years in Reedley, known to the rest of the county then as the *'Raisin Capitol of the World'* (at least that's what its city council members thought). Finally, a position opened up that offered a far better salary in a little dusty podunk of a town just north of Bakersfield, named Wasco (an Indian name, I seem to recall). When this occurred, I had just started establishing a comfortable cluster of little friends in Reedley. I had even managed to find a best buddy in Peter Peterson, who was the son of the local Methodist church's pastor. We soon became pretty tight friends, having similarly creative senses of imagination, and were quite a bit brighter than all the other local kids, seemingly. At the time, it didn't bother me at all that I seemed to prefer hanging with preachers' brats.

Pete was a rather thin, elfin like kid, with permanently arched eyebrows that seemed to be analyzing everything constantly. He also had absolutely no sense of style when it came to clothes and even in those days when 'style' was an almost unknown concept below high school level, Pete was a pretty dorky dresser (I suppose I was no better, for that matter). He had a weird way of sort of walking on the balls of his feet when he moved that looked pretty strange to me, but for unknown reasons my mother was impressed by that strange gait he affected and asked me why I couldn't walk as *smartly* myself (*WTF!?* I *never* understood the logic behind that critical remark and it bothers me to this day). I recall that Pete always wore long sleeved shirts that were hand-me-downs from his older brother Wayne, and never wore them with the collar button open or the sleeves rolled up (as I did). Pete also had brown hair and disturbingly green eyes that made his analytical gaze seem even more penetrating.

While the other kids were out playing baseball and basketball, Pete and I would swipe large cardboard refrigerator cartons from the local appliance store refuse pile and construct castles, submarines, airplanes, and tanks from them to play in. They were quite complicated affairs, with wings, turrets, portholes, and torpedo tubes, and were pretty sophisticated for cardboard weapons of warfare.

Unfortunately, soggy cardboard doesn't hold up well to the rigors of mock combat when it rains and every Spring these elaborate battlements and war vessels would slowly sag into sodden lumps of shapeless brown cellulose fiber, leaving us with the need for a supply of fresh appliance cartons to construct our war toys.

We had a million uses for cardboard, I remember, and one particularly brilliant idea was to make body armor patterned after that used by the ancient Greeks. I think this flash of genius occurred after a movie about the Trojan War had played at the local theatre, but whatever the source of the inspiration, we were soon both decked out in regulation Trojan armor (complete with cardboard helmet plumes and weapons) and ready to take on the Greeks at the least provocation. I remember having had some trouble trying to puzzle out exactly why the Greeks and Trojans wore skirts instead of pants, but peter's father, Pastor Peterson, reassured us that this was merely the regional custom of the ancients, who like the Highland Scots, preferred a bit of fresh circulation down below to the heated constraints of long pants.

Curiously, my buddy Peter came ready equipped with a friend named Jimmy Tomlinson. Whereas Pete was the son of well-educated parents (Peter's father was a graduate of some eastern University and his mother was also a college grad), Pete's friend Jimmy was the product of a hard-scrabble dust-bowl family that had immigrated to California from Oklahoma. Once in the state, his alcoholic father promptly died of cirrhosis, leaving his care to a mother who shortly also passed along. This left Jimmy temporarily an *'orfink'* until he was rescued from that awful limbo by a 'grandmother' who may or may not have been actually related.

Jimmy's granny, who was short, squat, a bit ugly and possessed of snaggled front teeth, was employed as the Methodist Church's janitor. I suppose Pete's family had given her the job (and use of a small one-room shack located right next to the church) out of a sense of Christian charity, but whatever the reason, Jimmy at least had a home and a guardian to look after him.

Jimmy's rough times showed up clearly in his face, where his family difficulties resulted in a permanent look of slight distrust of any and all he encountered. The skeptical affect contrasted rather badly with his babyish good looks and curly brown hair, which had a way of making the skepticism appear to be an imagined artifact in the eyes of the viewer. I remember Jimmy as being quite an earnest kid who always suspected he was being treated less well than other kids, due to his near-orfink status (and he usually was).

Although Pete and Jimmy were friends, their friendship was frequently disrupted by disagreements between his granny and the Pastor's wife. Peter's mother seemed to have been one of those somewhat haughty blue-nose women who think they could have done better with their lives by marrying slightly higher up in the social spectrum, and consequently work out their resulting disgruntlements on those who work domestically for them. Jimmy's granny, not without some irony, was named "Mrs. Bishop", and she was frequently the recipient of Mrs. Peterson's regular storms of irrational discontent. This in turn made Jimmy's life unbearable at times and he was probably the most persistently unhappy kid I knew at that time in my early life.

I well recall days when our refrigerator box submarine crew demanded the help of an extra rating on board, only to find that Jimmy was not *'welcome'* right now, due to the ongoing warfare between Mrs. Bishop and Peter's mother. You can imagine the fallout from all that needless angst on us kids, who had no clue at all as to what all the *hoo-hah* was about. All we knew was that we needed a deck gunner in the worst way and Petty Officer First Class Jimmy was assigned to temporary quarters duty by Mrs. Bishop's Shore Patrol.

Ma was worried about my not having a father for a role model, having been a firm believer in Dr. Benjamin Spock's then popular pediatric manifesto for raising children, so she launched me into the local Reedley Boy Scout troop. That was a very good thing for me, as it turned out, since I didn't have a dad to take me out camping and at the troop meetings I got to vicariously 'share' some of the other dads. It was probably one of the best decisions Ma ever made with regard for my welfare, as I see things now. Our troop met in Reedley's barn-like old Veterans Memorial Hall. Under its eves someone had strung up a couple of dozen old World War One German soldier 'coal-scuttle' bring-back helmets as suspended flower pots. It was a nice touch, planting red poppies in them, now that I look back on it.

I remember that out in front of that hall was parked a vintage 155 mm artillery cannon, permanently spiked so that no slightly inebriated local patriot could use it to celebrate New Year's Eve. The thing was absolutely huge (from my vantage as a little tyke) and the tires alone stood taller than my head. Many years of repeated paint jobs with olive-drab had caused great cracks to form on its long barrel, from its receiver all the way to the end of its plugged end. The Reedley vets apparently didn't want anyone to forget the sacrifices they had made in the World Wars and that huge cannon certainly caught everyone's eye to remind them, as they passed by their way to the Reedley post office. Of course, back then the Second World War was still very fresh in everyone's recollections and there was scarcely any anti-war sentiment to be found anywhere. Britain's 'Uncle Bertie' Russell was still regarded as some sort of anarchistic weirdo kook, rather than the patron saint of the anti-Vietnam protests he would later become.

As the 50s began, I started getting thoroughly immersed in my Boy Scout work, but for reasons that remain unknown to me, Peter was not similarly interested. As for Jimmy, he was so poor that he couldn't even afford the basic Scout initiation fees, let alone buy all the Scout uniforms and camping paraphernalia scouting required. Pete and I remained close friends (we are still close today), but sad little Jimmy somehow faded from our circle of *confreres* until one day he just seemed to vanish spontaneously. I never did find out what had happened to Jimmy, but it may be that some other long-lost relative finally took him after his granny passed away, a few years later. Or it may be that he finally reverted to *orfinkhood* once and for all. I'll never know, but I still reflect back on those days and wonder what sort of life fate had in store for him.

At any rate, the Boy Scouts were a positive association for me as a kid. I enthusiastically accepted the Scout way of life and Ma was happy that I was at least getting substantial training in being a good, upstanding little citizen, despite our modest (and fatherless) circumstances. It was hard earning a living and being both a mother and father to boot, so the Scouts really came along at the right time for both of us. Rising through the ranks was fairly easy for me as I quickly grasped woodcraft, merit badge skills, and the usual camp craft knowledge (especially the important knowledge of making a campfire by rubbing two Girl Scouts together...).

I started to take an appreciable interest in what we now call 'Native American' culture, since the Boy Scouts were big on Indian woodcraft and survival skills. The idea of running around in a loin cloth like a savage was also peculiarly appealing, for some reason (so was the war paint), but the summers were pretty hot in the lower Central Valley, so it seemed quite natural to me. I remember the white American's stereotyped vision of the typical Indian of that time as being pretty bare-ass *nekked*, anyway, and it wasn't until much later that I learned the Indians actually wore some pretty hefty layers of clothing (Buffalo robes, et al) during the winter months, while wintering out on the snowy Great Plains.

Peter's father, Pastor *Orville* Peterson, was a constrained, educated, and well filled-out fellow with a barely detectable streak of sanctimonious pomposity. He had been a chaplain in the Navy during the war and I recall digging around in Pete's attic one time and finding Orville's old shipboard battle helmet and black rubber Mk. IV gasmask in one of the boxes. Pete and I wanted to use them on our cardboard submarine to repel any possibility of another sneaky Japanese attack, but for some reason Pete's father had a strong attachment to those old war relics and quickly confiscated them. That was my very first encounter with a gasmask, an iconic symbol of the form of warfare that would much later (36 years later, in fact) take a substantial place in my adult concerns, as a chemical warfare defense consultant in the Middle East. Our antipathy to the Japanese foe of WWII notwithstanding, the Reedley Japanese-American Community regularly held festivals and bazaars in Pastor Peterson's Methodist Church social hall (that's where I first learned to love sushi, although at first it seemed rather odd to make edible stuff out of seaweed).

Mr. Peterson was not an outdoorsy type by *any* mean stretch of the term. I am not sure what his avocational interests were, actually, except that they didn't focus on camping, hunting, or fishing. His wife, Hyacinth, was also not much of a physically active person, preferring to play the piano, sing, and engage in parish social events. Pete's bigger brother, Wayne (who was a big, if somewhat smart, lummox), and his older sister Gaye, were fairly active outdoors types, by contrast. Peter, on the other hand, didn't seem to take much interest in the Scouts, so we grew a bit further apart for that reason, while still remaining the best of friends in other shared interests (like science fiction).

My own involvement with the Scouts took me to the usual camporees and jamborees, field trips, hikes, nature studies, and all the usual range of active Boy Scout activities. The monthly scout magazine, *Boy's Life,* came to my mailbox regularly, with the same punctuality as religious bulletins from the local church, and I would have to guess that this early association with the Boy Scouts (in combination with the lack of a fatherly presence) resulted in a distinctive 'Boy Scout' quality I have today, as an adult. Little did I realize that the Boy Scout spin on social reality I enthusiastically absorbed was only about 50 years out of date and evolving at the speed of an overmedicated banana slug. Think of it, looking back on this, as sort of like studying ornithology in order to understand rocket science and astrophysics. The result was that I grew up as straight as a choir boy (unmolested, that is), as ashamed as I am to admit the fact that I was never at any time a bad little boy like all my peers.

Speaking of choir boys, that's exactly what I was in the real sense. Not only was I hauled off regularly to Sunday church services, I was also pressed into service as what they call an 'alter-boy' [Note: NOT *'altered boy'*] for the Anglican Sunday services. In the Anglican (read Episcopalian) 'high church' service that held sway back in the early 50s Episcopalian Church, the celebratory rituals were not always easily distinguished from those of the Roman Catholic Church. The principal visual difference between the two faiths was that the Anglican service was read in plain old English, whereas in the RC service, Latin was still used. Otherwise the vestments, cassocks, mantles, surpluses, rituals and so forth were pretty much on par with the old and traditional RC priestly accoutrements.

As an alter-boy (sort of a pre-pubescent male version of the pagan *Vestal Virgins*, I guess—disturbing thought, actually!), we had the task of lighting the candles before the service, carrying the cross during processionals and recessionals, waiting on the priest during the offering of the communion, and generally fussing around the alter during the reading of the epistles and such. It always struck me as a bit odd, observing all the ceremonial *falderal* at close hand while trying to act appropriately solemn and contrite throughout.

Somehow or other, throughout a period of several years, I gained a growing feeling that all the religious mumbo-jumbo was just a bunch of superstitious malarkey. I just couldn't connect personally with the idea of there being some sort of great invisible higher presence out there that *personally* cared a fig about us human beings. Despite all the Sunday School lessons, despite undergoing all of the substantial socialisation that ends up making good little god-fearing Christians out of ignorant and immature little male savages, the end result was that I early-on made a decision that life as a Christian simply wasn't a viable option for me. In fact, the more I learned about the world we live in at school (and the vast universe it exists within), the less possible such a highly projective human *faith* in divine deities seemed.

My mother, who probably sorely needed a substantial spiritual shoulder to lean on, maintained an absolutely unshakable faith in her Christian God that would remain strong and (to my personal distaste) doggedly resolute until the roof of an Idaho gold mine collapsed upon her somewhat later (in the course of some geological exploring she was doing). For my money, however, Jesus, God, and the Christian Trinity were about as substantial, according to my perceptions of reality, as the boogeyman, the tooth fairy, leprechauns, Santa Claus, and honest egalitarianism in politicians.

Fortunately for the sake of my subsequent lifelong career as an unbelieving pagan, events conspired to remove me from my status as an alter-boy in the Reedley Episcopal Church forever, when that teaching position alluded to earlier opened up a bit further down the Central Valley. My regrets were few and included mostly having to leave behind a hot little number named Candace Russell in Reedley, whom I had run into at church choir practice. Aside from that, my fairly profitable weekly lawn mowing enterprise, and the need to temporarily part company from my good friend Pete, I was not greatly remiss over departing the *Raisin Capitol of the World,* as we once again migrated to an entirely new communal aggregation of post 'Dust Bowl' *Okie* and *Arkie* expatriates.

Since Ma also substituted occasionally as a teacher in some of the smaller communities outlying (Orange Cove, Lemon Cove, Dinuba, Parlier, and Sanger), I'll never know what sort of impact losing the one link to true literacy she constituted had on their drab little cotton-picking lives, but I secretly suspect that Ma was no sadder than I to leave them all in our dust as we headed south towards a whole new bastion of rural small-mindedness and provincialism named *Wasco*, just off Highway 99 and north of Bakersfield.

FAREWELL TO WATSONVILLE (The Last Supper)

It was, of course, a sort of *'Last Supper'*, except without Christ, or the 12 disciples, or even an unfairly maligned Judas skulking in the shadows. *Imura's Japanese Restaurant* was deserted, the only such eatery in Watsonville that served Asian food. In its window, the soft pink blur of a neon sign spelled out the *Imura's* in luminescent *curlicues*, minus an 'i' at the end. Inside, all the simple tables sat about in orderly, tidy rows of shadowed disuse, as if in anticipation of ravenously hungry hordes of hard-core soba noodle fans that had mysteriously failed to materialize. The hushed emptiness was perfect and palpable.

It was a fitting 'lonely guy' scenario to walk into, as Wingnut knew it would be. Silently, Wingnut congratulated himself on having picked the perfect *'Noe'* place to celebrate his personal, lonely farewell dinner ritual on this brilliantly moon-lit Spring evening.

The lone waitress, wife of the owner, greeted him with hot tea and a tentative smile that expressed undisguised puzzlement as to why this solitary *Hakujin* had walked in through the door to interrupt an otherwise completely quiet and uneventful evening: Watsonville was unused to crowds and loud groups on Tuesday evenings and sometimes even a solitary person was a *crowd*, to her manner of thought. Mrs. Imura was *Nisei*, as was her husband who bore an astounding resemblance to the Japanese-American actor *Mako*, plus 20 years.

Wingnut reached into his windbreaker and brought out his stained, bleached-out old *hachi*—the same pair that had, up until the occasion of *Ono the Honda's* adoption by another owner, ridden around sticking out of Ono's battered old dashboard ashtray. Mrs. Imura noted the well-used chopsticks Wingnut had placed on the table, partly hidden by the menu. With one raised eyebrow, she silently acknowledged their presence. Wingnut simply twisted his lips into that sad smile of his and nodded that, yes, he would use his own pair instead of the single-use disposable pair provided.

Mr. Imura, out in the kitchen, gazed abstractly at their sole customer. The dinner would be Chicken Terriyaki, he thought. Mr. Imura would have been willing to make book on *that.* Most Hakujin ordered Terriyaki in Japanese restaurants, he had noted, with as much certainty as they tended to order Lemon Chicken in the Chinese restaurants. It was a fact that long years of observation had verified.

Since the Chicken Terriyaki was already served up and warming under a heat lamp, it was soon sitting on the table in front of Wingnut. Wingnut always ate in the fastidious Okinawan manner, each course separate from the next and rice last. Mrs. Imura noted this from the small kitchen window, which commanded a hidden but panoramic view of the main dining room, and wondered to herself where he had picked up that habit...eating his rice *last* like one *Japonee.*

In the back-ground a rustic Japanese samisen & koto orchestra made a half-hearted effort to wheeze its way over and around two American songs: the theme from the motion picture *'Love Story'* and that from *'Gone with the Wind.'* Wingnut allowed himself another slight smile, thinking how ironically appropriate these two dreadful selections were as he munched thoughtfully on the noisy pickled cabbage. He redoubled his effort to evoke that sense of profound nostalgia which was always so fulfilling for him at such moments of deliberately self-engineered melancholia.

Somehow, despite his best efforts to capture that delicate mood of sorrowful dudgeon, the melancholia managed to elude him the same way the pickles were managing to elude the unsteady grasp of his chopsticks. Reflecting on that fact, he continued to pluck at the stringy pickled cabbage, hopefully.

Elsewhere, on a small visual soundstage set in his imagination, the door to Imura's Japanese Restaurant was opening to admit a muted but gradually increasing backdrop of animated female conversation.

Reflexively, Wingnut turned to see who the voices belonged to. In the small window, Mrs. Imura's face framed itself briefly in the opening. A young woman walked in.

It was not Mitsuko. Of course. It *could* never be Mitsuko...*would* never be Mitsuko, he corrected himself. *Not* Mitsuko.

But it *was* a young Sansei woman. She was somewhat flushed as she finished what she had been saying, coming through the doorway. Her gaze, which had been directed over her shoulder and thereby hiding her face, suddenly reversed itself as she darted a quick glance around the room. The empty room that Wingnut sat in by himself, was devoid of others, with no one but himself for company. The young woman looked about briefly with some uncertainty.

It is difficult to inhale an average size piece of Chicken Teriyaki whole, although many likely have unwillingly tried, throughout history. Perhaps the chicken morsel was smart enough to realise that its passage down the main bronchi was physiologically inconvenient, for when Wingnut suddenly gagged and turned blue for the merest second, the recalcitrant bit of fowl smartly did a 180° course change and sailed across the floor with the inertia of a Kabuki actor lunging at a foe to land almost *exactly* at her feet.

The young woman in the doorway, who had stopped dead in her tracks during this whole maneuver, stared at Wingnut. Perhaps it was the bluish tinge of his face that caught her attention, for you certainly don't see many blue Hakujin. Wingnut for his part, had stopped choking and was staring vacantly back at her, for it had been her sudden appearance that had prompted the chicken fragment to explode out of his mouth with rocket-like gusto.

Both stared at the other for a full heartbeat. It *wasn't* Mitsu, but it *could* have been Mitsu's *sister*. She had the animated look of a stone etched into her expression.

The young woman, who was Mrs. Imura's daughter, had turned then, and, after muttering a few brief words to her mother, walked back out the door she had come in. Wingnut watched her exit with a blank store. She did not return. Nor did Wingnut's choking sensation.

Twilight on Steroids

Despite the dysfunctional moodiness at Imura's, it was one of those rare, but beautiful and charmingly moody nights in which the whole moon-lit world seems to be holding its breath. There was not the merest hint of a gust outside the small beach cottage, nor the slightest suggestion of a breeze. The clear and coldly luminous moon poured its dispassionate grayish beams down upon the quiet coastal landscape with the detached but demented obsessiveness of a dairy farmer who had gone quietly insane and decided to methodically pour his cows' milk back into them...through their ears.

Outlined by the pale lunar illumination that quickly pushed twilight off the horizon, it was a contemplative, evocative moonscape that cast its spell upon the ocean's sandy doorstep. Further below on the beach, the breakers churned and muttered in low voices, gossiping about the myriad mysteries of Monterey Bay's shallows and speculating upon the submarine depths of the deep submarine canyon abyss that precipitously yawned, just offshore.

Wingnut walked slowly from the house down to the rickety old platform that perched precariously upon the verge of the precipice; the steep plunge below it pitched sharply down the sandy rise to the vast blackness of the beach, at the bottom. He was still drinking in the mood of quiet melancholy, savoring the bittersweet thrill of the semi-desolate, semi-cozy ambience and absorbing it as deeply as possible. His gaze swept the unusually docile breakers that stretched out before him. A seething mass of shadowed fluidity, they rolled ashore in muted ranks before disappearing into the fogbank that lived permanently in that littoral place. It was too peaceful, too gentle, too.... *'pacific',* he thought poetically. And yet it was perfect for the sort of semi-masochistic sense of nostalgic yearning which he wanted so desperately to feel, to conjure in himself, to isolate and minutely examine in the convolutions of his emotional wallowing.

Far out to sea, above the benign and noncommittal fogbank, the lights of a swiftly coursing jetliner marked out the streak of a 0.85 *Mach* winged aluminum projectile, as it voraciously consumed the miles stretching along the LA-to-SFO domestic flight corridor. Its multiple 200,000-watt strobe lights gave it the strange appearance of being another set of competing stars in Orion's girdle; except that this part of the girdle was falling, hurtling off, abandoning its stellar cross-dressing mimicry in hot sexual pursuit of the GCA beacon at San Francisco TCA.

The small tendrils of fog that were visible in the immediate area formed a soft halo around the lucid opacity of the moon as they slowly, silently and not without a little mystery, wafted seaward from the shore. There was a gentle off-shore breeze up higher, although here below the draught was no more turbulent than the eye of a typhoon...or the 'third eye' of an existential hurricane.

Wingnut swept the horizon with his gaze, huddling down a bit more into the warmth of the old windbreaker. On its back were the words *'Santa Cruz Senile'*, a cynical reference to the local paper, in flocked white fuzz that glowed strangely in the moonlight. All was quiet on the western front of the Monterey *deep*.

Behind and below him, on all sides, stretched darkened acres of immature Brussels Sprouts. Framing the edge of the sky, pines and cypresses rose like silent sentinels. Nothing was moving except the lights of the airliner slashing through the night, far off and 30,000 feet above. It was hushed. Everywhere it was perfectly silent.

Even the waves were whispering for some strange reason. Wingnut suddenly felt a slight rustle of movement within himself, a hint of the feeling he had been so carefully searching his emotional repertoire for. It started with a slight tug on his heart. An odd pair of extra-systolic beats which punctuated the moment, much as the upside-down exclamation mark of a sentence in Spanish precedes the remark that it brackets. Then the flood gates of a million virtual hellish waters of darkness opened and swept through him with the fury of a monsoon. This new, emotional abyss yawned bottomlessly and spewed forth raw emotion from its turgid depths. Then, *finally*, the toilet of his soul noiselessly *flushed*!

Oh God! He *was* lonely. He was so lonely he began to regret having paradoxically *wished for* the feeling of loneliness. He was suddenly so lonely he felt he no longer knew or cared about the difference between life and death, or whether either even mattered at all. He swam in the wonderful agony in a frusty, perverse way, but the unforeseen extent of the hurtfulness contained within it gnawed sorely at his guts (or perhaps it was the Chicken Teriyaki and *Wasabe*...?).

Of course, in the pall of this immense tidal wave of carefully nurtured solitude such thoughts counted for absolutely nothing. They simply did not exist. What is the character of a thought when no brain existed to consider it? What *did* exist was the crushing, but gratifyingly painful misery of this Frankensteinian parody of despair that he had so deliberately set out to conjure forth and coax out of himself. Substantially co-dependent, of course, was the conducive moodiness of the clear, neutral and disturbingly appealing moon-lit solitude.

He shivered as he let his body soak up every last bit of the wonderful angst of the splendidly cathartic emotional anguish. Sweeping the horizon, his eyes caught another spectral stratospheric intruder blazing through the cold and hostile fringes of space, lights flashing and engines throttled back to cruising detents.

Another cargo of impatient souls, bound in from nowhere, he reflected, *headed out for nowhere.* In a hellish hurry to ignore the cruelly implacable reality of the present *moment*...*second*...*nanosecond,* all biological life continued to ignore the requisites of Universal emptiness. The furiously impatient pursuit of the *elsewhen* and *otherwhy,* that they all hoped existed at their destination, continued unabated.

And then, quite suddenly, Wingnut felt the profound sense of loneliness lift as quickly as it had settled in. Mildly disappointed, he retraced his steps up the hillside path back to the house. Bathed in moonlight as it was, it had all the visual appeal of a shadowed mausoleum in some dead and forgotten burial ground. Walking up the dirt driveway, he opened the rear door of the crypt and entered.

Unknown to Wingnut, who thought he was completely and utterly alone, the *fog* had followed him. Dogging his foot-steps like the most tiny and persistent little shadow of a hungry mouse, it crossed the verge unseen and sat there, nibbling noiselessly upon a fragment of pale moonbeam cheese...

Kalikiano Kalei

A WHITE RAVEN

May 3rd (Tuesday)

It's hot, muggy, and slightly overcast. The sea is choppy and the wind arrives and departs with small, unenthusiastic gasps. I'm reduced to my last 'Diet Coke with Lime', as I forlornly scan the blazingly hot horizon for a friendly sail. If they don't find us before tomorrow on this lonely, desolate spit of land, we're goners. Oops. *Wrong journal, wrong scenario* (takes another slug of Diet Coke, notes ripe smegmatic aroma rising from unwashed shorts, and finds the *OTHER* journal to continue narrative in...).

Left 90-year-old old Romero to enjoy the cool breezes that drift through the covered walkway that separates Blanca's home from the semi-detached room I stay in and took the car out to the east end of the island this afternoon. Had the strangest experience out there. Having told Gunter I missed seeing the old Ilio'ilio Pae Heiau at about Mile Marker 15.5, I acted on his advice that there was another old and much more easily found ancient stone heiau (a fish heiau, dedicated to a minor god, Kulua) out on the east end, near Mile Marker 20 (close by Murphy's Beach).

Once there, it was as he said, relatively simple to find the old site, which lies on the makai side of the road between the roadway and the shore. There seems to have been an old hut built on the spot at some point in the recent past, covered in palm fronds after the ancient manner, and it had a few conventional picnic benches outside to indicate people may use it for occasional gatherings. Although it is simple to locate, it can't be seen from the road either, so one must park and get out, lock the car (why bother? Old mainland habit, I guess), and hike up a couple hundred yards to where it perches unseen just over the downward side of a protruding spit of hillside that overlooks a beautiful greenish-blue lagoon.

When I finally found it, it was late in the afternoon, but there was a nice trade blowing to cool things off and chase away some of the afternoon's mugginess. I was sitting there on one of the benches, enjoying the freshness of the breeze and gazing at the stones that must have formed the base of the old heiau when I noticed a brief movement behind me, just out of the corner of my eye. The sun was now behind the hillside and long shadows were being cast by the trees; thinking it had been a bird, I paid no more attention. A few moments later, I again saw some movement from the same corner of my eye, so this time I swiveled around on the bench in time to catch just the faintest glimpse of a slender woman who was gone behind some trees before I could see much of her. There was no mistaking her gender, since she had had long dark hair with some curious gray in it and seemed to be wearing a white and green fabric skirt, wrapped around her hips in the style of a Tahitian *pāreu*. I didn't actually see her face then, which had been turned away from me, but she had a dark complexion--clearly a local. There is a native Hawaiian settlement close by.

The sun was getting lower yet, so I thought about getting back, but suddenly this same woman appeared behind me on the other side of the hut. This time I saw her face distinctly and she appeared to be young, about 20 or so, but there was that strange silver-gray highlight scattered about in her dark hair. I said hello, but she simply smiled--the flash of her teeth suddenly catching a few odd rays of the departing sun that still skipped through the trees--and then turned around to disappear again into the trees. Her face was quite pretty in an austere sort of way and she had a look that was at the same time maidenly, but also strangely mature. When she had smiled, it struck me as odd that her eyes seemed to glow for the briefest instant...or was it my imagination and the odd angle of the departing sun? She had no flower on either side of her hair, but there was a green leafy bracelet around her left wrist. As a normally equipped red-blooded male whose eyes are instinctively drawn to certain gender characteristics, I couldn't help but notice that she wore what looked like a purple bikini top. Her hair glistened as if she had been swimming. She was pretty and she was nicely 'built'. Then she was gone and that's the extent of my recollections.

Odd, but *oh well*... I've never been a chick-magnet by any conceivable stretch of the imagination, so I mentally shrugged and felt as I always do at such a time...a bit lonely and somehow once again cheated out of a simple Vladimir Nabokov moment with a lovely young woman. A little wave of chagrin swept over me; always the same thing...a repeating theme of my life. I am not, sad to say, a Brad Pitt. Not even his younger and congenitally disfigured brother.

I stayed out there a bit longer, vaguely hoping that whoever that had been would return and stick around for a few minutes. There certainly had not been any guy with her. She did not return, however, and so after a few last looks about I headed back to the car in the dimming light. Looking back, I didn't see anyone, but then what had I been expecting, anyway? A lovely mythical Lorelei right here on this single person's null zone of an island? The trades were just starting to pick up when I finally left.

The drive back to *K'kai* (Kaunakakai) was uneventful and it finally occurred to me that I had not had a chance to look over the old heiau site, so preoccupied had I been with the appearance of this girl (woman?). Funny how she had been so graceful, making no noise at all on the stones or through the trees. I thought I felt a little pang of most ungentlemanly lust rise up in me.

After I returned from the drive, it was already getting quite dark, but I looped by the Kaunakakai wharf and managed to find Gunter sitting on his boat, the *'Little Toot Too'*, opposite the side that lists and cooking on a small hibachi on its deck. I pulled a few of the *Papeete* beers from the back floorboard of the rental car, where they had managed to get very warm, and we shared a brew. The boat was rocking a bit lop-sided in the water...like a drunken sailor, I thought, to my mild amusement.

"Well," Gunter said in his thick North German accent, *"So soon back. Did you find the heiau?"*

When I told him I had, I also mentioned the girl I had seen, giving him most of the details and not holding back the fact that I had found her more than a bit attractive, despite her brief appearance. He was gazing out at the water boundary where the Kaunakakai reef juts out into Kailohi Channel currents.

"Oh, you saw her then, eh? Nice breasts? Purple top? Congratulations! She doesn't show herself for everyone."

I hadn't mentioned the purple swim-suit top. In answer to my puzzled look, he took a long draw on the warm beer and glanced over at me, beaming a shark-like smile.

"'She' is a local woman that everyone swears is a ghost. According to the locals, she died some 13 years ago just off that point the old heiau sits on, while diving for Ahi. Accident of some kind. Her name is Corinne Popolohua...um, Hu'elani; they tell me her family lives just north of Kawelo way. It's said she's buried there in the local cemetery. They say she only shows herself when she is not frightened by strangers who show up at the old fish heiau. I think she must like you, yes? Have you ever had a dead woman for a friend before?"

He took another draw on the beer and soberly gazed seaward in the direction of twinkling lights on Maui's north shore. He was not smiling when he had finished telling me this. Nor was he was smiling when I took my leave, a short while later, to drive back to Manila Camp.

I am, of course, going to return to the Kawelo cemetery tomorrow and see if I can find a headstone that will convince me this is only another of Gunter's frequent expressions of dark German humor, but the fact that I have been searching so eagerly for my 'white raven experience' makes me less than pleased to have this pleasant mystery laid to rest as a prank. Just for curiosity, I looked up the meaning of the name *'Hu'elani'*. The direct Hawaiian translation is *'Opening up to Heaven'. 'Popolohua' means 'Purplish blue, as in sea or clouds'*. Brrrr. We shall see what tomorrow's trip to the Kawelo cemetery brings. A strange experience! A strange experience, indeed, for someone who does not believe in ghosts...either that or Gunter's sense of humor is darker than I thought.

May 4th (Wednesday)

If I had to take one single impression home with me of Molokai, it would have to be of endlessly barking dogs and run-amok rooster noise at night. Of course, this is Manila Camp I'm in and seems not to be characteristic of other less 'urbanised' parts of Molokai. Oh, how I wish we were able to afford a place on the more remote east end, rather than a compromise on the *makai* (seaward) side of Kam 5 highway where my property is located. The good news is that I already know my left side neighbor and my right-side neighbor I come to find is the nephew of a local fellow (nephew lives on Maui at the moment). The big task that confronts me is to secure the services of someone reliable whom I can contract to finish clearing my property and then make monthly return visits to keep it cleared. I guess I'll head for the Molokai Vistors' Bureau tomorrow and see what I can find. The classified ads in the Molokai Island Times were no help. First call to what was advertised as

'BD's Vista Advantage' seemed to be some neighborhood school kid with big aspirations (lawn mowing yes, property clearing no). Second call to 'Tropical Inspirations Landscaping' turned out to be a wrong number. Hmmmm. Back to square one. Maybe tomorrow will be more promising. In this search for just the right combination of capabilities, I am reminded of something *pake* (Chinese) real estate broker Margaret Hui told me: *"All Hawaiians are congenital liars."* [Makes mental note: Not good, since I've heard many times that local Hawaiians are also indolent. I feel like a missionary must have felt, heading off into the unknown to save heathen souls for Jesus, difference being I am heading off into the unknown to find an honest, hard-working heathen to wage herbicidal warfare for me.)

Just got a return call from BD, who apparently used the phone 'trace caller number' feature on his phone to contact me, after I switched off. Turns out that BD is the father and the school-kid I talked with is his son, 'BD, Junior' (who had answered the phone and in response to my question *"Can I talk with BD?"* replied with *"I'm BD"*). At any rate, we meet tomorrow to take a look at the lot and 'Big BD' will give me a quote for the job. 'BD' is actually a fellow called Bruce; I had called his home number, hence the confusion with his small son, and will use his cell number tomorrow. Ain't life interesting? Never a dull development, it seems.

Since I never have occasion to get any pictures of myself these days, I have fallen back to a old schtick I used to resort to in KSA--taking a few expat 'self-portraits' (the modern term for this is now *'selfies'*). Now, while this may be considered an extreme expression of vanity by some, I look at it more as a sort of historical document recording changes in the old self. Besides, it's my life and I am interested in it much as an entomologist would be fascinated by a curious bug stuck to his collection board on a pin. Nothing really wrong with this, I think, since by so doing I only risk running afoul of my own disapprobations. The pictures are, on examination, fully as bad as I had feared: receding chin, barely kept in check with the Abraham Lincoln style goatee, gray hair gaining a noticeable foothold, eyes reflecting a sort of flinty uncertainty about them (note: have to remind myself to squint more often, like Clint Eastwood did; hey, it worked for him!). Other changes not so noticeable in the pictures: loss of skin elasticity all over, due to the savaging effects of the sun exposure in KSA (collagenous cellular destruction), some pre-cancerous (actinic) skin changes on the cheeks (around the edges of the eyes--not good!), and perhaps even a bit of recently added adipose (too many chocolate toffee Macadamia nuts over the past week) around the midriff.

The oval neck amulet is a small section of tiger shark skin, with a tiger shark tooth affixed to it (from Aussie friend, 'Dr. Shark' in Oz); the other item on silver chain is something Sooks brought back for me from New Zealand, which I have always very much liked (it's a good-luck charm): a beautiful piece of jade-like stone carved into what the Maori aboriginals call the 'Path of Eternity' (the stone is shaped in the form of a highly stylized Moebius loop, without start or finish, and beautifully worked by hand-very unique item, actually). The hat, of course, is one I wore during the 1991 Gulf War in KSA; it's an old friend (lots of *mana*) that I take whenever I'm out somewhere 'adventuring'.

Breakfast was again library paste (Quaker Instant Oats) with the last of the dried cranberries, coffee (no bananas left), and the usual handful of vitamin and mineral supplements. Old Romero is out in the back yard, puttering about the grounds, raking-up small leaves that have fallen from the Mango and Papaya trees. I guess this is what helps keep him going, despite his 90+ years! Tough old bird who obviously worked very hard during his younger days, perhaps on the plantation.

Note on coconut carving: I managed to carve that coconut I picked up last week. I was reminded that carving coconut shells is much easier when the outer husk is still fresh and green; once the outer husk has become hard, they are a bitch to carve without screwing things up radically, through haste or impatience. This is good therapy and I find I enjoy it, although the small degree of dexterity I used to enjoy with my hands is greatly diminished from previous years (reason I don't attempt plastic model kits anymore). Wonder of I'd be any good at trying to make a hula *pahu* from a sectioned slice of coconut trunk? Just tried to reach Robert Kamatsu, the pahu master, again. No joy. Maybe later. Only 4 days left to get this taken care of.

One thing about Molokai is the fact that fresh fish are commonly available every day. If not your own catch, someone else's. There are more highly edible species in the local waters than most can imagine. While I wouldn't want to tempt fate by doing any underwater spear-fishing (plenty of *Tigers* in local waters), it's reportedly easy enough to drop a line in the water just about anywhere on the island and easily catch your limit within an hour. I've never been much of a fisherman (even trying to learn the knack of fly-fishing under Uncle Charlie's expert tutelage in Sun Valley, while vacationing next to Hemingway's Big Wood River lodge in the late 50s/early 60s, but without much encouraging evidence of real piscatorial skill either then or now). Much later, living in Santa Cruz, I even bought a surf casting rod & reel (still have it at home, in the garage), since I recall Dad formerly used to engage in that sport, but never once caught anything with it. More proof of deficit talent in the Ichthyologic Department, I fear. Not much of a hunter/gatherer or fisherman, and definitely not much good at the ancient Neanderthal sport of clubbing women over the head and dragging them home. Impression: would have made a lousy stone-ager (also known as an easy meal for a Saber-Toothed Tiger), I'm afraid.

If I ever end up retiring over here, I would probably look forward to kayaking around the reef and fishpond areas. Maybe then stop and drop a line over the side, earlier in the AM hours before the trades pick up and make the waters a bit choppy. I haven't the extreme motivation to take up serious outrigger racing (like some of the buff men & women I mentioned I ran into, yesterday), but at least I am fairly adept at splashing innocently about in a sea-going (keeled) kayak (thanks to former youthful days spent as an expert canoer and sailing instructor).

Arrr, matey. We be castin' off soon for fearsome adventures with our rubber ducky. Avast! Yessir, the scourge of the local duck pond, that's our Crusty Cooleridge. Beat to quarters, Mr. Cuthbert! Arrrr-arrrr-arrrr! (I think that's how blood-thirsty pirates are supposed to talk, anyway). *Step lively, young cabin-boy Jamie. A man's got to do what a man's got to do, Jaimie me boy! Arrr, etc., etc.*

Email from the other Aviation Museum board members informs me that our museum's Convair F-106 *Delta Dart* has now been successfully taken apart at AMARC (Aircraft Maintenance and Regeneration Center, located at Tucson, AZ) and is in the process of being loaded up for shipment to us in Sacramento (they said that there were still 30 gallons of overlooked JP-4 left in one of its wing-tanks, surprise!). Just my blasted luck to miss out on this once-in-a-lifetime adventure, retrieving a rare surviving specimen of my favorite aircraft from its hibernation out on the desert wastes for display resurrection at the museum. The process was delayed so many times, fraught with so many setbacks and broken deadlines (due to technical difficulties and political/bureaucratic hurdles at AMARC), that by the time the plan was finally cleared for take-off, I was over here on Molokai. I'll probably arrive back in Sacramento at just about the same time it rolls in on the truck. At least I'll get to participate in helping put it back together.

Took a bit of time off to return to the Kawalo area just now, to check on that cemetery, as related yesterday. I searched the whole area over several times and found no such grave for a *Corinne Popolohu Hu'elani*, although there two other *Hu'elani* graves (both men). This is probably sufficient evidence to conclude that Gunter was having a bit of fun with me about the ghostly girl at the heiau, but he persists in maintaining a straight face when he assures me that this is in very real fact no joke! That also doesn't explain away the perplexing fact that I hadn't mentioned the purple color of the swim-suit top she was wearing! I suppose I'll never really be sure, one way or another, but I know that what I saw was no day-dream. She appeared as solid and real as anyone can be. You just can't imagine visual details like that and others aren't able to routinely read minds, either. At any rate, I guess I owe Gunter another 6-pack of *Papeete* beer for at least giving me a most unusual experience (and unforgettable) that I cannot explain away with logic, reason, or any other conventional science-based process of rational understanding! I'm greatly tempted to return to the heiau and see if I can repeat the experience.

Thinking about that lovely vision of (spectral?) beauty, I am reminded of the way the ancient Hawaiians instituted what passed for marriage in their traditional (pre-missionary) culture. As I observed earlier in my journal narrative, nothing approaching a conventional western ‘sacrament of marriage’ was carried out when a man & woman decided to mate. The only officiation of their status consisted of having them 'sleep with each other' (according to the references) in the presence of the local priests. Whether this 'sleeping together' consisted of simply falling asleep and sawing Z's next to each other under the same kapa (native paper-like fabric made from tree-bark), or whether it meant *getting it on coitally* under the approving gaze of the elders, is left to speculation. I can't personally imagine feeling comfortable enough to screw someone (no matter how beautiful or alluring) as the grandparents watched, approvingly (but on second thought, perhaps that's just my own hang-up, based on cultural socialization under western customs and practices), so I'll assume that the 'sleeping together' was actually that and not wild coital debauchery.

One of the unique characteristics of the ancient Hawaiian culture that continually had the Christian missionaries sorely vexed was the perfectly natural native custom of what they (the missionaries) called 'an extreme act of apostasy'. By this, I mean the 'incestuous' practice of brothers and sisters 'marrying' (or even fathers and daughters, and sons and mothers). Although from a western scientific (genetic) standpoint this sort of behavior can have some very untoward results in terms of recessive genes being passed along to any offspring produced by the pairing, the custom was resorted to when a woman or man was considered to be of such 'high birth' (among the high Ali'i, or Hawaiian royalty) that a suitable mate of equal status could not be found. In that event, it was considered that the mating of a man and woman of the same immediate family bloodline was preferable to the mating of social un-equals. Thus, a brother and sister could (and frequently did) screw each other without much to-do. The curious thing about this is that there appears to be little documentation on the practice that survives today, despite the fact that even by non-scientific (i.e. Christian) standards, such behavior was regarded as being extremely reprehensible by the missionaries.

I am guessing that due to the extremely 'delicate' nature of this practice, the morally conservative and easily scandalised Christian missionaries were more than a bit reticent to discuss the matter, except within the most objective and figurative (religious) context. This is in all likelihood the chief reason why there was not much information on this subject recorded by those worthies that has survived to be passed along in their otherwise fairly comprehensive chronicles of heathen life. Too bad, too, since the speculative symbolic imagery of a brother and sister enjoying each other's healthy natural sexually is an attractive one, as long as the scientific and religious proscriptions have been carefully excised and set aside (observing good aesthetic surgical technique, of course). [A note to any righteously anointed Christian readers, here, who may be reading this: Remember, folks, I'm no God-fearing Christian myself; life is boring enough without removing some of the fun that such possibilities offer. If I had an absolutely *drop-dead beautiful* sister and was marooned on an island paradise, I'd probably waste no time exploring her upthrust mountains and lush, moist valleys myself.]

Another common ancient Hawaiian cultural practice that was NOT quite so pleasant to contemplate was that of infanticide. According to many sources I have accessed, unwanted infants (there being no absolutely reliable birth control, per se, available--although some Kahuna-prescribed herbal preparations were used for this purpose) were not uncommonly killed at or shortly after birth. Apparently, if a child was born with less than perfectly normal features (and due to incestual mating customs, this was likely fairly common), that infant would be disposed of immediately. This apparently was routinely done by burying the infant alive in the sand, from what I read. That seems more than a little heartless, given the fact that even sacrificial adult victims were usually strangled first, before being offered up at the heiau. However, I am reminded that human life mattered very little in a greater, overall context to the Hawaiians since theirs was a culture in which the social needs of all came far ahead of the needs of an individual. As Americans, who have been brought up from earliest childhood to subscribe to and embrace the ascendancy of individual rights over those of the majority, such an attitude seems grossly wrong. From my own personal viewpoint, as a person who has always felt the needs of the group should properly outweigh the rights and privileges of any individual member of society (within reason, of course), the practice in reference is slightly less shocking. In the absence of an artificially formulated religious proscription against such a practice, it undoubtedly made perfect sense to the early Hawaiians to kill a baby born with congenital defects of any discernible kind. The manner they used for killing the infants is still somewhat disturbing, however.

There's not much on the record concerning how the ancient culture treated mental illness, except for a few references to various individuals who were apparently so inflicted (again, such references as exist had to be passed along via oral histories, since there was no written language with which to record incidents of any possible relevance here), and the existence of several Hawaiian words that translate to ‘sick in the head’.

It is also a fact that it was not unusual for Hawaiians (at least during the later Ali'i period, after the arrival of the kahuna priest *Pa'ao* (who incidentally was supposed to have been 'white', and thereby assumed to be 'Caucasian', curiously enough) to regard very elderly members of the family as useless and not worth taking the requisite trouble to sustain, in the event they were incapacitated or incapable of supporting themselves. While this information conflicts somewhat with oral history information passed along about pre-Ali'i family customs on Molokai, it may in fact have some bearing on changes in ancient Hawaiian society that were due to or brought about by changes in the religion that occurred after the arrival of Pa'ao in the 11th or 12th Century. At any rate, the mention is made in several places that this was the later custom.

Naturally, as a western-raised person, the practices of infanticide and geriatricide seem unfortunate and somewhat disturbing to me (*Haole kapu?*), but seen strictly within the cultural context of their own civilisation ('Primitive cultures basic rule #1', as the cultural anthropologists are always reminding us), such customs appear perfectly functional and pragmatically practical.

I can hear the solar-heating water system cycling on the roof overhead. Many small, individual solar heating systems are routinely used on Molokai to provide hot water. Seems almost every home has some sort of solar water heating array on the roof, and why not? Now if they could simply harness the wind to tap into that cheap power source (the trade winds are always blowing here), they'd have the perfect little home-based closed system. Mainline electrical power on Molokai is provided by petroleum-fuel powered generation, as might be expected. There have been a few attempts to harness wind power on the other islands, but the cost of mechanical maintenance for those early and less efficient systems were so high that they ultimately failed. I am advised that with today's available state-of-the-art technology, such wind driven power generation schemes are once more cost-effective, but there has been little development of individual (residentially appropriate) private systems done, to my knowledge; most of the research has been done in terms of larger area-wide generation systems.

My friend the bumble-bee has been absent for a day or two. He is now back at his usual habits of buzzing ponderously about the awning, just outside my window. It's a good thing I enjoy writing, as otherwise I'd be hard pressed to stay amused during my stay here. Reading & writing are two favorite pastimes, of course, but neither is very demanding physically. I'm glancing down at my waistline, something I've never paid much attention to owing to the fact that I've always been on the slender side. However, these past 28 days or so have not involved much physical activity (aside from the volcano climb already mentioned) and the cumulative effect of this lethargy and the delicious chocolate covered toffee macadamia nuts that are a particular failing of mine has been a noticeable bit of added padding around the gut. Not much, but enough to make me take notice. *Horrors!* My worst nightmare is (and always has been) being fat and out of shape. I can't wait to get back to the daily bicycle ride and a muscle toning work-out at home on the *OwFlex*. If I end up retiring over here, I'll have to devise some sort of daily exercise regime to help stave off these prospects that are so especially loathsome to me. Maybe running, but that's not good for the knees at this stage of life. Bicycling would be best, but given the traffic habits here and the routine DUI pattern that prevails among the locals, bike-riding is not without considerable risk from DUIs on the island (from what I have seen and heard).

One awareness seems to be vaguely developing within me, thanks to the reflection pause this past few weeks has afforded me. That is, perhaps life in the islands is not as perfectly suited to me as I may have earlier thought. It may well be that I need a life on the mainland in the northern part of the state, perhaps somewhere along the north coast of California, as much as the tropics. I've always enjoyed the mountains and cooler climates, so maybe what I would really like is that sort of a bi-polar climatic venue. Molokai would be wonderful, if I weren't so concerned about exercise, getting old and fat, and suffering from the sort of indolent lifestyle that characterises life in the islands. Further, my far too idealistic and enthusiastic preconceived notions about a sense of 'community' here may also have been slightly premature, given the wide divergence that seems to exist between several different groups that one finds on the island.

An additional concern is the contamination of the island's adolescents by mainland pop-culture (and American mainstream attitudes), that is already noticeable, may just be the tip of the iceberg. If this process continues to develop unchecked (and there's no reason to suspect it won't, given the immediate access of media, with its unhappy and highly exploitative commercial effects, accessed through electronic technology), Molokai won't be half as insular and/or remote from these progressively deleterious influences are I would hope it would remain.

Whatever the final impact on my perceptions after I fly back to the mainland, I have definitely rushed into my purchase of the parcel here a bit prematurely (that is, without giving this a lot of wise reflection beforehand) and I am now faced with this unavoidable and concrete reality to deal with in future as best I am able. If I am very, very lucky, the value of the land may rise significantly in the 4 years ahead, that I have left before retirement. Meanwhile, however, I have to gear down to some serious meeting of the added financial responsibility that this new drain on my income poses. Perhaps I should investigate going on a regimen of *Prozac*, to help me adjust to the unhappy realities of life that I thought were pressing in on me too much back home. Hmmm. (Strokes graying goatee absentmindedly for a second, but successfully stifles the unconscious urge to reach for another chocolate covered toffee macadamia nut).

In any comprehensive contemporary assessment of Hawaiian civilisation, from earliest origins through the latest period, one cannot but literally concur with the view that the early Christian missionaries were both a harmful element (in the broadest sense) and a helpful one, considering the radical changes that the new religion brought to the Hawaiian islanders. It seems to be equally popular to take either one or the polar opposite other of two attitudes in this matter. There are those who will opine without restraint that the missionaries had, in their earnest desire to save the heathens' souls for their Christian God, by far a positive effect. There is another equally outspoken sentiment that the Christian missionaries bore ultimate responsibility for the falloff the Hawaiian monarchy (and the resulting loss of Hawaiian autonomy).

Both seem to carry equal validity, in my consideration, since there as many positive as there were negative aspects of the early Christian missionaries' work. Among the most positive were the efforts they made to study and record the ancient culture and history, and the devising of a written language for the islanders--something that the Hawaiians lacked, prior to 1820. The worst impact they had would probably have to have been their immense efforts to suppress the ancient morality and expressions of traditional cultural interactions with nature (in their efforts to save what they perceived as primitive godless heathens by converting them to the Christian religion).

As a proudly non-Christian heathen soul myself, I can never forgive them (the Christian missionaries) for their one-sided, mindless conviction that they had an iron-bound franchise, or absolute insight on understanding of the universe, but I can acknowledge that given the mean, ruthless, degenerate, and largely amoral nature of the non-religious white people who came to the islands (traders, whalers, sailors, soldiers, and commercial businessmen), the Christian missionaries are probably most wisely regarded, retrospectively, as the better of two evils.

Robert L. Stevenson commented on the grossly exploitative nature of those non-Christian white settlers, remarking that it was *that* sort of 'white person' who made him regret being of the same ethnicity. This opinion frequently mirrors my own feeling about modern American society, although you don't have to be white to be common-minded and totally lacking in higher ethical awarenesses, certainly. God knows (ironic use of the words, of course) that no one culture, race, or creed has an exclusive lock on the baser aspects of human behavior. It's just a matter of the purest coincidence that I am white and the people responsible for Hawaii's ultimate downfall (as an ancient and proud people, possessed of a unique and distinctive culture unlike no other) were also (as anyone with intelligence would hasten to confirm).

All other things being equal (my Ivy League, button-down collar and Harris Tweed jacket wearing college political science instructor's favorite utterance), the missionaries probably did somewhat more good than harm, in the final assessment. That doesn't mean that I am willing to completely absolve them of the many harmful effects of their evangelical Protestant religious fervor (since this has been a common theme with all religions since the dawn of recorded history, each of which believes its distinctive concept of 'God' is the one and only legitimate one), but I am at least willing to allow that for all their very human failings, the Christian missionaries meant well. I suppose you could use that same sentiment to say that despite all of Adolf Hitler's heinous outrages (or Mao's, or Pol Pot's, or Saddam Hussein's, et al), he meant well. However, I think my intended meaning stands sufficiently well qualified within the supportive context of these paragraphs to allow those words to be safely used here.

No religion has ever had, nor shall ever have (in my humble opinion), any more truly sagacious insight into the deeper, ultimate mysteries of human experience than that of the average frontally lobotomized individual. For that reason, any seeking after absolute 'truths', when it comes to the Biggest Questions (e.g. *"What's it all about, Alfie?"*) is destined to wither on the vines of intelligent human inquiry. By virtue of that belief, I regard anything and everything accomplished anywhere in 'the name of god' as being nothing more than the inspired application of latent human abilities. They seem to arise solely out of the life circumstances of all biological life that are as sentient or non-sentient as logical possibilities allow for (and not from any party-line connection directly to 'God').

Against that Kevlar®-like backdrop of my own doggedly maintained personal prejudices, I am very sad to find that the ancient Hawaiians lost so much of themselves not to one group or another, but to the fact that whenever a weaker group (i.e. possessed of a lesser quality of weapons technology) meets a more powerful group (i.e. possessed of weapons technology of a higher level or quality), the weaker group is doomed to be subjugated. That is ultimately what happened to ancient Hawaii. Western man with his advanced weapons (and only slightly less coincidentally, with his religion) came along, contact was made, and the more rapacious, overwhelming force came out on top. In that sense, the end was already foreseen the minute Cook pulled into the Hawaiians' parking lot, back in 1778, and the early Christian missionaries simply tossed a few low-yield tactical theological weapons into the cultural battle here and there. Add all of these to the introduction of western diseases against which the Hawaiians had no natural immunity and you have the near-demise of a complete culture.

Drove into K'kai to take a break and pick up some things at *The Friendly Market*. In the hottest part of the day you you'd expect things to be pretty slow and surprise...they were! On a whim, I dropped in at *Kanemitsu's* to check out their remaining bakery goods and bought a couple of apple fritters. Didn't notice Frank at first, an older artist whom I had met at the art mart, last Saturday, sitting behind me at one of the tables. His wave caught my attention and after I bought the stuff I sat down to talk story for a while. Frank is the fellow whom I have mentioned earlier in my journal had had surgery for skin cancer on his face. As we chatted, it came out that he has also had abdominal surgery for metastasized CA, and was on dialysis for years before finally getting a kidney transplant. Some medical history, I reckoned. He's only 66, too. Makes me reflect anew on the importance of having good genes.

Frank is an artist and as we talked about this and that, the subject of George of 'George's Gallery' came up. When I expressed some regret over the fact that George refused to sell any of his personal works on display in the gallery, this seemed to be a hot button for Frank, who vehemently volunteered a few things about George that I'd never have guessed. Apparently, Frank had offered to help George renovate his old building some time ago and had (rather rudely) never even received a word of appreciation for his help. I told Frank that although I hadn't met George personally, I had gathered from this and that that he was somewhat of an arrogant individual. This Frank confirmed and went on to say that he thought it was ironic that George won't sell any of his local art to interested parties, while on the internet he seemed to have quite a trade (apparently with customers in the Far East) going in works that Frank expressed as 'pure pornography'. Frank doesn't strike me as a blue-nose Christian conservative, so his opinion of what he termed 'pornography' is of substantial interest. George advertises a lot in the island papers for models that he wants to paint 'fully clothed' portraits of. Given this new bit of information about George's apparent erotic art side-line, I can't help but wonder about the emphasis on 'fully clothed' and how that may tie into his other interests. Just goes to show you that despite what the appearances seem to indicate, there's never such thing as a fully complete understanding possible, no matter who you are dealing with (e.g. President Bill's fellated dalliance with Monica Lewinsky in the Oval Office).

Frank apparently needs some money, since he offered to paint a picture similar to one I had briefly admired last Saturday (of a bull fight in Spain); at the time I admired it, he had said he was holding for someone else. Now, Frank is one of those souls I would call a talented dabbler, despite the fact that he tells me he teaches art at the local community center. Anyone with even modest ability can, of course, teach anyone of lesser ability, so that's not saying much. The proof in art is in the viewing and not in the self-pronouncement of one's 'instructor' status. This doesn't change Frank's stature as a good fellow with whom it is fun to chat, needless to say, but an artist is not truly an artist till his peers refer to him as such.

As we were talking, an exceptionally good looking young lady walked in, took a look at the baked goods and then walked out. She definitely caught my eye and I tracked her out of the corner of my eye as she walked down the street, thinking to myself: *"Holy shit, can it be that a lovely unattached young woman has somehow ended upon little old Molokai?"* I should have known better, as in the next 5 minutes she returned with a hunky, buff boyfriend. Alas, there's no justice in life! She had a great set of chi-chis, too, standing out nicely against her T-shirt. [Note to self: What is it about women's breasts, anyway? Is it the latent infant still trapped in us grown-up men that they excite? Or the recollection of the last good lustful suck we had as babes? Wonder what a psychologist would have to say about men and their fixation with firm, full female breasts, anyway? Ah, the marvels of blind sexual instinct.]

Since Frank knows Gunter, I decided to ask him if he knew anything about that old heiau out at Murphy's Beach that Gunter had steered me to. *"Oh yeah,"* he replied, *"Been there. It's a fish heiau, supposedly dedicated to Kuula (a minor fish aumakua). Did you know it's haunted?"*

Ah! I told him that I did and that I had in fact seen what could only have been the ghost in reference. *"Wow...you saw her, huh? She's supposed to be nice looking, young, but hardly anyone ever sees her. How did you luck out?"*

I couldn't explain it any better than he could, of course, but asked him if the story about a haunting was really legit, or whether this was more of Gunter's humor? I told him also about finding no grave, as Gunter has suggested I would at Kawelo.

"Nope, supposed to be at Pu'uko'o, not Kawelo, from what I've heard. The locals there could probably tell you more about it, since she seems to have had family there. You really saw her, or are you just pulling my leg? Story goes she doesn't show herself unless she isn't afraid of you. Never heard of anyone I know actually seeing her before...must be afraid of everyone...but from what you said, that was one pretty lady...um, at one time, of course." At that he stopped and looked at me with a puzzled expression. *"Strange stuff, that! You really saw her, huh? Wow!"*

I assured him I at least saw someone there. Whether a ghost or a real person was beyond my ability to say, since there was no indication of any ghostly behavior (or at least what I think would be ghostly behavior), as far as I could tell from those brief glimpses. She simply looked like a really good-looking lady to me, I guessed perhaps just walking back up from the sea, since her hair was wet.

I left Frank shortly afterwards to take my things back up to the place in Manila Camp. Judging from Frank's reaction, I'd say that either this is a larger joke than I thought, or I saw something I simply cannot explain (there's that bit about her purple top and the translation of her name; everything else can be rationalized but those two tantalizing details!). Amazing and here I am, back at square one, a non-believer who doesn't know what to make of this whole thing. [Makes mental note to buttonhole Gunter again and ask him for more information. Maybe with some more warm Papeete.] I did learn one interesting further thing: it was the custom for local Molokai families to put a small circlet made of Maile vine on the left wrist of a very recently deceased person. I recall that she was wearing something on her left wrist, but the encounter was too brief to know what, other than it was green in color and seemed to be made of leaves. *Brrrr.*

Sitting here, thinking about the above developments and feeling a strong need for one of those apple fritters I bought earlier in the day (dripping with saturated fat and fried, to boot--death wish?). Bruce (of BD's Vista Advantage) tells me he has a conflict in that his daughter needs to be at the library at 6PM to pick up some sort of award she won for reading. We've agreed to reschedule our rendezvous to check out the property for a cost estimate tomorrow. That's the Molokai way; nothing ever written in stone and always subject to the needs of the *'ohana* (or 'family', which is, of course, as it ought to be).

The last couple of days have been quite warm and humid. Lots of moisture-laden clouds developing late in the day, without a lot of the usual wind to cool things off. Since my room faces the sun (away from the trades), it gets fairly warm by about 4PM.

Another of my books sheds an interesting perspective on the early missionaries I have been holding forth about. The book was apparently written as a sort of response to all the less than positive insinuations James Michener made about them in his fictionalized novel *'HAWAII'*. By Michener's reckoning, the missionaries were all a bunch of holier than thou blue-nosed prudes who had a greater number of human failings that most people, religious or not. The thread of hypocrisy runs strongly and centrally through the book. Apparently, some of the more 'God-fearing' brethren among us have felt Michener slighted their evangelical forebears a bit too much, even though Michener's book is fiction that was based approximately on actual people. The book *('Hawaii: Truth Stranger than Fiction'*, by LaRue Piercy) takes pains to delve into the actual history that Michener researched so diligently (in typical Michener style) and contrasts the fiction to the true events that took place, since the parallels are quite real (just names, places, and actual events changed to make them seem purely fictional) and fascinating.

It makes interesting reading, but one gets the feeling that the author is trying hard to vindicate the historic figures that Michener used to model his characters after. He makes a remark in the preface expressing his pleasure in having received so many compliments from readers who felt such a book was 'long overdue'; one gets the distinct feeling that the 'grateful readers' are not modern-day godless heathens, either. At the very least it makes for interesting reading, since Michener's books are so well known and widely read. An amusing image comes to mind: Michener decides to do a similarly expansive and terribly complicated book with a bit sharper focus: *'MOLOKAI'.*

I can see parts of it in my mind, as I write this. One unforgettable chapter features a particularly strong minded (but intuitively brilliant) heathen high chief named *Kalika* (Hawaiian for 'Cooleridge'), who has a rep for being a stupendously well-hung lover (his *'Ule'* is legendary, and in fact it's the real-life model for the *sacred Ka Ule o Nanaha*), and 6 wives, each of whom is more gorgeous than the next. As I see it in my mind's eye, Kalika has just sacrificed a particularly arrogant missionary (who bears a striking resemblance to *George Dubya Bush*) for mouthing off at him, is about to lead his people up against the missionaries to overthrow them and successfully reclaim the islands for the Hawaiians. Oh yes, in this he is assisted by a couple of passing friendly alien UFOs, who decide to trade him some of their older (last lightyear's model, actually) *photon torpedoes* for a load of coconuts (which just happen to be made of the EXACT chemical ingredients from which their interstellar fuel is synthesized...what a coincidence!). It gets even *better*...

Of course, there's already a book (several, matter of fact) by that name, as well as a movie. The subject matter focuses on Father Damien's work with the lepers in the *Kalaupapa Colony*. I haven't mentioned much about that particular aspect of Molokai, since it is well known by most of the world and besides, the guy had a 'saint complex'. Not my kind of mensch, really. Oh yes, while on the subject of Hansen's Disease, those insinuating rumors you may have heard about Father Damien, Mother Marienne, and Baby Ignatz are not true ... Father Damien is on the road towards R.C. *saintdom* (along with *Mom Theresa*) as I write this, which is great, because he really was a marvelously committed human being (somewhat STRANGE, but still a really wonderful, selfless guy). Someone once remarked that the only real state of selflessness is achieved after one dies. Think about it.

Hmmmmm. That was an 'off-handed' remark, if I ever heard one. Then there's the leper who left the prostitute a tip. This of course, reminds me of many more tasteless jokes one hears about lepers, but I'll spare you. They were questionably amusing originally and probably would not be much improved in the retelling here.

It's getting later, my humor is getting more tasteless and cynical, and that apple fritter on the kitchen table is still sitting there, staring at me balefully as it continues to ooze saturated fat in the afternoon heat. Come back tomorrow: I promise it'll only get better in these truly inspired (perspired?) pages.

May 5th (Thursday)

Absolutely wretched night last night. The earplugs kept loosening and falling out, and the rooster/dog chorus began earlier than usual and lasted the rest of the remaining time, until well past dawn (it is now 7:42 AM and they are still at it). Had to take Benadryl instead of Actifed for sleep before bed and that usually imparts a groggy sensation on arising. As if that weren't enough trouble for the start of a new day, I also woke with a headache. Made my usually strong *cuppa* and popped the standard handful of vitamin pills, including some native Noni herb. Then, after the coffee took hold, the ASA went to work, the Noni kicked in, and I had consumed one of those gooey, drippy death-wish apple fritters, I was finally in better shape and ready to rock & roll.

The small electric coffee grinder I have here is made by the Braun (correctly pronounced *'brown'* and not *'bronn'*, as most non-German speakers assume) Company (GmBH); I brought it with me and have used it continuously for more than 21 years now. Cylindrical and bright orange (my favorite color), it still grinds away perfectly, although the blade is doubtless far duller than it used to be, having sliced through God only knows how many thousands of pounds of coffee beans over the past two decades. This is a meaningful measure of how seriously I take my coffee habit, I suppose, but every person has items in which he invests sacred significance. Some have crucifixes, others have pagan totems; I have my sacred coffee grinder and it certainly is a *wholly relic* in its own right *(wholly* my salvation each morning). Well worth worshipping the product it helps create, I think, since coffee, after all is GOD!

I went out early this morning, after scrubbing the accumulation of sweaty dreck off my body in the shower. Ever since talking to Frank about that strange happening at the old heiau, I had been meaning to go back there and do some further investigating into that place. Taking my camera, I drove east along Kam V Highway toward Murphy's Beach, traveling at the posted 35 mph speed limit and constantly having impatient locals zip up behind me at near twice the speed. Strikes me as more than slightly ironic on this 'slow-mo' island, that the locals are the most blatant violators of their own languid *kapus* against being in a hurry. I suspect that that these speeders in their jacked-up pickup trucks are not the long-time native locals, but impatient *haole malihini* who have migrated to the east end within the past 10 years.

After a half hour or so I passed the 'Neighborhood Store & Counter' and reached Po'oku'u. The graveyard was supposed to be there somewhere, but I had no idea exactly where, so I finally ended up asking an old *kanaka* (local native) who was walking on the makai side of the road where I might find it. Expecting pidgin *patois*, I was pleasantly surprised to find he spoke regular English (or close enough to it to be able to understand him without first straining the words through a #4 transliterative filter).

He directed me to the site, which was on the *mauka* (toward the hills) side of the road, and not far from where we stood. After a short while I found the exit off the roadway and turned down the dusty road cut from the crumbled volcanic earth. The crunch of my tyres was the only sound that broke the stillness in that otherwise silent repository of human remains, and I parked under a large Koa tree at the distal end of the cemetery. Half expecting to feel some sort of strange sensation (due to an over-active anticipation, no doubt), I slowly walked down the rows of graves, taking care to not step on the graves themselves (I have these funny little attitudes about this, that I can't really explain...respect for the dead?). There weren't too many of them. Most appeared to be very old, with sadly withered floral arrays long since dried out in the sun; a good number had ancient wooden markers on which the names and dates had long since been weathered off. Large flies and bees droned here and there in the morning sun.

The graves were not arranged in neat, orderly rows, but appeared to lay scattered about. One section had children's graves clustered together. I recall having read that this was an ancient practice that was done to allow the spirits of the dead children to play together and thereby be less lonely in death. Some of the children were newborns, more than a few less than a day or two old, according to the markers that could still be read. Near the graves was an incongruous bright blue waster barrel with the large letters OIL emblazoned on its side.

A thorough search of the graves produced no grave identified as being that of a Corinne Popolohu Hu'elani, but the skeptic in me had half-expected this outcome. After taking a last look around, I walked the short distance back to the car. The sun was already getting noticeably hotter, despite the early hour (10 AM) and I found myself getting thirsty.

The old heiau was not far off, so I drove back to that point and parked. There was no one else about within eyesight as I walked up the slightly inclined slope to the crest of the mound and peered down at the heiau wall, with its nearby old and tattered hut, some 100 yards away. The volcanic rock (*a'a*, which is the crumbly, jagged type-as opposed to the rounded *paho'eho'e* type) under foot crunched satisfyingly as I walked over to the hut. The view to Maui across the Pailolo Channel was clear and beautiful, as always. On the east end of the reef, where the shallows ended and the deep lay nearer to shore, the waters varied from a lovely turquoise shade to the deepest cobalt-blue. The whiteness of the breaking surf was startling. I could see why this would be a favorite diving spot, and it was conveniently close to the dazzling stretch of sandy beach that lay just at the foot of the old heiau.

Someone had been in the water already, as the light impressions of vaguely discernable footprints leading to and from the water suggested. As I neared the old heiau I looked carefully around; part of me, hoped, but didn't really expect to see the figure of the strange young woman I had seen before. There was no surprise in store for me (sadly) as I sat down on the same bench I had originally been seated on, several days ago. The sun was by now shining fully on the spot and there was only the vague murmur of the surf, breaking on the reef beyond the lagoon, to interrupt the silence.

Suddenly, my gaze was arrested by something breaking the surface of the water, out in the lagoon near the reef's edge. It was definitely the flash of a dorsal fin; probably one of the small black-tipped reef sharks that sometimes come in close to shore. A *'mano'*, as the Hawaiians would term it. The fin was soon gone as quickly as it had appeared, however, and the small dark shadow accompanying it quickly vanished. The stillness persisted. Clearly this was not a day for unusual sightings that couldn't be explained. After 15 minutes or so, hoping that I was wrong, I grudgingly admitted to myself that Gunter had been pulling my leg, after all. Somehow, I was being exposed to this joke as perhaps all newcomers must, by informal custom.

It was then that I spotted it. Out on the beach, along the track of those footprints from the heiau to the water and about halfway up from the edge of it, lay a shockingly purple flower of unusual size. It was quite large and I felt a little tingle of excitement as I walked over to it. The flower was still glistening with moisture. I picked it up and examined it more closely, all the while thinking somewhat perplexedly about how the color purple seemed to be a common thread running through all this. I turned the flower over, and registered the fact that it had veins of subtle, slivery-grey shading on the indigo under-surface of its velvety petals. That sent a slight shiver through me as I placed the flower back on the beach and gazed out at the lagoon. *'Another coincidence?'* I thought, as I tried to dismiss the odds against this further strange turn of events. A recollection of the woman's silver-streaked black hair flashed through my mind briefly.

Clearly, though, there was nothing more to be gained from lingering further, so I walked back to the car and drove slowly back west on Kam V Highway. Stopping *en-route* at the 'Neighborhood Store and Counter', I walked in and picked up a chilled carbonated coffee drink from the cooler. The auntie at the counter had been chatting in an animated fashion with a local, as I waited to buy the item. The banter went on for an unusually long time, it seemed. Probably trying to underscore a subtle point for the benefit of the haole tourist about what the local 'lay back' attitude concerning the flow of things is.

Finally, she waved goodbye to the local and turned to me, but the happy relaxed look was gone and instantly replaced by an *'Oh, one a'dem'* look. I decided to take a chance on being treated like an unwelcome haole and after paying for the drink asked "*Good morning Auntie. Do you know anything about an old fish heiau, back there, that supposedly has a ghost?*"

Her look hardened immediately as she asked me why I wanted to know. She knew something; it was easy to see this, from the slight change apparent in her attitude, but she wasn't about to admit anything to a strange haole.

"A friend told me about a young woman who apparently died out there in the lagoon while diving, a few years ago. Some story about her ghost returning to that spot."

She looked hard at me for a few seconds before replying *"Eh! Dat's jus' one ole chicken-flesh story dey tell the keiki. Keep dem out of wattah dere. Not real."*

I briefly told her about the girl, the purple flower, and what I had been told by others. She looked a little startled for just the briefest second, but said again. *"No girl name a Corinne, no ghost. Jus' one ole kine story, you know. We all Christians here; don believe any dat ole stuffs anymore; keiki chicken-flesh story, you know...das all."*

Someone had come in and there was no further time to continue our conversation, for she had handed my change back to me and wished me a good day before turning to greet the new customer (a dark-skinned, older local Kanaka). *"Hey ole Tom, wassup, bruddah?"*

I drove back to K'kai, more bemused than ever and no further along the path towards any sort of resolution in my mind on the subject. After I got back I ran into Gunter on his old bicycle (this is how he gets around, since he lives on his boat) and told him what I had experienced earlier. He was on his way to the local community disadvantaged adult center, on the hill near Molokai General Hospital, where they operate a sort of continuous garage sale of old recycled items, and didn't stop very long.

"Well, I tell you that the woman was wrong. They don't want to admit these things to outsiders. She knows. And you say you saw a purple flower there today, didn't you? How do you explain that, eh? That woman at the Neighborhood Store may say she's 'Christian', but the old traditions out there on east end are not yet all dead. I introduce you sometime to a local guy who knows these

things; doesn't allow himself to be called "Kahuna 'Ike Kuhohonu" ('seer' with deep spiritual insights), but he knows about these things. Tschüss, eh!" Then Gunter was off, peddling up the street on the old bike and somehow managing to still look dignified, despite his trademark faded aloha shirt and dingy white ball cap.

No closer to any sort of understanding, I spent the following few hours reading through some more of my accumulation of books. In a very good collection of strange stories written by various authors about the Pacific islands, I ran across a quote by a very readable author (of the 30s and 40s) named Clifford Gessler. Gessler had been a journalist for the *Honolulu Star-Bulletin* (newspaper) back in the early 30s, before getting bored and running off to the South Pacific islands.

In one of his stories, called *'Phantoms and Physicians on Tepuka'*, he strikes a resonant chord with the following excerpt: 'Part of the celebrated lure of far-away and primitive places no doubt is a response to the boy in man; in such surroundings (as the Pacific islands), among child-like peoples, he regains the play-world of his childhood. Where the pursuits at which he played as a boy are the serious vocations of adults, he finds a satisfaction of some instinct as old as the childhood of his own race.'

The truth of this simple statement of fact comes across quite clearly to those of us possessed of a more vivid imagination than others. I have long joked with friends about the fact that you 'scratch the man and find the boy'. I think it is a lucky woman who recognises, accepts, and is able to appreciate this inescapably latent quality in her husband, for aren't we all child-men (as opposed, say to perhaps '*child-ren*'?) in some manner or another, despite all our manly self-regard?

I decided to skip the bi-weekly email answering session at the local library and in the hot middle of the day I again ran into Gunter (Molokai is really just a very small 'community', after all). This time he found the time to take me to the house of a local named Joe, who was a traditional herb master in the old Hawaiian manner (he would have been called a *'Kahuna La'au Lapa'au'*). Gunter assured me that Joe was also supposed to have additional gifts befitting one who is a *'Kahuna Ninau 'Uhune'*, or 'communicator of spirits', although that fact was not advertised widely, except in the local Kanaka circles.

When we arrived at his simple, old style single-walled home, Joe was sitting out back in a tattered old yellow plastic deck-chair, sipping a beer under the shade of his car-port. He was somewhat portly, with a grey beard and long slender fingers that seemed somewhat out of character with the rest of his ample girth. The well-worn white tank-top he wore said HARD ROCK CAFÉ: SAIGON, in faded script. *"Ho, Gunter! Wassup, bruddah?"* He greeted us with the obligatory *shaka*, as he dispatched another dead soldier into the nearby waste can with the perfected aim of a sharpshooter. I decided that in addition to his ancient knowledge, he had also been 'in country' ('Nam slang for a tour in that war) at some time in the 70s.

Gunter introduced me and we both found cold beer cans thrust in our hands as we sat down on an old couch in the cool breeze-way. *"So, Gunter tell me you meet da kine wahine lapu (ghost woman) at Pu'kuo fish heiau, den wen gon' way on you, hm? You mind me aks you wat she look like?"*

Joe listened very attentively as I gave him the full extent of my observations, the *pāreu*, the purple suit top, the floral bracelet, dark hair with silver-grey streaks, and finally the large purple flower I had seen on the sand earlier in the morning. The mute testimony of several nearby empty beer cans seeming to have had absolutely no effect on his ability to concentrate, he listened carefully, observing me with a calm and steady gaze as I spoke. Joe certainly didn't look out of the ordinary to me...just another pot-bellied Kanaka...but his keen dark eyes told a different story. For my part, I certainly must have looked exactly as a pale-skinned haole should, as I finished up my story. Joe took another slow draw on his beer before replying.

"I tell you now dis wahine you see, not many see her. Dis no jokey stuffs, here. Dat wahine genuine akua lapu (ghost) at dat fish heiau. Mebbe um Hanehane, but good stuffs no pakalaki (bad luck) fo you. Dis wahine lapu seem like you or she not let you not see um." Joe shifted in his dilapidated old chair, took another draught, and thoughtfully scratched his ma'i for a minute with his other hand.

"Should not bodda you, brah. Dat wahine lapu gotta rep foe be 'olu'olu akua lapu (gentle, unharmful spirit), mebbe even aumakua (ancestral or familiy spirit). Sum kine nani koki wahine lapu (beautiful ghost), eh? You aks me, I return dere, take La'i (Ti leaf) an put on beach, wheh befo you see flowa. Don take flowa wid you, if you see anudda dere, doh: dat be pomaika'i nui (very unlucky)!"

Gunter had been listening quietly as he worked on his own beer. There was no smile on his face and no indication that this was simply another phase of what might still be a complex and well-rehearsed joke. When Joe had finished, I asked him about the missing grave.

"Ho, brah! Dat simple enuff. Dey no foun body wen dis wahine go stay missin'. She prolly join mano aumakua ('shark ancestor', protective family shark spirit) who out dat way. Wen take La'i, not hurt you say prayer: 'Auhea 'oe, e ke kanaka o ke akua, eia ka kāua wahi 'ai, ua loa'amaila mai ka pō mai; no laila nāu e 'aumakua mai i ka 'ai a kaua!' "

There was little to be said after that. Joe confirmed the *wahine lapu* existed and there's no reason to doubt that, since it all seems to add up in a strange (but very Hawaiian) sort of way. We downed another can of the now warm beer and took our leave after a bit, leaving the remainder of the 6-pack for Joe to polish off. Joe waved a parting shaka at us, but he was not smiling, either, I noticed. He seemed to be staring out at the distant bulk of Maui, rising out of the mists across the channel.

The part about the purple top and the flower can't be explained away, but it is worthy of some reflective bemusement that I seem to have a ghostly friend who took a fancy to me on that lonely stretch of coast. I am not ashamed to admit I did in fact take a Ti-leaf offering and place it on the beach, where I saw the foot prints and purple flower. I had written down the prayer Joe suggested and I repeated it aloud when I placed the Ti-leaf there; there's that healthy streak of rebellious pagan heathen in me that really wants to believe what I saw was actually inexplicable by any means known to westerners; perhaps this experience is that *'white raven'* I've always searched for. The Hawaiians, of course, believe in the importance of putting thoughts into spoken words—especially when praying.

Sooks, waiting for me back on the mainland, would be frightened to hear of any of this; she had warned me before I left specifically not to have anything to do with the old legends of the island, since she knows of my burning curiosity about such things. The woman I saw at the old fish heiau, whether real or not, was unquestionably beautiful and an interesting memory to take with me from Molokai. One final mystery also remains: according to Joe, who knows much about such things, there are no indigenous large purple flowers on Molokai, such as that I saw there in front of the old heiau...go figure, eh?

It's late in the afternoon now and the humidity is not as noticeable as it has been over the past two days. There are a few clouds starting to gather, as usual, but the breeze is enough to keep the heat from being oppressive. I had another of my cheap & dirty peanut-butter & jelly sandwiches (a perfect 'Sandwich Islands sandwich', it seems to me) and was able to successfully fend off the urge to eat that other apple-fritter (saving it for Friday).

I was staring at all my books just a few moments ago. That's a heavy load of stuff and I hope they won't hit me with a baggage surcharge, owing to it. I think about the fact that I only weigh about 160 pounds soaking wet and a number of other passengers (probably hefty local types) typically weigh twice that amount. Surely the combined weight of me and by books won't unduly exceed existing figures for the average passenger, in light of such a fact? Guess we won't know until the moment of truth at the Island Air ticket counter on Sunday.

Looking back over the past month or so, I am thinking that there isn't anything I couldn't have gained just as easily in two weeks here as I have in twice that amount of time. Except the lengthy bulk of this journal, which at this time is just about to exceed 100,000 words (exactly 98,889 words at this juncture). This will cost me about 160 hours of hard-earned vacation time, and since the water line installation didn't really require my presence over here to begin with, it may have been a bit of an extravagant excess on my part (not that I can't afford to spend those 160 hours, what with a grand total accrued of over 450 hours).

Aside from the strange experience at the old heiau, nothing I have seen or done here has really been too startling. It would have been more stimulating to have someone along with me, with which to share the time. Perhaps a gorgeous & ravishingly sensual female (like Sooks) to while away the hours with (but alas! I have to make do with the mere suggestion of one and you can't easily get it on with a ghost, can you?) would have helped a lot. Molokai remains, after all is said, read, and done, NOT a place high up on the list of *'Sierra Hotel'* (note: military aviation slang for *'Shit Hot'*) singles watering holes (not that I normally or customarily play that game, as someone in a fulfilling relationship, of course). I didn't come here for that purpose, after all, since my main intent was to experience some long-overdue peace and quiet in which to read and write.

The wind is picking up a bit outside now and there is a lovely wind-chime that someone has hanging nearby. I keep thinking about all the hundreds of different kinds of flowers on the island. but the fact is that among them all (Molokai is, after all, a botanist's *Fantasy Island*) there are absolutely NO large, velvety purple blooms to be seen anywhere (visualize: a sudden outburst *of "Look Boss: da flower, da flower, da flower!"*, followed by the scornful response in a deep Ricardo Montalban accent, runs through my head*: "Oh shut up, Poo-poo, you disgusting little scum bag! Go out and greet our new guests..."*).

The above is all true; I'd swear it on a stack of Holy Korans any day.

SEARCHING FOR HAUMEA

The reef rash on my shoulder still stings occasionally. I can be sitting there in the big wood-paneled room facing the stormy ocean on a frigid January day, struggling mightily to force some deep-seated thoughts out and into the laptop. Or find myself totally preoccupied with thoughts of the boundless Pacific Coast kelp fields, flooding my senses with the sight of echelons of graceful pelicans riding the ground effect over the waves in a search for small fish. The monstrous blue-gray swells topped with spuming plumes of spray roll in, like relentless fluidic juggernauts of doom, demanding total awareness. Plenty of stuff out there to divert the focus of my attention from any connections my brain normally makes with limbs, guts, and bodily sensations of any kind. Yet, suddenly the immense oceanic display of all that powerful wintry natural force splits right down the middle and twinkles out, as my left shoulder starts to twinge...

If it hadn't been for the *noni* and aloe *Haumea* had slathered on me, I'd probably be covered to this day with rows of angry ridges of inflamed skin, where the sharp coral had raked my shoulder and back. It all happened many years ago and would be now deeply buried and lying near-forgotten in some chest of memories, if it weren't for this occasional stab of fleeting pain.

I had been on a day trip to Makaha with Uncle Phil and Auntie Lilinoe, my adopted Oahu parents who had taken me in after Ma died. That locale on the West Coast of Oahu known throughout the surfing world as the home of the monster waves of winter was just an hour's drive west on the bumpy roads from Pearl. Although the summertime at Makaha is marked by mild surf and nearly flat wave conditions, by my reckoning as an adult today that visit now has as much significance to me as a *Haji's* pilgrimage to *Makkah*. A visit to a sacred site among holy places. A walk near the still waters of the pools fronting the *Taj Mahal*. But at that time, I was just a kid, a *keiki* in the local island language. *"Holy"* had no meaning for me at all, unless it was somehow the combined effects of unlimited sun and waves, and no homework to have to study.

I was just this small, adopted haole kid, tagging along with my relatives as they took care of some *'ohana* (family) business in Makaha. Overhead the sun was fierce and unbearably hot. The dry nature of Oahu's western summer shores made itself felt in the palpable currents of heat rising from Makaha's volcanic hillsides. Under such conditions, the cool ocean beckoned like a haven of refuge from that thermal beast of nature. Paddling well out from the beach on a borrowed board that was *way* too big for me, I had tried to find a few waves worth riding, although the surf was typically non-existent. After what felt like hours (minutes often dragged by like hours for me, filtered through my kid's perspective) of waiting astride my board, a few small swells finally struggled in from the ocean, showing seeming reluctance to rise up from the vast uniformity of all that beautiful blue-green water.

Haumea had apparently been watching from the shore when I pearled ungracefully at the bottom of the only mediocre wave that had offered itself up. The large longboard flipped under nose-first and then shot out and upwards as the crest steamrolled me under and smashed me to the bottom. Shore breaks are always a bear for the unskilled at Makaha and if the bottom isn't smooth and sandy below you, a wipeout in the wrong place can grind you into bloody hamburger faster than you can say *Quicksilver...* or ground-round! That goes double for kids, even when the summer seas at Makaha are almost perfectly flat.

Haumea wasn't watching from the shore to assess my technique, since I was clearly a tourist kid and typically about as graceful as a Manatee with cerebral palsy on a longboard. She might have stopped by there on her way to somewhere else, to briefly amuse herself with the antics of the tourist haoles who hadn't a single drop of Hawaiian blood anywhere in their pasty white, grossly sunburned bodies. Or she might have been sent by some unknown protective spirit to watch out over inexperienced haole kids who were clearly out of their realm of comfort. I'll never have an answer for that last question, despite my fervent need to believe in *aumakua* (family protective spirits, that are often departed ancestors).

Haumea could afford to indulge herself in this manner, since she was everything on a board or off it that my race wasn't and likely could never be. Haumea's bloodlines reached back hundreds of years, to the ancient Polynesians masters of the waves who had come to the islands in the second influx of migrants from the *Marquesas*. With the effects of long exposure to the sun darkening the patina of her island heritage, reflecting back on that moment today, my guess would have to be that there were just enough *pake* (Chinese) and *haole* (outsider) ancestors in her family's mix to segue her genes into the perfectly lovely amalgam of prescient wisdom and strong *makuwahine* (strong nurturing womanliness) stature she so perfectly embodied.

It was only many years later that I found out who Haumea really was; that among her other many accomplishments, she was a champion surfer and a true *'waterwoman'* (an all-around natural in the water—diver, surfer, paddler, swimmer, *and lifeguard*) with few peers, either male or female. With sun-streaked long dark hair tied back, the unmistakable smile she always wore while sliding over the swells was visible for hundreds of yards (I am told), like the dazzling flash of a lighthouse beacon through the gathering coastal dusk. It was a singular thing with her, that smile, for it just developed naturally whenever she was on or in the water. To say she was an amazingly adept *water-woman* is understating things the same way someone might casually compare the liftoff of a space shuttle booster to the spurting explosions of a roman candle. A true surfer of the soul, Haumea, a sacred bearer of the aloha spirit, was only truly *at home* in the ocean waters surrounding Makaha's point. The spirit of aloha ran deep in her veins. But I didn't know all this at the time. I was simply a water-logged *keiki* who was out where I shouldn't have been—out of Auntie Lilinoe and Uncle Phil's sight and looking like a drowned *poidog* (Hawaiian for 'mutt').

Slender, graceful, superbly-toned and smoothly muscled in the manner so many surfers tend to be, Haumea was...even from my immature *haole keiki* vantage...about as handsome a woman as you can find in the islands. And she was a local, which meant that someone like me--a non-local *haole* kid--could normally expect to be forever relegated to the sort of second-class citizen status that is the modern island norm among locals. Everyone knows that locals and haole tourists don't mix socially, especially *hapa* (half) haole military families from Pearl Harbor.

But I digress. I had just swallowed a ton of salty brine and come up gasping for breath. Once the ocean finally released me and spat me out on the shore, I was simply grateful to be breathing again and all in one piece. The battered old longboard I had been using hadn't had a leash, since it was almost as ancient as Uncle Phil, and besides...leashes weren't even invented until the late 70s. My *katonk* (island slang for 'mainland Japanese-American') friend Calvin Nishinaka had left it with me just before he and his family had departed Pearl for an assignment in Japan, and now it floated forlornly in the soup nearby, more waterlogged than floating, due to all the dings.

Crawling out of the water, I noticed that I was dripping red stuff. *The coral!* My back had been raked raw by the living coral and only inexplicably good luck had kept me from having my face ground into the reef instead of my back.

My white skin and the bright crimson blood must have made a strange contrast for onlookers. I surely must have looked pathetic to those gathered on the shore, such as Haumea, who routinely stop at Makaha State Beach to watch the m*alihini* sliders try their luck on the 'wild and raging' (one foot high) summer crests of Makaha. There was little solace at all to be found in the fact that there were at least seven or eight other equally pasty white haole carcasses falling off boards on baby waves out in the tranquil waters. They were all adults, however, and I was this little kid all by myself. Just another little *haole keiki,* vicariously imagining himself a tiny dot on the thundering walls of winter surf. Those towering swells that can make a grown man and experienced surfer wet himself just *watching* them smash in to shore.

The sandy beach at Makaha rises up steeply from the water's edge and I stopped for a moment to look back at the small surf that most *kanaka maole* (native locals) would regard as mere bath water, suitable only for the local *keiki* (children). It was then, as I stood with my crimson shoulders turned *mauka* (facing inland), that Haumea probably noticed the severe reef rash. Fortunately, I couldn't see the extent of the wounds myself, but the saltwater was starting to make me painfully aware of just how badly I had been lacerated by my collision with the sharp coral growths.

Typically, the intense pain isn't apparent right away, since it takes a while for the body to check itself over, tally up the score, and communicate with damaged nerves before alert signals run screaming to the brain's pain centers. They say it is the same way with surfers who have lost an arm or leg to a marauding tiger shark; at first, there's no pain at all. Not even slight discomfort. Until the extreme shock of what the bloody waters reveal settles in, to run insanely down the echoing corridors of the human brain.

As I stared out at the baby swells that had dislodged me from Calvin's ancient borrowed board, I heard a voice behind me ask *"That has to hurt, eh!"* The voice, soft and low, but very definitely *feminine* voice was my introduction to this amazing woman. Since haoles have been falling off surf boards for almost 100 years now, I had not been too surprised to immediately place the voice as a 'local voice' even before I saw her face.

Locals at Makaha usually reserve only their most austere disdain for the tourists, at most. They do not normally choose to mingle voluntarily with the *malihini* (mainland) tourists and Makaha is definitely a *local* area that hews to strongly established *local custom.* Unless the visiting tourists lack the good sense to stay off the better waves and out of the way when the local *hui he'e nalu* (local surfers) are out. Then add alcohol or meth to any encounter between the locals and the tourists at Makaha and things can get pretty ugly in no time. This is especially true if one of the outsiders has the ignorant audacity to try to *poke squid* with a local *sistah.* But then, unmindful of all this adult awareness I would later gain, I turned and faced the singular woman I came to find out was *Haumea.*

Viewed in the eye of recollection, many years later, she had been slender and tall, but regally proportioned; not the usual economy sized island wahine. As an impressionable kid, I recall she had seemed to tower over me with some sort of undefinable *presence*. I recall also that Haumea had worn a yellow *pareau* (a Tahitian style wraparound garment affected by women) over a green tank suit. Her long dark hair tied back gave evidence of having been very recently in the water and her dark sun-burnished skin accentuated the soft green of her suit with startling contrast. *"Come over here,"* she said, motioning towards her. *"I have some aloe and a bottle of noni lotion up there* (gesturing back up-beach) *and you really need something on your back right away."*

I must have appeared semi-stupefied by her appearance, for clearly Haumea was about as intensely impressive a woman as any I can ever recall having seen until then. Despite my dazzled state, I could sense a sort of natural authority mixed with benevolent concern behind her words, and it totally demanded my full attention. To this day I seem to have this special ability to sense spectacularly vital female 'presence' like that and as an adult I am notorious for turning into a quivering blob of speechless jelly, capable only of croaking pitifully, when confronted by it.

There is a sort of ill-defined recognition that dawns within me at such moments that I am confronting a primal source of life force that shakes me to the core. I felt it as a keiki then and I feel it as an adult now. Too, in my years of adult experience, I have found I am directly confronted by truly substantial women usually only about once every ten years, so that sensibility must have been triggered early on by this singular local wahine. [Years later, a *pake* (Chinese) friend, learning of this encounter from me, said *"Go buy one lottery ticket now, brah! Neva too late!"* I will never figure out exactly why he said that, but clearly this childhood experience of mine meant something deeper to him that eluded me then, as it still does.]

"You were in the wrong spot, eh! The break over the coral is bad unless you are very, very good on the waves. Safer to stay over the sandy bottom in the center of the beach. Judging from what I just saw, you are clearly NOT 'very, very good' right now, but...good news! You stay go out

there regularly and it will come to you." Haumea had said this without any ambiguity, smiling through her eyes with sincere empathy over my discomfort, clearly concerned with my raw shoulder, so there could be no misunderstanding of her intent. Too, I could readily sense that her words came from her heart and that she meant every single word of it. *"Good thing this is July. Makaha's no place for anyone except the best of the best, when the big swells of winter roll in."*

Still somewhat tongue-tied, out of breath, and bemused by her sudden appearance, I briefly waded out to grab Calvin's old longboard and with her help I wrestled it up the beach to drop it just out of reach of the docile surges of the ocean. Then, following Haumea as trustingly as I imagined a small child (like me) would his own mother, I trudged through the sand towards the coco-palms and the pile of towels and clothes near the lifeguard stand she had pointed towards.

The lifeguard had clearly recognised Haumea, waving a big *shaka* at her as we passed by his covered orange and white perch. Haumea's big white smile flashed back in return. Remembered through the filter of decades of adulthood, I still swear it could have peeled wax off a surfboard at 100 paces or cleared the fouled bottom of a fishing ketch of a lifetime of barnacle growth in mere seconds. It was that kind of smile and it communicated volumes of warmth and unforced, natural goodness. It engendered in me, as I understand it now, the same sort of overwhelmingly powerful imperative to respect life and all of creation that watching a monstrous winter storm wells up deep inside me.

Flashing a sidelong look at Haumea, I had no idea that she was in her 40s at the time, since the ability to guess at or even be concerned with trying to gauge a woman's age would not affect me at all until *well* after I had reached puberty. There had been a white flower tucked behind her left ear, island style, an indication I now know of the fact that that she was married, and she possessed a natural confidence and presence that suited her mature female beauty perfectly. Reaching the pile of towels, she gestured to me, as she had picked up a small squeeze bottle full of some fluid and removed the cap. *"This is aloe juice; it will help take the pain away. Noni will also help lots, but if you don't get something on that rash right away, you'll have scaring there that won't eva go 'way.'"*

Looking directly at me and smoothing the jelled fluid gently on my raw shoulder with her strong hands, she continued, *"Your family staying at Makaha Shores, mebbe? Where you from? Visiting from the mainland, perhaps? Not local haole, anyway. Where's your mom and dad and where did that battered old board come from? It's not yours: too big for you!"*

I had admitted the obvious, that I was just passing through for the day while Uncle and Auntie ran some errands in town. I didn't admit we were all from Pearl Harbor, since I had heard even as a kid that that admission could provoke some displeasure by locals on the island who lived well away from the military base and who still resented the *Makua Valley* intrusions.

"Well, haole boy, the surf isn't much in the summer, but you managed to wipe out pretty badly in dakine baby soup, nonetheless." She was smiling again. *"That's a distinction of sorts, I guess. You keep at it, before you know it you'll be way bettah. Need lot of practice to become good on a surfboard, though! You can call me Auntie Haumea, by the way."*

I wasn't so overawed by her radiant vitality and powerful strength of her personal warmth to miss the fact that she had referred to me as a *'haole boy'*, but I took that as a friendly compliment, coming from someone as impressively local and healthy as she was. *"Thanks. My name is Kaliki",* is what I managed in return. Lame for an adult, perhaps, but adequate for a kid.

"Ho, you have island connections? That's a nice Hawaiian name...means 'Christian'. Once you catch the wave, stay back on the board more, but if it helps make you feel better, blame that pearl-dive on the board. Everyone takes that cheap shot from time to time. Sometimes better than aloe to take the sting out, eh!" More smiles.

"I have to go now, but try to stay out of trouble, OK? I'm not always here to take care of stray ilio (dogs) and haole keiki." The big white smile flashed again as she laughed at my embarrassment and further explained: *"Makaha can be tough on outsiders and the water is no place to get into trouble of any kind that you can avoid. Learn to read the water first, eh! Now you go find your Uncle and Auntie and don't stray too far from them, OK? Not my day to be lifeguard today, eh!"*

So saying, she turned her head to grin at me one more time and that great big smile defrosted all the ice off my preadolescent self-esteem in an instant. Then, with a flip of her long dark mane she had gathered up her things, waved to the lifeguard on duty, and began walking back up to the parking lot adjacent to the Makaha Shores condos. A tawny colored *poidog* ('mutt') came out from behind the lifeguard and stand ambled along with her as she left. Thoroughly entranced by this impressive woman, I permitted myself to stare after her, unabashedly slack-mouthed as I noted the way she seemed to dance lightly uphill, through the sand.

Thoughts of my own lost mother mixed confusingly with my child-like feelings of being an adopted *orphink* at that moment. I admit that as an adult I'm quite unusually moved by displays of singular female nurturing of this type, but even at that early point in my life it was clear this was no ordinary *makuwahine.* There is in all of us, after all, a primally fierce compulsion to love and respect one's mother, something I had been denied by fate and forces beyond my youthful understanding. Sadly, only in a few of us does that deep formative need transform itself into a passionate surrogate regard for our ultimate mother: *Nature*, the *Mother of all Creation*. Strangely enough, I recall having something approximating that exact thought as Haumea walked out of sight and my youthful life on that day (either that or I have imposed this thought retroactively on the experience, not that it matters either way).

That short and embarrassing ride, I am ashamed to admit, was just about the best one I had had at Makaha that day and two hours after being patched up by Haumea, I left again for Pearl with Uncle Phil and Auntie Lilinoe. It would have humbled me greatly to reflect on my amateurish wipeout on the baby waves at Makaha had I been a grown-up, since I've always subsequently thought of myself as the proverbial surf legend in my own mind. But confronted by the undeniable reality of that primal encounter with lovely Haumea, I realised only too well that we are all simply what we all are…and very little *more*.

Each of us develops very differently from one another in ways that are largely unmanageable, and no amount of retroactive self-delusion ever changes that basic poker hand our genes and formative environment deals us early in life. Some are gifted by genetics and environmental influences with greatness and mastery, others are not. Despite this immutable fact, the great salvation of our kind is that we are nevertheless capable of being inspired by examples of greatness around us. To say I was inspired that day is the greatest understatement!

Haumea would continue to live the idyllic island life I imagined she had always led at Makaha, after we left. She with her *makuakane* (husband) and keiki, engaged in many community concerns and activities associated with love of the ocean and life, would doubtless inspire many others like myself, who by natural inclination continually search for goodness and the aloha matrix in all things. Unknown to me then, I would someday in future end up frequenting the cold North California coast, where an occasional twinge in my shoulder would forever force me to look back, yet again, and dream about the warmth and beauty of that strangely impressive island moment. Despite regular immersion in the coast's year-round 53-degree water, it would never fail to exert an effect something like the catalysing shock of a cold cresting wave, but with less explicitly sexual overtones.

Afterwards, I actively thought nothing more deeply about that experience with Haumea until about 6 months ago, when I happened to be watching the *Quicksilver* professional surfing contest on Oahu's North Shore via satellite link. Midway through the women's pro heats, the CNN camera panned the judges and I could swear I caught a glimpse of Haumea standing near the commentators, chatting with them as if they were *'ohana* (family). Come to think of it, they probably *were* and to this day I will continue to marvel over why she took an interest in my chewed-up shoulder that hot summer day at Makaha, so many years ago. Surely there can't still be that many genuinely *good* women like that walking around on the tough Wai'anae Coast Oahu beaches, who *routinely* express loving concern over haole tourist kids as if they were their *own*?

To my supremely good fortune, Auntie Haumea, as I came to understand later, was one of the most revered and highly respected local women to be found anywhere on all of Oahu. Lovingly regarded by nearly everyone in the islands who knew her (and most did), she was (so I am told) every bit the genuine living legend that my juvenile *Munchhausen* persona could only remotely dream of being. Meeting her that day was for me sort of like winning a lottery of the soul, now that I reflect back on it.

That encounter with the essential core of pure Hawaiian warmth and spiritual female *mana* (spirit) possessed by lovely Haumea still greatly beguiles me when I think about those days. A few rough scars remain on my shoulder from that pounding on the reef that I took some years ago, but I regard them rather proudly as trophies of a unique rendezvous with primal forces of the eternally female human spirit Haumea possessed that transcends my limited *kane* (male) understanding, but that shall forever fascinate me to my very last days on Earth.

There are, of course, innumerable oedipal currents running around buried deep within many of us, although most of them are so profoundly submerged in submarine canyons of the conscious psyche that most will never even be vaguely aware of them. As for mine, sitting here in front of one of the most spectacular displays of nature's ordered chaos conceivable (the Pacific Ocean), I recognise my own glimmer of those archetypal instincts as vaguely luminescent shapes, like abysmal creatures lurking in the darkest anthracitic reaches of the ocean's stygian bowels.

At my bidding, they rise upwards towards the surface, towards that solar brightness, where they take archetypal form as mythical *Haumea*, the prototypic *Earth-Mother Goddess* and traditional source of all womanly fertility in ancient Hawaiian eyes. The same *Haumea* I have little doubt who revealed the smallest part of her myriad mysteries *in human form* to me briefly, as a child on that Makaha beach, many years in my past.

[I share all this now with you, well mindful of the ancient Hawaiian saying: *"I 'ole 'ola no ka huewai i ka piha 'ole".*

It translates directly to *"The water gourd gurgles when not filled well"*, but I won't reveal the intended actual meaning. That is for you to wonder about, unless you have a well-developed familiarity with Mary Kawena Pukui's seminal collection of traditional Hawaiian proverbs and poetical sayings, *'OLELO NO 'EAU'*, eh!]

Aloha kakou!

MAILE AND THE LITTLE GREEN MENEHUNE

There is a 'new' ancient story being passed down in *mele* on the island of Molokai, as the Irish in Hawaii prepare to honor their revered patron saint, *Kahuna Naomh Pádraig*. It is the story of Maile and the little green *menehune*. This is a true story and one I know is true because my great grand-tutu told me this when I was still a child. At the time she was renown across the island and beyond, as one of the most skillful women story-tellers to be found among the people of Hawaii.

In a land where there was never a written language, and therefore no means of passing down a recorded event from generation to generation, the task of collecting and transmitting histories of the people fell to Hawaiians who were gifted with the ability to remember tales and stories told to them and retell them to others. According to the ancient custom, these individuals became highly regarded masters of the spoken word in their communities and were accorded revered status as *Kahunas* of the oral history of their people. To this day, 'talking story' remains one of the most ancient customs kept alive through individual contact among the people of the islands, a land where skillful speaking is still very greatly respected and the spoken word highly regarded.

Our story takes place on the island of *Molokai nui a Hina*, or *'Molokai blessed to Hina'*, for that is what it translates to in the language of the *Haoles (whites)*. The time is very, very long ago, in a past dimly remembered only in the stories of aunties and great-aunties that are told to beloved children who have been well-behaved and who deserve to hear them.

Thus it was that *Maile*, a young and comely maiden of 16, lived with her family on the great bay at the far end of Molokai's *manae* (east end) that is known as *Halawa*. Maile was a shy and gentle girl, who, as a child, usually obeyed her father's and mother's wishes without question. She was always, however, somewhat lonely, for there were few other girls among the families who shared that area near the Halawa taro fields. Her usual companions were local boys from that small community and especially her two brothers, who begrudgingly assumed responsibility for watching out for her and keeping her safe from harm (so they thought!).

After years of playing with the boys and enjoying their rough and tumble activities, beautiful Maile became bolder and more assertive herself. Her confidence grew especially from riding the waves (*he'e na'lu*) on the long board with which she learned to glide so gracefully across the wave-tops. When not on the water, she excelled in climbing the coconut palms with the best of the boys and was exceptionally light and nimble, showing much grace evident in her slender frame as she quickly scrambled up the trunk to reach the biggest, yellow-green nuts at the top of the palms.

Maile's mother was frequently concerned for her, since despite the fact that Maile was always offered as much taro, fruit, and fish at meals as she could eat, she remained unusually thin for a Hawaiian girl, where the norm was more often to be big-boned and full-bodied. But thin and agile she remained, with beautiful, rich dark skin, and flashing brown eyes that would unconsciously blink with surprise at the slightest unexpected commotion near her. Of her youthful beauty, it was said that the quick flash of her white teeth when she smiled could instantly melt the sternest man's heart and make him soften his fatherly admonishments, whenever she was being more willful than the adults thought she should be.

Maile had received her name from that uniquely pretty and fragrant, wandering and entwining forest vine that is found higher up on the rain-saturated slopes of the mighty volcano Kamakou (the highest point on the island, at 4428 feet). Known as the sacred vine of *Laka* (Pele's sister), the ancient Hawaiian Goddess of the Hula, the *Maile* vine with its shiny, sweet-smelling leaves was highly prized for its use in making beautiful leis.

Like the sweet scented and twining vine that was her namesake, Maile was also fond of wandering and roaming about by herself, taking great enjoyment in going off by herself to explore *Halawa Valley*, much to her parents' consternation, who wanted her to stay and tend the taro patches. Sometimes she would even take her *papa he'e na'lu* (surfboard) out into the cold, deep waters that well - up off Halawa's beach and wait just beyond the big, crashing breakers that constantly swept in from the sea. There she would sit on her board, looking out away from shore and seemingly lost in wonder at how vast the open ocean seemed. But soon her keen eyes would spot a particularly large wave rolling towards her and she would swim skillfully ahead of it before its swelling bulk caught her up. Catching the wave just before it crested, she would ride it to shore with an effortless style born from years of practice and smiling unconsciously with the pure joy that filled her at such moments.

Bare breasts glistening with sea water and wearing just her long, dark hair gathered together and thrown over her shoulders, she would reach the beach laughing with delight and clearly as comfortable with the ocean as any creature that lived in or under it. Maile was, at such moments, at perfect peace with her world, a world of ocean waves and currents that rolled in to Halawa's waiting sands in unending rows. Despite her slenderness, her supple feminine strength was more evident in how easily she lifted the heavy longboard out of the water than in the presence of any discernable muscle she carried on her frame.

The other women of the community who might have been nearby at such times would glance over at her and unconsciously feel sorry for what they regarded as her unhealthy slimness at such times, for by their standards, she was far too slender for a young woman of her age.

"That Maile!" they would say, clucking their tongues as she ran up the beach ahead of the waves. *"She will waste away into nothing if she doesn't eat! How ill she must feel!"* Maile, for her part, was completely unmindful of these well-intended criticisms, for she was content just as things were.

And so the days and weeks passed slowly and peacefully at Halawa Valley, as they always do in the islands. Before long, the rough winter weather had disappeared and the Kahunas announced spring's arrival, with its fair seas and gentler climate. As the weather improved, Maile's mother and father found themselves thinking about their only daughter and the fact that she was now a very grown-up young woman, ready for a husband and a family of her own. Maile, of course, had little thought for such things, since she too much enjoyed the simple beauty and languid pleasures of the seacoast around her and had almost no awareness of her own maturing female form.

Thus it was, late on one spring day, that she was wandering on the slopes just above the valley and out of view of the village, when she came upon a most unusual sight. There was a swift motion in the grass just ahead of her near some large volcanic rocks and she started involuntarily, the quick flash of her eyes betraying her surprise as they always did. Standing very still, she gazed intently at the bushes and rocks nearby, from where sounds of movement had issued forth.

After several long minutes, the strangest little green hands parted the bushes and a small head looked out at her with big yellow eyes! The little man (for that is what he was) was entirely green-hued and wearing only a garment of leaves and vines wrapped around his middle. A wispy white beard wreathed his face and his features were soft and sun-darkened, with an upturned nose and thin lips.

They stood there, Maile and this little green man, each eying the other with an intensely quizzical stare until finally the little man smiled and motioned to her, indicating with both his small hands that she should not be anxious.

"You must be Maile" he addressed her, to her great surprise! With a deep voice for such a perfectly miniature person, he grinned as he said her name, and crawled out from behind the bushes to sit on the top of a nearby rock.

"I have watched you often as you have walked about this area. You are the daughter of a family from that community of Kanaka Nu'i (big people) who live down there, near the taro fields, are you not?" So saying, he motioned down towards the flat verge of the bay at the end of the valley. His manner was almost familiar in its unmistakable tones of casual friendliness.

Maile, who had by this time somewhat recovered her wits and tongue, now looked keenly at the little man, fascinated by the fact that she estimated his size to be less than half of her own.

"Yes, that is true. I am Maile and I live down there, as you have observed, but who…or what…are you? Is your skin really green, or have you rubbed something from the forest upon it? And you are so small…!"

"Oh yes," he replied, *"I am actually…as you say…green like leaves of the Ironwood and Koa trees. My people have lived in the highest parts of this island for a long, long time, and have been very successful in not letting ourselves be*

seen or known, except perhaps in your children's stories and tall tales."

Here he paused to smile, as if thinking it all very amusing. *"We are called the Menehune and we have lived here long before your forefathers landed on this bay in their great ocean-going wa'a ia-ko* (outrigger canoes)."

Maile had heard the ancient fables that told of small people many times as a child, of course: small roundly shaped little people living secretly and far removed from the community, high up the volcanic slopes, but she had always regarded them as any child would…as the mythical subjects of delightful stories told by aging aunties in the gathering dusk of evening, after dinner.

"Keiki wahine (woman-child), *I am probably older than any of the oldest, most ancient aunties in your little community down there,"* the little green man continued with a smile, as if reading her thoughts. *"Since you have discovered me, I have something to share with you that may surprise you, if you will but listen carefully to me for a few minutes."*

"You have grown to womanhood almost unmindful of this fact, but shortly you will cross over into another part of your young life. Your skill on the papa he'e nalu (surfboard) *is great and all the creatures of the ocean deeps regard you as one of their own, such is your skill in the water. You will find soon enough, however, that there is even more to life than these delights…more to fascinate you than the playful waves you love so much."*

"Go now, back down the hill and contemplate the ancient wisdom of the manoakua (shark spirit) *that guards you and your family from harm as you he'e nalu* (ride the waves). *Shortly, that new life shall come to you by way of*

the very ocean you daily glide upon. Now go! And remember my words in the days to come!"

Maile glanced briefly at the sun's slanting rays, as he finished saying these words and when she glanced back at him, there was nothing to suggest she had ever been other than alone and by herself, for the little green man with the white beard had vanished as if into the air itself.

"Such a strange thing!" she thought to herself before turning and walking bemusedly back down the hillside to the valley.

Several weeks then came and went, each one bringing warmer days and smoother seas. Before long, she had forgotten her encounter the little man almost entirely, almost willing herself to believe she had imagined the whole thing. After sharing the secret only with one especially trusted auntie, her Tutu had simply smiled wonderingly at her and shaken her head, as if to say *"What an imagination this child has!"*

It was early in the morning, not long afterwards, that she had taken up the large board and headed back to the waters of Halawa, eager to swim and ride the ocean swells. As she reached the coursing surf's spent surge she made to throw her board in, but something at the edge of her vision caught her eye. Looking full at the object, she was startled to see that it appeared to be a man.

But this man, who had two arms, legs, a head, and hands like any other man, was as *white* as the underside of a shark! That is, his skin was not dark like hers, but pale and ashen. His hair was not black, either, but red! And yet, there could be no mistaking his being a man, for he lay on his back on the sand, unclothed and seeming to be asleep. The sea lapped at his feet and she then realised that he had been cast ashore from the ocean, perhaps fallen from a canoe or boat that had passed by the bay.

Dropping the board on the sand, she slowly walked over to him and knelt beside him. He was breathing she noted, and was still wet from the ocean, with bits of kelp on his back and legs. Looking with fascination at his strange red hair, she found herself remembering the encounter with the little green man and then also remembered his strange words. First a little green man and now a big red-haired man with pale white skin! This was certainly strange, she reflected, as she caught herself looking at his exposed *U'le*, which was large and very thick. Yes, all of this was very strange!

Maile then went to get the others of her village and soon the strange white man was brought back to a hut, where he shortly awakened. He spoke a few words after opening his eyes, or at least she imagined they were words since they had no meaning to her or any of the others. He did not speak her language at any rate; that much was clear to everyone.

Her father and mother kindly took care of this stranger over the following weeks and soon he was strong enough to get up and walk around. Not surprisingly, he seemed confused and uncertain of himself for some time, as any stranger in a strange land would, but did not take long to realise that wherever he had originally come from, all ties to that origin were now cut as completely as the *piko* (umbilical cord) is cut from an infant after birth.

As the months went by, Maile found herself increasingly fascinated by this great white-skinned man who at first spoke gibberish (at least she felt it so) in such an oddly musical manner. He, in turn, became quite devoted to her as well, for she had become truly a lovely young woman with all the fresh charms that maidenly beauty inspires in a woman.

For his part, he came to learn some of Maile's language with her help, and she then learned in turn that he came from a country far beyond the ocean's end that he called *E'ire*. He had by then remembered that he had fallen from a big boat he was sailing on, after being caught by surprise when the sail he was reefing unexpectedly filled with wind and threw him into the sea. Although the ship had sailed on, unaware of his plight, he had seen the island in the distance and had tried to swim to it. Only his good luck (he called it *'the luck o' Erin'*) had saved him by casting him up on the beach, where he had been found by Maile.

Over time, this strange red-haired man who called himself *'Pádraig'* fell deeply in love with beautiful Maile and they were pleased to discover that they both loved each other intensely and with equal passion. Maile, who had soon been brought into the full bloom of womanhood by Padraig's loving caresses, found herself to be bearing a child a short time later and in due course that child...a boy...was born on the island of Molokai, in the valley they call Halawa.

The child ultimately grew to manhood under the loving care and attention of his beautiful dark-skinned mother and his handsome, white-skinned, red-haired father and rose to prominence in the community, where his intelligence and gentle strength came to be appreciated and admired by all who came to know him. The Kahunas regarded him favorably as an exceptional person, despite his strangely colored skin and possessed of much *mana* (spirit), since his father had been delivered by the ocean. And so he was and had been.

This boy in time also found a maiden whom he loved among the Halawa people, and thus began the Molokai tradition of the merging and inter-melding of many races whose offspring have become the new *Kanaka Maoli* (locals) of modern Molokai.

It may amuse you to know also, that from this event a most unusual and uniquely Hawaiian *Saint Patrick's Day* story came into being on Molokai that is still repeated, both by the old *tutus*, when they regale the children with their many wonderful stories of the old traditional customs and history found on the island of *Molokai nui a Hina,* and by the locals when they raise a glass to old *Naomh Pádraig* every 17th of March on the *haole* calendar...

Or so I have been told by my own ancient *tutu* who says it is all as true and certain as the endless waves that sweep our island shores!

ZIPPING FLIES WITH PAPA HEMINGWAY

This probably sounds like a fish story already and I haven't even really begun it yet, but it's a true account of part of my childhood that leaps out of the polluted stream of my life like a ghostly mutant Koi from a toxic and stagnant backwater of past remembrance.

I was just a kid at the time the events described here took place, a precocious young under-achiever of an orfink-to-be. You'll recall perhaps that *'orfink'* was what Popeye the Sailor Man called little *'Swee'pea'*, the *orfink infink* adopted by him and *Olive Oyl*, but it's more likely that the term won't make any sense at all to attention-challenged Twitterers, those totally possessed by the evil commercial spirits that haunt their cellphones, individuals who think that ball cap visors are meant to shade the eyes (not the back of the head), kids who regard gang signs as *rilly kool*, and 20-somethings with multiple frontal lobe piercings to complement their full-brain tattoos.

But let's not dwell on these inalterable facts, since today you can be an orfink and still have a living biological father and mother present (well, the term 'present' is arguable, of course, and subject to highly variable interpretation) in your own home! My own orfinkhood came about some time after this story took place, but that's an entirely different tale.

In 1950, my own Da—a career military officer--shuffled off this mortal coil about 4 years into my post-VJ Day life as an infink, leaving Ma to keep on keeping on as both a parent and a wage-earner despite the sudden and unanticipated absence of our primary familial income. Fortunately for both of us, she had gotten her undergraduate degree as a teacher in Idaho some years before being swept off her feet by Da's highly corrosive Irish charm. After his funeral, was able to leave the San Francisco

Presidio officers' quarters without further delay (where we had been not uncomfortably ensconced) and take an available teaching position in the San Joaquin Valley with me in tow.

Since Ma spent most of her waking hours driving herself crazy in a hopeless effort to come up with meaningful (emphasis, emphasis) lesson plans for the education of vicious little inbred idiots (the offspring of Dust Bowl agricultural workers who'd settled in Steinbeck's wrathful bowl of grapes), she was in no mood to spend a lot of quality time with me (her own little vicious, inbred chile), most of the time.

To this day, I well recall how the daily ritual of 'coming home after school each day' played out. She'd walk in the door looking like she'd been hit by a Greyhound Bus, muttering about how abysmally stupid the *'Oakies', 'Arkies',* and '*Ozarkies'* were, how 'fat people' (one of her favorite subjects of disdain) were to be pitied, and how the swarms of little Black *pickanninies* were taking over the town's school classrooms.

Ma, you see, was the product of a higher-aspiring, upper-middle class Caucasian Presbyterian family (from the classic 'WASP' mold) of French-German Huguenots, the college educated daughter of a college educated mother, who had fallen for a handsome, already once previously married Irish-American Army officer in that uncertain lead-up to the outbreak of war with Japan. She had inherited strong artistic sensitivities and a considerable amount of graphics talent from her own mother.

She was broadly educated, but finding herself suddenly cast adrift in the uncertain vagaries of Central California life in the 1950s had somehow fueled a smoldering sense of resentment within her over being forced to cope with the proletarian necessities of survival in the male-dominated working world as a female school system employee and single parent.

Not in the least helpful was the fact that Ma's family took inordinate pride in their pedigreed line of Anglo-Saxon ancestry, a family that wasn't just satisfied with an ancestor on the Mayflower (no less than a relative of Captain John Smith) and being a cousin to the notorious Boston Witch Trials prosecutor (and scientific genius), Reverend Cotton Mather, but that claimed another, earlier one (Sir John Tewes) who actually helped finalise the much-amended Magna Carta, back in 1297. You just don't get much more hoity-toity as a honkie than this, but let me further intrigue you with the fact that Ma was also a fervent, card-carrying member of that arch WASPish organisation of blue-nosed American female flag-wavers, the *'Daughters of the American Revolution'* (who still think their archetypal, patriotic red/white/blue knickers don't get dirty like everyone else's). Last, but by no means least, her recently demised husband (my Da), had been a regimental drummer boy with Teddy Roosevelt's Rough Riders when they had stormed San Juan Hill in 1898 and she drew a widow's pension (small, but noteworthy) for that. Taken together, it was a heady mix of pedigrees for an impoverished school marm down on her luck to be mindful of in the midst of middle-class impoverishment.

All of Ma's subconscious sense of resentment, dented dignity, and impugned self-worth (I am convinced) came pouring out of her in her daily ranting disparagements of fat people, 'savage' little Black kids...and even worse, apparently...the ignorant offspring of White, trailer-trash agricultural laborers that had filled up the Central and Coastal California schools (and thereby given John Steinbeck with his immortally enduring subject material). And I, despite my feeling that as an only son I deserved some loving nurturing from me own mum, found myself the unwilling audience for these daily, post meridian diatribes that began (5 times each week) immediately school had ended for the day. You see, by the time Ma got home each afternoon, she was 'taught-out' and had little energy left over for sharing much of her wealth of insightful knowledge with me. For her, I suppose, it was energy conservation, pure and simple.

Despite my attempts to largely block, or at least divert these poisonous rivulets of bias through construction of a virtual *Grand Coulee Thought Dam* in my mind, I have no doubt that I nevertheless eventually became quite heavily contaminated by all that emotionally toxic sludge that flowed my way. It probably explains, at least in part, why I have a hard time relating comfortably to Blacks in my own life today (despite being one of those *"liberal white bastards"* everyone loves to vituperate), as well as the sharp stabs of deeply subconscious, liberal guilt I feel whenever I am confronted by the arch forces of politically correct reactionism (in all their indignant righteousness).

It definitely had something to do with my obsessive efforts to keep myself lean, not to mention an almost palpable dislike I still harbor for excess body fat (on myself and others), but hey...we all have our little personal demons and shoulder monkeys, eh? As long as those little wraiths don't whisper hateful things into our ears and encourage us to commit random acts of gratuitous homicidal rage, I figure they're relatively harmless on the broader scale of human buggaboos!

Of course, being a teacher's son (with no father), I also had the unfortunate handicap of being mercilessly bullied by those same little 'diverse' thugs in school that my mother so intensely disdained. Since they all likely thought of my Ma as a hateful representation of the dominant White culture that made their little disprivileged lives so wretched (her being all that and a female teacher, as well!), and in view of the fact that she also represented relatively unassailable educational authority, I became the logical scapegoat for all their reactive frustrations and delinquent resentments in my own classes.

But all of this is just some requisite background upon which to build the story that follows. Suffice it to conclude all the foregoing remarks by saying I didn't have a very happy or secure childhood in California, a fact that still lurks in my nature like some sort of rough beast that has learned in that darkly repressed sanctum of my lifetime to pull all the right strings that cause self-hurt, personal guilt, generalised insecurity and free-floating unhappiness.

As an intelligent and sensitive little guy, even disregarding the liabilities visited upon me by my attention-deficit affliction, and without a male role model to fall back on for pugilistic advice, I was left largely out there on the raging battlefield of male post-pubescent adolescence to my own devices. With no Da handy to coach me on how to land a good left hook on a bully's chin and lacking (apparently) any vestige of my Irish blood's vaunted heritage of giving back as good as I got (or worse), my usual impromptu defense was a verbal disparagement of my tormenter that had far too rich an eloquence to be ignored, and which invariably prompted more black eyes. Thus, I silently endured more than my share of completely undeserved abuse for being their hated teacher's smart (and vulnerable) little kid with an unnaturally large vocabulary (here I am reminded of poet jack Spicer's ostensible last words: *"My vocabulary did this to me!"*).

Despite all the emotional and ancestral baggage that came with being me in the childhood phase of my life, however, the one great saving blessing I could be grateful for was having an uncle (Ma's younger brother) named 'Charlie'. Uncle Charlie, as I unfailingly addressed him, was a successful physician and surgeon in the small Idaho farming community of Burley, a town located about 24 miles southeast of Twin Falls and situated just 75 miles or so above the trashy little pit-stop of an Idaho/Nevada border portal illustriously named 'Contact'. [At the time, Contact was a bump in the old frontier trail that had only a last-chance gas station, combined with a part-time Indian souvenir shop.]

The road through it, from Nevada to Idaho was originally a stage trail that back in Indian days was routinely attacked by renegade Shoshones; when we passed over it, parts of the road were still oiled gravel. Some sections of it, just past Contact proper, were surrounded on both sides by large rock formations that would have been perfect for ambushes by redskins looking to add a few blond scalps to the trophy collection! Today, Contact has grown into a large, somewhat sprawling little complex, full of neon and glitz, shops and stores, crowding the edges of several large Indian-owned gambling casinos. Now the Indians collect dollars instead of scalps! *Redskins' revenge!*

Burley was in fact my mother's home, having been born there along with Charlie after Granpa and Granma had (in the 1860s) left Savannah (Missouri) by wagon to settle in southern Idaho. Since Granpa was a pharmacist by profession (and therefore able to make a quite respectable living amidst all the dirt-poor farmers and cattle-poor cowboys, selling patent snake-oil and remedies), he operated a drug store that he later upgraded by associating it with the nation-wide Rexall Drug Store chain of the early 1900s. Grampa, whose given name was 'Charles Alfred', had named his son (my uncle) Charles as well and packed him off back east to Northwestern University, where Uncle Charles Alfred II soon finished up his academic studies by taking honors as a graduate of their (at the time VERY) prestigious medical school.

After graduation, Uncle Charlie returned to Burley and set up his practice as a physician and general surgeon on the town's main drag, just down the street from his father's pharmacy and sandwiched between a house of ill repute coyly named the 'Lee Rooms' and the local Grange office. Between father and son, they pretty much had the town of 3000 or so's health care business completely wrapped up. It was a cozy arrangement that brought the family quite a bit of both money and local prestige, but it didn't much help Ma's composure or self-regard as a suddenly widowed mother with a small dependent son who lived almost a thousand or more miles further west and awkwardly removed from any direct support by her family.

But since Ma had already been relocated out there in California for some time and with her eye directed towards eventually collecting a significant California State Teacher's Association retirement pension, she decided to remain where she was and settled for spending her available vacation time in Idaho. Since despite relatively modest pay, California teachers have traditionally (and up until recent decades) had the priceless benefit of a fully-paid three month annual vacation during summer recess, this meant that every June we'd pack up Da's prized old 1937 Oldsmobile and leave clouds of dust across the sere Nevada alkali wastes (some of the main roads were actually still unpaved then) in our haste to get back to the JR Simplot owned potato fields of beautiful, bucolic, rural (and intensely Mormon) southern Idaho.

As Uncle Charlie's less economically blessed older sister, Ma was grateful for being able to stay with the family for three months every summer. For this reason, most of the really close childhood chums I counted had been in Burley and not in California, since in Idaho I wasn't identified as the onerous offspring of a poor, single parent/teacher, but a first cousin of one of the wealthiest and most reputable families in town (and therefore not as heavily subject to prejudice by my peers). Those languid, relaxed and idyllic summers in Idaho almost made up for the bitter rigors of adolescent life in the Central Valley of California and since Burley was such a small town, despite our staying at Granma's relatively modest wood-framed house (Granpa had since passed on), Uncle Charlie's expensive brick mansion and my three first cousins were only a few blocks removed and easy to visit.

Uncle Charlie's life had, like that of most Americans and my mother, been substantially affected by the uncertainties of the Second World War. Following the lead of the majority of patriotic Americans immediately after the 1941 attack on Pearl Harbor had taken place, Uncle Charlie offered his medical expertise to the US Army, receiving a commission as a Captain in the medical corps. After a number of adventures serving as an army surgeon (first in the North African and later in the European campaigns) he finally mustered out of the Army in 1946 as a Lt. Colonel and returned home to Burley with a fairly generous separation bonus and plans to start Burley's first formal hospital (named '*The Cottage Hospital*').

Now just before Uncle Charlie had gone off to sew arms and legs back on wounded American soldiers (and about the time Ma had been swept off her feet by Da), wealthy American businessman (and Chairman of the Union Pacific Railroad Board) W. Averell Harriman had decided, in view of the great success of the Lake Placid Winter Olympics in 1932, to create a hybrid American counterpart to some of the most famous European winter resorts (like those found in Switzerland and Austria) known. By the end of 1936, his magnificent and exclusive new, year-round vacation resort of the Union Pacific's *'Sun Valley'* was ready to open (at least in its early phase) its doors to well-heeled, wealthy members of upper-class American and international society.

Located in Idaho's beautiful but poor Blane County, a vast range of sheep and cattle lands some hundred miles north of Burley and nestled just below the spectacularly beautiful Sawtooth and Salmon River Wilderness regions of the Challis National Forest, Sun Valley was at once a sensational recreational success with what soon became known in the 60s as 'jet setters'. Equally attractive to summer or winter visitors and providing a broad range of varied sports activities for the wealthy and well-connected, Averell's Sun Valley Resort was at that time principally accessed via his Union Pacific Railway, resulting in considerable profit for both the resort and the railroad. With some of the finest hunting, golfing, fishing, skiing, and riding available anywhere in the entire country all clustered together near the spectacular backdrop of the Idaho Rocky Mountains, Sun Valley instantly became the favored 'watering hole' of the nation's wealthy spoiled darlings, Hollywood movie stars, and upper-class members of society. A number of movies were shot there (one most memorably named *'Sun Valley Serenade'*, starring Sonje Henie and featuring Glenn Miller's band) and before long, the name 'Sun Valley' had come to be firmly associated with leisured wealth and upper-class society.

Although public use of the facilities was restricted temporarily during the war while Sun Valley was pressed into use as a US Navy casualty recovery hospital by the government, as soon as the war had ended the Union Pacific Railroad resort of Sun Valley again opened its doors to the pleasure-seeking privileged members of affluent American society in an even grander and more expanded form. It is worth noting in passing here that Harriman's Sun Valley, aside from proving to be positively visionary in its concept, later served as the singular inspiration for all of today's modern outdoor super resorts (esp. Vail, Aspen, Sugar Bowl, and other major recreational resort enclaves across the country.

At any rate, Uncle Charlie had returned home after the war, more than ready to forget all the sadness and violence he had witnessed and again resume civilian life. Endowed with a separation bonus that, combined with his normally substantial income as a community surgeon, provided considerable wherewithal, he enthusiastically plunged back into civilian medicine. As one of the founding members of what eventually became the Idaho Chapter of the American Medical Association, and in addition to being highly regarded by his medical peers, Charlie was known for having quite a bit of personal *savoir-faire* and was immediately attracted to the breathtakingly scenic rural environs that surrounded Sun Valley. With a keen and lifelong passion for fly fishing, golf, and skiing, the convenient location of the small little post silver-boom town of Ketchum, located directly adjacent to Sun Valley, prompted him to purchase a site there on which to build a vacation home for the family to enjoy.

Although the small-town site of Ketchum (present population now about several thousand) is today as ritzy and expensive as Sun Valley itself is to settle in, at that time it was a very small community of a few hundred souls who were mostly left-over dregs from the silver and lead mining boom that had figured chiefly in the region's economy, a few decades earlier. Property was reasonably inexpensive and all the wealth of Sun Valley's world-class recreational gate-way lay virtually at Ketchum's doorstep. It was a lovely place for a 'summer cabin'.

His appetite considerably whetted by the promise of the great shooting and fishing recreational offerings to be found near Ketchum, Charlie finally bought a piece of property located right along the water's edge of the Big Wood River and directly at the foot of Bald Mountain, a 9150-foot-high peak of spectacular natural beauty that is regarded by skiers and winter recreation sportsmen as perhaps the all-around best ski-mountain to be found in the entire nation. On this strip of scenically blessed land, Uncle Charlie contracted for a local fellow to construct a two-story 'log-cabin' that we would thereafter come to regard as our summertime home-away-from-home. While I reference it as a 'log-cabin', it would be more appropriate perhaps to describe it as a 'log-mansion', since it incorporated every modern convenience and luxury then known (1948) to a post-war America that was just discovering the joy of consuming unlimited amounts of material stuff.

The new digs included a separate 2-car garage and a ski loft fitted out with a pair of brand new 'Head' metal downhill skis for my aunt and my three older cousins (John, Corinne, and Charles Alfred III, who also became a surgeon like his dad). [I myself felt lucky to be able to borrow a pair of the beaten up old bear-trap binding, ex-10th Mountain Division surplus skis my cousins had formerly used. To his credit, Charlie had promised me a pair of the new Head skis if I made straight A grades at school, but that was as unlikely as Joseph Stalin suddenly becoming a Franciscan monk!]

At that time and prior to the introduction of the new metal ski technology (resulting from wartime advances in aircraft metal fabrication), all snow skis had been made of wood and had been fitted with what we now aspersively refer to as 'bear-trap' bindings (since they'd break your leg just about as effectively as a bear-trap, in the event of a fall). In fact, *most* skis then available were white-painted surplus relics of the Amy's 10th Mountain Division ski troops. With the new metal technology that sandwiched aluminum upper and lower layers over a wood core for maximum strength and flexibility, Head Skis overnight and single-handedly revolutionized the sport of downhill skiing and established the company as the premier, leading-edge supplier of high-quality winter sports gear for the well-to-do. Here then was Uncle Charlie, with a scenically sited, to-die-for river front vacation home at the foot of Bald Mountain, surrounded by nothing but the splendid solitude of a thick, luxurious pine forest and the soothing rush of water down coursing down one of the finest trout streams to be found anywhere. Best of all, it was located just a spit out the window from America's newest and most stylishly fashionable vacation resort development.

I don't think it would be hard to believe me if I stated that in having access to all this, I counted myself as perhaps one of the luckiest kids in the world (despite all the unhappy circumstances of life in California as a hated teacher's brat). Almost as soon as we arrived in Idaho each summer, we'd start getting things together to relocate to Ketchum for several weeks at a time, making the long drive up from Burley through the spectacularly desolate Shoshone volcanic lava fields (*Craters of the Moon National Monument*) and ready to settle back into Charlie's new digs. The first thing I usually did on arrival was to rush out to the river's edge and check out the prominent rocky spur situated above 500 feet above the cabin and across the river, on the side of Mt. Baldy.

Each year I'd delight to find the same family of American Bald Eagles comfortably nested there in a huge and well-protected nest that was safely inaccessible to any ground-based predators who might have a taste for unfledged eaglets. My attention would usually next turn to the prolific *'water skimmer'* and Mayfly nymph populations that inhabited the slow-moving shallows (along with the myriad other little water critters living amongst the rocks). After that, the local horsetail (*'Equisetum'*, a vascular plant that is essentially a living fossil often found growing in damp areas) patches demanded inspection, and the list of subsequent diversions was endless. It was, you see, a kid's paradise for discovery and it was...*all...mine.*

As for Uncle Charlie, as circumstances developed, his new post-war practice in Burley kept him typically so busy that he hardly had any time to get away to the psychically healing environs of his new cabin, but when he did manage to briefly tear himself away from his surgeries and AMA affairs, he was in his element. The trout fishing in particular was sensational, since the Big Wood River held healthy populations of large, fat Rainbow, Golden, and German Brown trout. Fly fishing was the name of the game, naturally, and all one had to do was step out the front door, walk across the lawn to the river, and wade out into its shallows with a creel and pole in hand. A few flicks of the wrist later and the wicker creel (filled with wet rushes) would soon be gorged to capacity with these beauteous piscatorial prizes. With hardly any game wardens to patrol the area, it was every fisherman's dream of an unfettered paradise and in retrospect it sometimes seemed as if we'd had trout for breakfast, lunch, and dinner...all fresh and right out of the sparkling waters of the river. *Fortunately*, we all loved fresh trout.

My own fly fishing techniques left a lot to be desired, of course, since I was only this California-raised kid who more often than not had only read about fish in books, rather than caught them in rivers with a real hook and line. For the most part I was satisfied with an ordinary spin-casting rod and reel my uncle bought me, since I'd used one at Scout Camp to lake fish and knew a bit about spin-casting. And so, armed with cheese balls and a bottle of salmon eggs, I'd set forth to try my luck. Given the fact that I've never been much of a Nimrod (I was more like a numb-rod, actually), I usually felt fortunate if I caught a couple of Rainbows over the course of a few hours, out in front of the cabin.

The one faded Kodacolor picture I still have of myself thus outfitted as an ace fisherman (at age 11--posted at the top) shows me wearing a broad grin that belies the actual difficulties with which I managed to get something on my hook that didn't regularly wiggle off and escape. [The smiling elderly woman on my right in that picture is Granma, who graduated Summa cum Laude from Lake Erie Women's College back in the 1800s, a time when most women were lucky to be allowed to attend high school by parents who sternly believed they should be mothers and not intellectuals. Granma was quite a world traveler, having ridden camels in Egypt at age 85! She even knew Gertrude Bell, famed post-Victorian adventurer and mentor of T. E. Lawrence, whom we know today as *'Lawrence of Arabia'*.]

Sometimes, if Uncle Charlie had been able to join us at the cabin, he would let me accompany him in a perpetually unsuccessful effort to learn how to fish with artificial flies, which was then one of those arcane mysteries of the male sports world that the fishing adept took much secret pride in. At such times, we'd wander up and down river, trying various prime fishing holes along the way, and Charlie would share 'instructive' stories with me about local fishermen who had drowned due to various careless acts of aquatic impropriety (such as wearing laced-up hip waders and stepping into an unexpected river hole). *Brrrrrr!* Great confidence-building stories for little kids! Mostly I learned to keep my trap shut and just try hard not to scare the fish away for Charlie, since just about everything I did was somehow disruptive of the unspoken rules that govern fly fishing in streams by groups of fishermen.

Since Gary *'Coop'* Cooper and *'Papa'* Hemingway were great friends and shooting partners, they were often to be seen in and around Sun Valley, either hunting or fishing together, but aside from Uncle Charlie's family and one or two other physicians' families who had built cabins near Uncle Charlie's property (after hearing of his real estate acquisition there), we rarely ran into others fishing along that long and serene stretch of the Big Wood River that lay at the foot of Bald Mountain. Thus, when we did run into a few other fishermen, it would more often than not be Papa Hemingway with some of his buddies.

Big Wood River's bountiful fishing wasn't just a local secret, naturally, as over the course of years from its inception through the 1960s, the absolutely great angling opportunities to be found therein drew large numbers of economically well-off seasonal visitors who regularly sought out exceptional fishing and hunting venues across the country for personal recreation. Among them were an appreciable number of the most well-known American and international motion picture stars and entertainment celebrities, as well as many well-known luminaries from the world of writing and literature, politicians of note, and a wide array of prominent public note-worthies.

Chief among the latter ranks was renown *'Lost Generation'* author Ernest Hemingway, who had completed *For Whom the Bell Tolls* (considered by many to be his greatest novel) while originally staying in suite 206 of the Sun Valley Lodge in the fall of 1939. At Sun Valley's inception, Averell Harriman had invited Hemingway and other celebrity friends (principally from Hollywood) to the resort to help promote it. With all his writing and screen-writing successes, Hemingway had quickly cultivated a following of a number of Hollywood's favorite stars, who were in turn soon captivated by the man's larger than life personality. Gary Cooper was a particularly frequent visitor and favored Hemingway hunting/fishing partner, as were Clark Gable, Errol Flynn, Lucille Ball, Marilyn Monroe, and a number of members of the extended Joseph Kennedy family (just to name a very few).

As a kid of 11 I had, of course, no clear idea of who precisely Ernest Hemingway was, other than a vague impression based upon the sparse information Uncle

Charlie gave me in answer to my naïve questions. He'd simply pass it off with a casual *"He's a well- known writer"* remark and let it go at that, but since he had personally attended the big man (and other celebrities) at Sun Valley for miscellaneous odd ailments and aches on the occasion of Papa's frequent returns to the resort, Charlie knew Hemingway on more than a casual basis. Mostly their associations in the river were limited to the sort of masculine bonding conversations that characterise just about any male sports activity, consisting mostly of brief discussions and exchanges on the effects of weather on the fish, the day's catches, how they were biting, the merits of certain baits and flies that seemed to work better than others, where the fish were feeding and so forth. Since Charlie didn't drink and Papa did, they were not accustomed to socialising over a bottle of expensive Cognac after a days' catch, as were most of Papa's other buddies.

Hemingway towered over me, even as an older man in his early 60s, but then so did everyone else, my being this little kid to whom all others were usually adult and therefore large-sized people. I well remember a couple of occasions when Charlie and I were on the river fishing, when around the bend came Papa with a few of his well 'lubricated' close confreres. On one occasion, it was Gary Cooper that Papa had in tow, a particularly familiar confidant of Papa's from what I was told, and Coop stood so tall that it seemed to me in person to be every bit the gaunt, laconic, giant cowboy he came across as in the movie *'High Noon'.*

Being a small boy, I rarely spoke to anyone unless spoken to, since that was the adult etiquette of my time spent in Burley with stentorian Uncle Charlie and I was also a sort of shy little guy by nature. One time when we were out there, we rounded the downstream northeast bend in the river to stumble upon none other than Papa, poised in the shallows and artfully framed by the day's fading sunlight, taking a *whiz* by the water's edge. Totally unconcerned about the sudden invasion of his privacy, Hemingway nodded at my uncle, flashing his famously broad and toothy smile, shook a few last drops from his prodigious *willie*, and zipped up his fly with the natural satisfaction of someone who has drunk a few too many glasses of lager before happy hour had officially begun. [Now you will perhaps better understand the title of this piece: *'Zipping Flies with Papa Hemingway'*.]

With that, he reached into his creel with the same coarse brown fingers he'd just shaken his willie with and pulled out a couple of the biggest Brown Trout I'd ever seen, saying *"Here, take these Brown Trout off my hands, boy, but don't be surprised if they put up a fight in your frying pan! Even dead, they're due respect with each bite"* (or something approximating this, since it's been almost 50 years now since the incident occurred). Taking the big fish from him a bit tentatively, I smiled my best little kid smile at Papa and glanced anxiously back at Uncle Charlie as if to say "OK...now what?" We had the fish for dinner that night (along with some Rainbows Charlie caught) and I still remember how good they tasted. In the background while we dined on trout, Charlie's old Zenith phonograph was playing a 78 RPM recording of Gershwin's *'American in Paris'*, a song that would doubtless have pleased Papa greatly, had he been there to share our moveable fishy feast.

At any rate, Hemingway had also fallen under the enchanting spell of the Big Wood River's relaxed ambience shortly after discovering the recreational paradise that was Sun Valley and it wasn't long before he also bought a home situated a bit further downstream and not too far from the old Warm Springs Resort (since closed down) on Big Wood River. We could walk to it easily from our own cabin and would occasionally pass by it as we ambled along in the shallows of the river. I recall that the Hemingway place had had a sort of strangely modern appearance, being of a squat and incongruous concrete construction and not quite the perfect woodsy setting I would today imagine as suitable for a man of Hemingway's illustriously outdoorsy affect. Uncle Charlie pointed it out to me on several occasions during the course of our now-and-then fishing excursions, since in the intervening several years I had studied literature in my first year or two of high school and by then had acquired a somewhat better idea of exactly who and what 'Papa' Hemingway was in the world of modern literature.

Some years later, when I was 15 (1961), Ma and I had once more returned to Sun Valley and Ketchum for a summer stay and were installed in Uncle Charlie's cabin in the shadowed lee of Mt. Baldy when Papa decided to bring the final chapter of his storied life to a premature and spectacular climax. Having long suffered from the combined effects of alcoholism, depression (undoubtedly augmented by his many years of ETOH abuse), free-floating fears of aging, the latent after-effects of electroshock therapy, fears of his own fame, and perhaps a little-known form of metabolic disease known as 'bronze diabetes' (hemochromatosis), in the quiet and peaceful early Sunday morning hours of July 2nd, Papa got up before his wife Mary and went downstairs.

Reaching into his gun cabinet in the cabin's hallway, he put the barrels of his favorite double-barreled shotgun to his head and pulled the triggers. Startled awake by the resounding blast in that solidly constructed house, Mary Hemingway hurried down the stairs and found Papa dead of a single 12-gauge shell's discharge (only one of the two barrels had fired). It was a particularly gruesome scene (according to medical reports), for he had rested his forehead on the barrels, braced the butt of the gun on the floor, and blown the upper half of his head entirely off. At the age of 61, Hemingway had scripted the final chapter in his life's story, joining several other members of his family who at various times would also choose suicide as an exit from life.

The first those of us at Charlie's cabin had known of this event was when the wail of the local sheriff's squad car broke the peaceful languor that had settled in on the river that morning, but nothing definitive in terms of what had happened was initially circulated, other than a rumor that *"...it appears as if author Ernest Hemingway has died from an accidental gun injury".* As we later found out, that was Mary Hemingway's desperately hopeful interpretation of what had happened, albeit a false hope entirely understandable by virtue of the shock she had experienced over the violent nature of his death. The actual truth of Papa's suicide was kept obscured from public scrutiny for a significant while after that, although no one who knew him was really fooled by the 'gun accident' cover story. Eventually everyone came to learn the unhappy facts behind the circumstances of Papa's demise.

After all the hubbub had subsided, Papa Hemingway was laid to rest in the Ketchum Cemetery near a large old tree. Mysteriously, almost as soon as his remains had been interred, it was noticed by locals that the level of his grave appeared to be sinking rather more precipitously each day, or at least a lot more than one would expect from mere subsidence of freshly dug soil placed on a recent grave. This bizarre circumstance continued over the next few weeks despite the almost daily replenishment of dirt over his plot by cemetery caretakers and stories soon began to circulate speculating on all sorts of strange and mysterious causes.

Finally, it dawned on locals that someone was physically removing dirt in some quantity from the site to sell as macabre souvenirs of the literary giant and his near-legendary life. One unconscionably clever fellow in particular was in fact observed actually making off with the grave's soil by the bucketful for that purpose. After this fact came to light, the gravesite was quickly enclosed by a suitably protective fence, although eventually that was removed as soon as the public's rabid fascination with his violent demise had lessened. Papa's last wife, Mary, was eventually laid to rest near him.

Today, the grave remains a quiet and unremarkable place of calm and picturesque serenity, flanked by two large sentinel trees and backed by the natural beauty of Idaho's Sawtooth Range. The last time I was there, a number of years ago on a foggy morning, in my imagination I fancied I could see Papa's grizzled ghost standing there behind one of those tall, dark trees that stand guard on either side of him, zipping up his trousers with gusto and saying "*Boy, there's only one thing better than catching a Brownie and that's taking a whiz downstream with your best dog, on the banks of your favorite fishing hole...*"

Papa would be the first to affirm the simple pleasures of those possibilities, were he alive today, I remain convinced...

* * *

[Note: I returned to Sun valley and Ketchum a few years ago, on a nostalgic trip to that best-loved part of my childhood. The changes everywhere were palpable and dramatic. Ketchum and Sun Valley are now well beyond the economic reach of most 'ordinary' people to enjoy and predictably Ketchum is now an art colony and haven for high-roller realtors and wealthy families who apparently need *'artsiness'* in their expensive lives. As for Uncle Charlie's cabin on Big Wood River Road (it's now a paved street), it had been so 'improved' as to render it almost unrecognisable and had been put on the market for sale at a modest 3.5 million dollars. I seem to recall that Charlie had originally paid $9,000 for both property and cabin, back in the late 40s, and in 1976 he sold it for the princely sum of $125,000, dividing the return on it among his three children, my first cousins.]

A SPARROW IN THE STORM

It was really a very small hill. Green and grass covered, a modest mass that barely qualified it as more than an up-thrust hump. A geological odd fellow of no consequence at all against the grand severity of the surrounding peaks of the *Oberbayern* countryside.

Perched precariously atop the hill was a small figure. Despite his leather helmet, goggles and jacket, it was apparent that this was not a full-grown man but a mere boy. The boy hunched, tensely, in the seat of a flimsy, fabric-covered contraption with wings. A closer study of the object revealed its purpose. It was a glider. A rude, almost home-made one to be sure, but definitely designed to fly without a motor...if it got off the ground!

In the cool Bavarian air of the morning, all was calm. The trees stood quietly, uncritical and neutral witnesses to the scene that was unfolding. Small birds...*sparrows*...flitted about, chirping as they pursued their insect prey among the pine boughs. In the distance, the rising sun glimmered upon the snow fields of the craggy ridges which rose behind the *Kreuzeckhaus*. A distant tinkle of cowbells punctuated the pastoral peace which prevailed.

All nature seemed at peace...except on the grassy mound. The 14-year-old lad sitting at the controls of the glider was quietly sweating liters. He was grateful for the fact that his face was largely hidden by the awkward and poorly fitting padded leather helmet, the intensity of his gaze unviewable to the other boys standing near the wing-tips holding the rickety craft steady. His hands grasped the control stick grimly. It was important, he reminded himself, that he keep *both* hands on the stick, for to rest one of them in his lap would surely reveal the small tremor that his acute anxiety was producing in them. It would not do to reveal the fear that consumed his fluttering heart.

The small group of figures clustered around the craft were exchanging comments in a serious manner. Their somber, determined airs belied their youthful appearance, that seemed strangely out of context in this tranquil and beautiful alpine setting. Standing some distance away from the group was an adult, khaki-clad, holding a clipboard and staring intently upwind. His insignia revealed him to be a member of the NSFK, or *National Socialist Flieger Korps*. Attached to the under part of the glider was a rope cable. It joined the skid rail attachment which served as an undercarriage on this machine, just forward of the single bench seat which the boy fidgeted nervously upon. The rope ran from the metal connector on the skid in a line, straight and true, aimed along a tangent that led it some 25 yards, where it joined a heavier, woven cable of thick rubber cords. At a distance of several hundred feet directly ahead of the glider, the cable assembly fed into an awkward, metal pulley-device. Squatting below the large wheel-like mechanism was a naked petrol engine. The engine was smeared with grime but was otherwise very well maintained, from appearances.

And it had to be. For upon command from the boys' leader, the engine, which was running quietly in neutral gear, would be run up to maximum RPM and the clutch lock on the pulley wheel slipped. With massive force, the rope and rubber cable would quickly retract around the wheel and the soaring machine connected to it would be snapped forward with a strong jerk, gathering momentum as it hurtled down the hill. There would be little time for second-thoughts or anxious apprehensions once the craft was in motion, for within a matter of seconds it would be at that critical point whereupon, at the threshold of true aerodynamic flight, the small figure in the pilot's seat must perform quickly, precisely and without hesitation to both release the 'slingshot' cable and manipulate the control surfaces to steady the machine in its awkward leap from earth-bound thrall to air-borne release.

The leader was making a notation on his clipboard. In a minute or so the moment of truth would occur. In the glider's seat, the boy wrested his mind away from the disastrous possibilities which he knew all too well existed; he had studied aerodynamic theory quite exhaustively, along with all the other members of his troop of *Hitler Jugend*. He had flown model gliders countless times in the course of his study and had witnessed more than a few spectacular crashes and mishaps. The results had been sobering, even to a boy of 14 who thought--with all the characteristic indestructibility of youthful optimism--that he would live forever.

But it was now time to plant these fleeting seeds of black pessimism back in the ground; in split seconds, he would be in another element altogether: in a floating, wheeling and utterly free world which would allow him to race the birds over the tree-tops and scorn worries of the terrible war that was mercilessly destroying his native homeland. The boy looked briefly away from the wing, where his friends were checking the wires and stays and glanced up at the sky far over the massive crest of the *Zugspitze*.
It *was* a train! So real was the appearance, that smoke seemed to be coming from an outsized cropping of rock near the *Münchnerhaus* on the summit! He stared, briefly fascinated by another sight much higher up, of the lines of billowing white condensation that streamed high over the Zugspitze by the hundreds, toward the north. He knew this sight as well as any of the other members of his troop, for at this late date in the war, such spectacles of vast armadas of allied bombers streaking through the stratosphere were common.

Of course, he had no idea of the sheer magnitude of death and destruction which this remote sight symbolized, for the careful indoctrination of the troop's instructors spared them the awful reality of all that. At this moment, he felt instead of anguish, a detached, almost kindred affinity with those awesome machines which thundered so high and so serenely above the green earth below. He wished it were he up there, far above the clouds and free to soar beyond the horizon. All of these thoughts crowded into a single second of time as his attention snapped back to the imminent task at hand.

The leader's hand went up. It was a signal that the moment of release was very near. The boy shifted his weight in the insubstantial seat, placed his hands firmly on the control stick. Near the right wingtip a blonde, tow-headed friend of his was shouting something to him. He heard the words and moved the control stick forward and back, side to side. The surfaces of the rudder, wings and tail planes all worked as he knew they would.

It was only a few seconds now before the command to release the cable wind-up would be given. In the distance, he saw the puff of white smoke that indicated the engine was being run up to maximum RPM. He searched his mind quickly... had he forgotten anything? No. It was all a routine he had practiced countless times using a grounded training glider made of crates and boards. *Alles ist ordnung*. He was ready.

"Loss!" came the shouted signal as the leader's hand snapped down in an arc. The mass of fabric and wood that would now leap into the air jolted violently with the force which the cable transmitted to the glider. The boy gulped involuntarily. The sweat streamed down his neck, catching the bracing rush of alpine air through the openings in his jacket. The shock of the catapult left too little time to think about what was happening. Within seconds he was teetering unsurely, still linked to the ground but hovering on the

bumpy, uncertain verge of aerodynamic flight. Not yet neither bird nor flying machine, the glider shot forward, gathering speed. Far behind him, his troop had long since released the wingtips, running at top speed alongside as the taut cable pulled the accelerating machine off the hill.

Instinctively, the student pilot sensed that the craft was under the positive influence of lifting forces, felt the rough turbulence that marked off the edge of flight from laminar ground effect. He smoothed out the machine with sensitive motions of his hands on the stick. A few more seconds, now...

His right hand gripping the stick, he placed his left upon the metal cable release by his leg and waited, sensing the motions of the now fully flying machine through the contact of his body with the seat, eyes fixed upon the trees at the end of the run-out below the hill. *'Proprioceptic'* was the term his leader had used to describe this inherent seat-of-the-pants sensing of what the machine was doing.

All fear, all tension, even the greasy feeling he had had in the pit of his stomach just moments ago were gone...left behind as the release snapped firmly to the limit of its travel. Adrenalin was running the show now, controlled the moment and dictated completely the sequence of events that ticked off his mental check-list. The cable parted perfectly with a small thump. As it fell away, the small glider rocked gently like a dove flexing its pinions in mid-swoop and strained for the thermals of the ridge ahead.
The troop gathered below could see the spare outline of the white fuselage clearly in the slanted rays of the morning sun. It was a fair launch. The leader noted something on his clipboard and momentarily grimaced in the strong glare of the sun as the craft banked in front of it. The student's friends were enthusiastically caught up in the simple perfection of the moment, raptly watching the progress of the silent machine. As they studied it, they

followed its slow, almost floating, motion as it swept around, pointing toward the high pasture behind the *Kreuzeckhaus*. On the deck of the Alpenvereins structure, several people also followed the leisurely flight of the machine as it played hide-and-seek with the thermal currents of air sweeping up around the Zugspitze's massive bulk.

Of the six or seven figures at the umbrella-shaded tables, a small, spare and dark-haired Asian man sat apart, studying the spectacle. His features contrasted strongly with the fair-haired, sturdy Caucasian appearance of those not far from him. It did not occur to him to think too strongly of the differences his Japanese features painted in comparison to his companions, for he was also caught up in the quiet beauty of the soaring, man-made bird as it reached for the invisible pillars of heated air which coiled high up into the empty blue sky. *Masuo Yoshimura* was enjoying his visit to the glider training site, despite the cold and unignorable facts concerning the raging conflict which soon threatened to overwhelm Germany. He had been invited to view the training program, of which these young student fliers were part, at the behest of the German War Ministry and with the blessing and official encouragement of the Messerschmitt factory.

As he watched the small white machine slowly wheel through the heavy low-altitude density of the crisp, cool morning, he found himself recalling what the Messerschmitt people had said about Dr. Lippisch's advanced new design. The Me-163 *Komet*, they had designated the prototypes. It was, he recalled, a rather radical idea, but nevertheless, one that had a streak of brilliant if desperate genius in it.

The *Komet* was a glider. Of sorts. Rather, it was a fearsomely armed machine which, powered by a reaction engine that enabled it to streak through allied bomber formations at upwards of 575 miles per hour and shoot them down, before exhausting its fuel a mere 6 minutes after launch. With no propellant tank empty, it was then nothing but a very advanced and aerodynamically advanced glider.

The *Komet* was also a product of the hopeless pragmatism which Germany found itself compelled to resort to in the face of a growing threat of losing the war which they themselves had loosed upon the European continent. And it was designed with ruthless and daringly advanced technological skill which the German aircraft industry hoped would win the battle for the skies, thereby saving those who now desperate fought on the ground.

As an armed gun platform of blinding speed, the *Komet* had all the advantages going for it. All of them. Speed, surprise and power. The concept postulated that ultimately whole squadrons of these small, delta-winged and elevon equipped projectiles would be able to launch from sites directly in the path of the growing allied bomber formations, rocket up to 30,000 feet in a matter of minutes and wreak severe havoc and destruction among the boxes of slowly moving bombers almost before they knew what was upon them; six minutes from launch, fuel and oxidizer spent, the craft would drop back down to its base, hoping to land in the absence of any intruding allied fighters. During landing they would be quite literally helpless, sitting ducks in an Allied shooting gallery.

Yoshimura, as the representative of the Mitsubishi Aircraft Factory on liaison duty with the German Luftwaffe, and in the capacity today of an observer, was intrigued with the idea. So very much different from our own studies of piloted, flying bombs, designed for missions which included no provision for the safe return of the aircrew, he mused. *This one actually brought the pilot back alive!*

A woman at the nearby table was shielding her eyes as she looked toward the white glider. She was talking in an animated manner with the tall German officer seated next to her. He kept his eyes on the glider as the woman gestured just out of Yoshimura's earshot. Colonel von Strasser was the Luftwaffe's officer in charge of the glider training program; it was clear from the relish which he downed the delicious Bavarian beer in his stein that he did not particularly miss his old assignment in the East, nor did he particularly care to leave this beautiful haven of fragile peace in the midst of a world he had seen enough of...a world being ripped savagely apart.

Strasser suddenly glanced in Yoshimura's direction. Their eyes met for an instant, and Yoshimura flashed the 'thumbs up' recognition of a good flight to the Colonel, who smiled sparely before returning his gaze skyward.

In the distance, the glider waggled momentarily and dropped quickly for an instant before catching another updraft. It suddenly brought Masao's thoughts back to something one of the Messerschmitt flight test pilots had remarked upon a week ago, over perhaps one-too-many cognacs.

"They have an unfortunate habit, you know, of blowing up on touchdown." The pilot had been drinking with a determination that puzzled Masao. *"Something having to do with the hypergolic nature of the propellant and oxidizer slop left in the combustion tubes after the rocket engine shuts down. When the Komet hits the earth on its landing skid at the end of its flight, the residue often spontaneously ignites and blows the little bastard to tiny bits."*

The pilot paused, downing a quick swallow of the expensive French cognac he now had in his hand--*how did the Luftwaffe obtain these increasingly rare vintages in the midst of this horrible war? "I don't have to tell you how many pieces the pilot is often blown into…? Do you know that the original Komet test pilot was a woman? A woman!"*

The pilot was obviously relieved that he was not assigned to the *Komet* program and Masao quickly wondered how much of what this slightly intoxicated officer was telling him was highly classified information. In retrospect, it seemed like something that the Messerschmitt people had neither the time nor inclination to attempt to rectify, for their primary concerns were to get the pilot up to the bombers.... and of apparently lesser significance was the matter of getting the pilot back in complete safety.
This relatively unknown aspect of the *Komet* development program had very limited currency, from what Masao could gather in his casual conversations with other officials, more highly placed in the project. It was obvious as to why.

Masao glanced once again at the white sailplane being flown by the Hitler Youth student glider pilot, as it circled around for a return to the pastoral clearing which served as a landing site. These boys, he reflected, who were really not much more than children, were being trained systematically to be glider pilots. Once modestly trained in these simple craft, they would be immediately fed *directly* into accelerated flight operations for the *Komet*.

The *Komet* was really more of a deadly 'shooting star,' he found himself thinking. How *could* these young men know what *really* lay in store for them?

Their whole world, so tightly structured by the propagandists, did not include the very real possibility of suffering death through the conveniently overlooked technical problem that the unresolved *Komet* landing explosions presented.

The thought of these young men dying in such a coldly, premeditated manner brought thoughts of his brother, Yukio, to mind. He wondered how he was faring in the United States, in the lengthening shadow of the Pacific War. It had been a long, long time since he had heard anything about the welfare of his younger brother, his wife, and the other friends and relatives who had chosen to remain in the US prior to the outbreak of the war. Anything was possible these days, he realised soberly. What is another life in the unending flood tide of humanity?

Overhead, the fragile assembly of fabric covered spars and longerons was gliding back over the Kreuzeckhaus like a large, silent bird. The view from up over the Zugspitze had been remarkable. With perfect crystal clarity, one could see all the surrounding countryside effortlessly, despite the thick glass goggles. The student at the control stick had quickly become caught up in the lazy, un-hurried game of seeking updrafts, all anxiety and nervousness entirely forgotten in the thrill of pure flight. It had all been a slow-motion, utterly noiseless journey around and over the rugged rocky spines of the Zugspitze's jagged back, broken only by the whistle of the wind through the wire stays and past the wing struts. How marvelous it felt, and what promise it was of better experiences to follow!

The boy shifted his weight in the simple sailplane's seat and returned his thoughts to the task of bringing the graceful bird down within the narrow confines of the cleared landing area. Although he had not done so before, once again the drill was burned into his memory. The instructions leaped up on mental command as he reviewed the landing procedure in his mind. Trim for landing. Maintain airspeed. Adjust angle of attack. Run base-leg to final. Bank left, recover. Maintain airspeed. Line it up. Carefully. *Kiss the ground like a lover...*

He felt a trifle of apprehension return as the ground loomed closer.

The sweaty feeling was returning as he clutched the stick gingerly, ready to correct at the slightest hint of a cross-gust. As the ground neared he remembered the instructor's admonishment to come down at a fairly steep angle so as to keep the all-important airspeed up...a stall without power could be deadly. Despite this understanding it still seemed somewhat unnatural to maintain speed toward the earth at such a sharp rate of descent. The raw edge of nervousness was fighting his rational knowledge of final approach procedure for gliders as he brought the now rapidly dropping craft over the threshold of the cleared field, every nerve taut and ready to respond. He sensed rather than felt the embrace of ground effect airflow over the wings as he dropped lower still.

Just as he was starting to flare-out, scant feet above the deck, something flashed into the corner of the narrow field of vision the bulky goggles afforded. With the speed of desperation known only by the pursued as the pursuer closes in, a small brown bird, fleeing for its life from the sharp and merciless talons of a hotly trailing falcon smashed with full force into his eyes.

Despite the protection of the goggles, the sudden surprise of the blow to his face caused an involuntary jerk of his hands on the control stick, as the falcon narrowly swerved to avoid a similar impact.

The momentary movement of the stick to the left altered the even balance of the glider as it penetrated the cushion of ground effect and within a split second the left wing-tip had tapped the ground. The force with which it hit was not really enough to upset the machine, had it not been for a stubby growth of stunted tree branch which had been overlooked by a careless member of the troop. The wing-tip caught the branch with just enough force to tip the glider over towards the left at a fairly high speed. Once altered, the flight path deteriorated suddenly as the spindly glider impacted and broke apart in several large pieces.

Those watching from the Krueuzeckhaus deck leaped up, as did the troop of Hitler Youth who were watching their friend and troopmate bring his machine in for what had appeared to be a perfect first landing. All converged upon the tattered shreds of fabric and spars which lay desolately, abandoned by inertia and forsaken by the forces of lift. Through some miracle, the boy at the controls had been wrenched out of the seat as the restraint straps broke and had been almost gently lofted into the air at the moment of impact. After two complete loops, he had been deposited, although firmly and painfully, in a sitting position on a particularly grassy portion of the clearing. He sat, dazed, speechless and not quite sure if he were still altogether or not...but conscious and fully aware.

As the leader approached at a run, followed by the other students, the boy looked down at his left leg. A reddish stain was soaking his pants, and he recognized with a sickening shock that a piece of sharply splintered bone was protruding from the encircling, bloody stain just above the knee.

Looking up into the Leader's blanched face, he numbly heard the former speak: *"Mein Gott, Heinzie, that's no way to treat the Reich's property!"* Then the pain began...

Yoshimura, who had jumped up from his seat on the deck, observed the whole incident from afar. Now there, he thought to himself, is one very, very fortunate young man...he would be sent immediately to hospital for a prolonged recovery...and very far away from the deadly fighting.

The boy, 14-year-old Heinz Gross, born in Jena and ultimately destined to become a US citizen, owning a successful biergarten deli in Santa Cruz (CA), would have agreed completely, had he been able to foresee his future otherwise!

NOTES FROM THE BUNKER

This is being *tappety-tapped* at Underdog's *Fortress of Solitariness* on the North California Coast, at a secret locale roughly north of Fort Ross and Fort Bragg (i.e. in the Mendocino area). As much of an unfan of the whole Superman/fantasy hero shtick as I am, I still acknowledge the fact that in one specific of the Superman story, Marvel Comics Group had it right! Superman's *Fortress of Solitude* was a wizardly plot invention in the Superman storyline. While I am not sure whether all men value solitude as much as do I, from early puppyhood onwards I have had a strong need for a well-hidden kennel of refuge to which I can venture in periodic retreats from the stark insanity that so often passes for American life. In being of this particular sentiment, Michael Moore could be my older, smarter brother, since our socio-political outlooks quite often appear to be as congruent as Christ on a rough rude crucifix.

I usually refer to this place as my 'bunker', although it is in reality the vacation retreat of a very old and greatly valued friend who is as close as a blood-brother to me. *Mi amistad de sangre* uses it rarely, if ever, since he is usually far away, taking care of chemical and biological defense concerns on the other side of the planet. Therefore, I pretty much have it to myself, whenever the spirit (or diminishment of it, as the case may be) moves. It is small enough, (only about 750 ft sq total) to be mistaken for a large gothic doghouse, but thoughtfully located on a coastal hilltop overlooking the ocean and screened on three sides by a lovely private forest of Norfolk Pines. The house itself is simply designed in the shape of a square and has two internal rooms. No *fancy-schmancy* stuff here, just basic utility and a sort of rough, woodsy coastal elegance that blends in perfectly with the whole Northern California mood.

Set up as a bachelor cottage, with an interior atmosphere that is an eclectic blend of 1920s *'Bohemian Grove'* parlor and half University of California at Berkeley dorm room, it is perfect for reflecting tranquilly on the woes of this weary old world, perched as it is as an *ærie* overlooking some of the most spectacularly beautiful coastal scenery found south of the Oregon shoreline.

From my reckoning, it is just about as ideal a hideaway as any reasonably complicated guy could hope for and has all the requisite accoutrements that a creative throwback like myself needs to soldier on in comfortably spartan seclusion. Among its delights are a French press pot for preparing my frequent hits of caffeine, a telescope for Gray Whale watching, binoculars for checking out the bikinied wildlife on the beach far below (summers only), a library that would make the archetypal Cal Berkeley graduate librarian drool with envy and a porch with southern exposure that makes wintering over here absolutely splendid.

What it doesn't have is just as important as what it does have, and that includes NO landline telephone and no television (although it is equipped with dial-up modem landline access). The sleeping accommodations are also to my liking, with a nice thick futon in a sleeping loft providing either simple nighttime comfort, or romantic ambience (as the case may be). Cooking rituals are undertaken on a propane stove and beautifully pure water comes from a well out in the yard. Its one concession to modern comfort is a Grand Coulee Dam spillway of a shower that provides plenty of luxuriously hot water from a solar heating system, and I hope to shout that there're few things as wonderful on a chilly Pacific Coast winter morning than a hot mug of strong coffee, followed by a healthy shit, a hot shower, and a log fire (in that order). In fact, those four things have to rank so far up on the male scale of 'Good Things' (*sorry*, Martha...they may not be your 'good things', but they're definitely mine!) that prolonged, noisy, juicy sex itself arguably drops to 5th place on this list.

In short, 'The Bunker' is paradisiacal for all my intents and purposes, and when I'm not chilling on a Molokai beach, I'm usually up here on my coastal hill-top retreat. Actually, Molokai and Northern California are both equally important to me, since as a Gemini (in Chinese astrology I'm a 'Fire Dog'), there are two distinctly polar halves of my personality that require constant upkeep. Being a person prone to polar extremes is something I have long since gotten used to, but whether I am this way due to a self-fulfilling propensity urged into being by knowledge of the properties of my astrological sign, or whether the cause is more genetic and/or blamable on formative socializing influences, is anyone's guess. I like to excuse this nature on the basis of the traditional regard the Japanese had for people who do not fit the requisite mold of uniformity as being *'exceptional'*. Whether true or not, it serves as a useful ego-boosting rationalisation that I avail myself of frequently, on occasion.

This stellar duality is reflected in my near equal regard for both Molokai and the North California Coast as important elements of my geophysical life support matrix, since each has diametrically unique, yet spiritually important experiential qualities that feed my soul. I could no more thrive without the gentle Pacific Island trade-winds than I could without the cool coastal California convection fogs that regulate the microclimate found in this region. Ancient volcanic Molokai, with its unique South Pacific oceanic climate and culture has a special magic all of its own, naturally, that is unique in all the world (excluding other Pacific Island locales), whereas the same is true (at least in a climatic sense) with Northern California's wonderfully *saturnine* Sequoia redwoods and its rugged, melancholy coastline. Taken together, they constitute (as co-equal halves of a whole) my concept of heavenly paradise.

Today, as I look out over the wonderful Pacific coast, it is balmy and calm, with just the gentlest hint of an off-shore breeze. The swells coming in from the east are as smooth and undisturbed as the languid icing swirls on a chocolate layer cake. As the sun heats up the landscape and throws off the residual chill from the previous night, the sense of invigorating newness and freshness imparted is almost as palpable as the scent of pines in the air. Out at sea, a pod of Gray Whales is passing off the coast, lazily taking their time along the annual migratory route to the northern waters to graze on the rich varieties of tiny California sea life found here. Overhead, hawks and seabirds wheel and dive on invisible thermals rising from the headland, while further out to sea whole squadrons of immensely ungainly pelicans improbably fly single-file in close formation just above the surface of the water, fishing (they remind me of huge airliners like the new Airbus A-380, similarly monstrously large and seemingly un-airworthy by virtue of their vast bulk and un-aerodynamic weightiness).

My two Siberians are snoozing peacefully nearby, having returned a short while ago from a leisurely *sniff-and-squirt* excursion on the hillside and now perfectly content to drift off to doggy-dreamland (or wherever it is that dogs go, when sleeping), lulled to slumber by the nonstop *tappety-tap* clicking sounds from my keyboard. Raki (my big male) is having dreams, judging by the spasmodic jerking of his huge furry paws and the excited snorts he is somnolently emitting. Doubtless, he is chasing deer through the brambles that are found on the hillside, between the trees, and having the time of his life in unconscious pursuit of imaginary does that always somehow manage to elude him. Laika, my bitch, is more peacefully reposed and breathing heavily, the exposed pads of her dainty little doggy feet looking like graceful toe-shoes of a ballerina with no less than 5 points (well, perhaps you need a bit of *imagination* to see all *that* in her paws, but they *are* dainty for a working breed dog, and she does mince along with a sort of graceful sense of purpose when afoot).

Having these two magnificent beasts here with me to share this sanctum is a feeling that is a bit difficult to do adequate justice to, since the evocative mood created by their proximity is more spiritual than temporal. They manage to manifest a sense of intelligent awareness of what we three are about here that doesn't require words or even thought to qualify, so instinctively are they attuned to our mutual interactions. And for a person who regularly abuses, mangles, dismembers, destroys, alters, synthesises, and misapplies verbiage for personal amusement, such wordless, spiritual communication serves as a refreshing break from the daily norm. Just a look from them communicates all that needs to be acknowledged: *"OK, boss. Take your time. What-ever! There's plenty of time for another walk when you're ready."*

Outside the sun is starting to slant down differently, the shadows are getting a bit longer, and the shortened overhead passage of the winter sun makes itself known with a mere glance out the window. The weather this first week in December has been amazingly peaceful, warm and balmy during the day and yet crisp and cold at night. At such moments, it is all too easy to understand how critically important the solar warmth of the sun is to all life on this planet. At the same time, and removed as I am from all the distracting artificial detritus of our 'civilisation', it is equally easy to reflect sadly upon humanity's continuing insane fixation upon taking apart the entire planet to convert its scenic splendors into raw material for economic exploitation. The fact is that in the mad American economic pursuit of wealth, we somehow overlook even the most basic laws of nature: that even a *parasite* doesn't kill its *host*.

Ironically, that is exactly what we humans are doing each and every day as we devastate everything in our path like a stream of insatiably hungry army ants...a pattern of behavior that if unchecked will ultimately destroy our planet as surely as if the sun suddenly went *Super-Nova*. But enough of the tin-plated, evangelical eco-revivalism. When out here in the bunker, I strive to limit myself to thoughts unrelated to this tendency we humans have of shitting in our own kennels and crapping on our own doorsteps. Pity we can't even take a hint from our four-footed domestic companions (and I'm not talking marital companions here, of course, although some of them like doing things doggy-style too, heh-heh), who know instinctively that such behavior is not just unacceptable, but unnatural as well.

And taking that tangent a bit further, I am reminded of that modestly witty observation that *"...the more I know my dogs, the more I dislike people".* I haven't personally reached that bitterly final end-stage state of misanthropy myself...just yet, anyhow...but I would rather have this splendid solitude to share with the two big furry goofballs who are presently snoozing at my feet than with about 99.9% of two-footed critters I am acquainted with, back in the civilised setting I have temporarily escaped from. Behind every successfully persistent stereotype is a strong core of truth, naturally enough, and *doggone*, if that isn't *so* true in this case!

I wouldn't mind sharing this splendid setting with a woman on occasion, and have in fact often thought about that, but my prior experience has demonstrated well enough that tempting fate to destroy the entire selfishly unencumbered solitary ambience of the moment in that manner is not far removed from playing Russian roulette with a full cylinder of hollow-point bullets. While the prospect of having wild sex with a gorgeously alluring vixen in such an evocative setting is admittedly tantalizing, seldom have I ever met someone who can match their sensual assets equally with both the sharpness of their synaptical functions and the brilliance of their spiritual maturity well enough to warrant inviting a Lois Lane (*or* Polly Pureheart) into 'The Bunker'. Violation of that prime dictum would probably result in a contentious sparring contest the likes of which the ongoing *schlagerfest* between the Palestinians and the Israelis would seem like a spat between *Tweedledum and Tweedledee.*

Until such a coincident harmonic coital convergence occurs (and there's likely about as much chance of THAT happening as there is a chance for American-style democracy succeeding in the Middle East), I shall continue to solitarily mix my metaphors with my mercenary misological misapprehension, abrogate my allegorical analogies with anal abruptness, and scramble my synonymic syllogisms with studied stupefaction. 'The Bunker' will likely remain a *Fortress of Solitude*, rather than a *Fortress of Fornication*, and it is probably just as well for all that.

And now I'm going to sacrifice a chicken or two on the barby, down a good glass of some *Dôle* Swiss Rhone wine I imported from the Canton of Wallis, and watch the sun set into that great big pool of liquid gold that is shimmering magically just out the window. Tonight will be another gorgeous and brilliant full moon and I am at this last thought reminded of that famous Irish poem by Y.B. Yeats, titled *'The Song of Wandering Ængus'*. The last verse of it is worth repeating here as the fires of the sun finally extinguish themselves in the vast waters of the cold Pacific:

'Though I am old with wandering,
Through hollow lands and hilly lands,
I will find out where she has gone,
And kiss her lips and hands.
And walk among long dappled grass,
And pluck till time and times are done

The silver apples of the moon
And the golden apples of the sun….'

CHICKEN SKIN STORIES OF OLD HAWAII

Here follow two or so stories associated with the darker mana of *Molokai* and *Maui*. On the mainland, these tales would be called 'spooky', but on the islands, the term is 'chicken skin'. Hawaii, as a culture once dominated by the ancient traditional religion and associated *'kapus'* (we know them more familiarly by the Tahitian term 'taboo', more or less meaning 'forbidden'), is a culture infinitely rich in spirituality. In fact, every single object on the islands, both natural and man-made, was believed to contain varying amounts of spiritual power, in the perceptions of the old Hawaiian culture. 'Mana' (spirituality) is a uniquely Hawaiian term that has many possible meanings, ranging from its purer and more beneficial aspects (such as the influence of ancestral spirits, or '*aumakua*') all the way to the powerful spells and evil curses of 'dark mana'.

On Molokai, the priests and Kahunas were purported to possess immensely powerful mana. So feared was their spiritual ability that the island of Molokaiwas originally known as the 'island of powerful prayers' (in Hawaiian, *"Molokai Pule O`o"*), and it was believed that the priests of Molokai could literally 'pray' their enemies to death! In fact, several oral histories have been recorded in which exactly that happened, when the island was invaded by Ali'i (royalty) from other islands in the 1700s. Inhabitants of the other islands usually gave Molokai a wide berth, as a result of this feared reputation the Molokai shaman-priests had, and one consequence was that the island was not subject to the constant and unending inter island wars and battles between contending royalty (*Ali'i*) as were the others.

The last story appearing here concerns *'Night Marchers'*, generally acknowledged to be the ghosts of ancient kings and gods who march as phantoms across the island on certain nights of the lunar month. If one locates a Hawaiian lunar calendar and takes a look at the dates favorable to supernatural events, the nights usually favored by these departed spirits are usually marked out rather clearly. Night marchers also frequent specific parts of the island and follow known 'paths', so if one is eager enough to encounter this dark phenomenon, there is enough information available for anyone to set about that task appropriately (not that one should deliberately actively seek out such powerfully spiritual things, of course!).

A few years ago, a couple of young *haoles* on Oahu exploited the Hawaiian 'night marcher' legends to prepare a series of low-budget 'movies' about night marching spirits. They deserve some small credit for being imaginative, but their film-making effort was really quite poor in the final result, the acting quite terrible, and overall the result did a disservice to the small, hard core of truth behind the legendary phenomenon of night marching on the islands. In particular, in the second of these 'movies', the role of the heroes in the film was played by a couple of young haoles and the locals (native Hawaiians) playing roles in the film were made out to appear as stereotypically 'dumb kanakas', which was both grossly inappropriate and a racially contrived disservice to an extreme extent. More evidence that contemporary White racism is still alive and healthy on the islands!

The best stories about night marching may be found in translations of old original oral stories passed down from generation to generation, among the locals. In the past several decades, a few individuals have actively pursued many of these stories and written them down, publishing them in book collections. One such author named *Rick Carroll* has made a name for himself in Hawaii as a collector of Hawaiian ghost stories (generally called *'Chicken Skin Stories'* in the islands). Carroll originally worked for the San Francisco Chronicle and later relocated to the islands, where he then started publishing collections of spooky tales and stories—all of which are supposedly true and that actually happened to people in various parts of Hawaii. Due to the fact that Hawaii is a racially mixed locale, with a range of spiritually diverse ethnic influences (that includes Japanese, Chinese, Portuguese, and Filipino), the ghostly stories of Hawaii include many elements of these cultures in a unique mix that has come to characterise Hawaiian ghost stories. More can be read about author Rick Carroll and his books at the following URL, for anyone interested: http://www.besspress.com/ (Once there, Search for 'Rick Carroll').

At any rate, Hawaii is today still filled with much traditional Hawaiian mana, thickly overlaid by a layer of imported mythology and spirituality, despite the best efforts of Christians to eliminate what they regard as 'all that superstitious nonsense'.

Of course, the definition of 'superstitious nonsense' is a matter of outlook and interpretation, isn't it? For example, I myself regard most ancient Christian beliefs (among them the belief that the historical figure known as 'Jesus' was actually the 'son of God') as a lot of superstitious nonsense, so whatever 'truth' there is (and there always some, no matter how fantastic the stories may seem) with regard to this matter is entirely relative and depends upon the viewer's perceptions, doesn't it? That having been said, following are a few tidbits to tease you into taking a closer look at Hawaii's vast wealth of legends and ghostly stories.

A MOLOKAI HAUNTING: JUST SOME IDIOT HAOLE POUNDING ON A PAHU

Iao Needle on Maui is an evocative feature of the Iao Valley State Park on Maui. It is often obscured by clouds and fog, standing behind the bifurcation of the *Iao Stream* as it flows through the cleft of the *Pu'u Kakui* crater. In former centuries, Iao Needle formed a natural alter for worship of *Ku* (one of the chief deities of old Hawaii, among other things the fierce God of War) and other traditional Hawaiian gods. Today, aside from being a singularly striking natural monolith of up-thrust basaltic lava, it serves to remind many visiting *malihinis* (tourists) of a large erect penis (the Hawaiian term for penis is *'Ule'*). In a recent painting of it by a Molokiian artist, it does seem to point skyward like some like some sort of an advertisement for natural ancient Hawaiian *Viagra* or *Cialis*. [Shamefully, despite having had a number of daily conversations with the artist in reference, I neglected to record his surname; modest soul that he is, he signs his work simply as 'Wally'.]

It is acrylic on canvas and I bought it at the weekly produce market and crafts fair that you find on Kaunakai's *Ala Molama Street* every Saturday AM. Wally is a retired older haole who came to the island some years ago with his wife. He paints landscapes on Molokai and Maui, but also teaches art at the local community night school. Many of Wally's paintings appear a bit rustic, but a few of them are actually quite good, this image of the Iao Needle being one of them. He also had a beautiful image of *Fuji-san* (Mt. Fujiyama) in Japan, but he was holding it for someone else who had spoken for it already, so I passed on it.

Wally had a terrible bout with skin cancer of the face, due to overexposure throughout his life, so he wears a Panama style hat religiously. With a very fair skin (typical of many haoles such as myself) and obsessed with the usual haole desire to be brown like the kanaka locals, Wally practically assured himself of some later cancerous melanomas. He is lucky to still have a face, so severe was the damage he allowed the sun to inflict on him, by not wearing a hat earlier in life.

Molokai has a number of artists of varying skill. A few of them are virtual masters of their mediums, while many--predictably--are somewhat less talented (this doesn't mean their prices are much less, however). There are generally three places where you can view a good sampling of their works on the island. One is in *Stanley's Gallery* and Cafe on Ala Molama Street (Stanley himself is probably the best artist on the island). The second is at the *Coffees of Hawaii* gallery in *Kualapu'u* and the third is at the *Kamakana Fine Arts Gallery*in Kaunkakai (although that gallery has since been sold and has a new name--the *Molokai Fine Arts Gallery*--as well as a new owner--*Julia Keliikuli Peters*).

Among the most prolific of the local photographers is a chap known simply as 'Phil', who sells reprint enlargements of his many beautiful Molokai photographic images on the corner, during the weekly Kaunakakai produce and crafts fair. Next to Phil's slot are the racks of nice old 'pre-used' (love that quaint term, don't you?) aloha shirts sold by *Theodocia Wainwright*, a rather exotic looking Filipina woman who lives on the *Mana'e* (East End) with her contractor husband (like most guys who meet her without knowing she's happily married, I fell in love with her at first sight!).

Nearby, local *Paul Elias*, who is 100% Hawaiian, displays his hand carved Pahu and fish hooks; Paul's works are truly beautiful and authentically crafted after the traditional custom and he maintains the true aloha spirit courtesies of inviting you to his home to talk and eat (*E komo mai, e noho mai, e `ai a e, wala`au!*).

Then there is *Carlo*, a German expatriate who has spent the last 10 years as a sort of South Pacific vagabond, after leaving his intaglio art work in Europe and taking to a 36-foot sloop for his travels. Carlo usually ends up at his old, slightly lopsided sloop that is tied to the wharf at Kaunakakai, and can be spotted frequently during any given day tooling around K'kai on his dilapidated old single-speed, fat-tired bicycle. With a characteristic white goatee and seemingly always wearing a weathered old white ball cap, there's never any doubt that it is indeed Carlo when you spot him. Unusually, Carlo doesn't particularly care for beer--a strange predilection I found out one day, when I left two six-packs of Papeete (Tahitian) Beer for him on the poop-deck of his old sloop. A German who doesn't like beer is almost as paradoxical (in my opinion) as a beautiful woman who loves other women. But, each to his/her own drummer's beat, of course.

Carlo cleverly takes local items and makes them into objets d'art, such as the very appealing small *Aku* (Tiki) he creates from the island's local deer antlers. One of these I purchased from him a while back and I still admire it, carrying it along with my personal shark aku (*mano akua*) that friend Fast Eddie gave me. Carlo also paints in a unique style that derives directly from his previous occupation as an intaglio pattern artist for a fabric-printing business (in Europe). He lives aboard his sloop, which I like to call *'The Leaking Lena'* (although it is actually named the *'Vanda'* and lists about 15 degrees to port, giving it a permanent lean to that side) as a reminder of the *'Beany & Cecil'* TV kiddy cartoon series of the 1950s and 60s.

The art colony on Molokai is small, compared to that found on the other Hawaiian Islands (thankfully, since if it were too popular, the island would be over-run by tourists and artists; following this would surely come swarms of real estate investors, so how much better to keep Molokai's art colony a sort of well-kept secret!).

Since Molokai is the birthplace of Hula (every island claims this, but Molokai seems to be the *genuine 'Hula piko'* birthplace of this most Hawaiian dance), there are a few master carvers on the island who still carve the old *Heiau Pahu* and *Hula Pahu* (drums), hewn from coconut palm trunks. Local *Bill Kepuni* is one of them and his son-in-law *Victor Lopez* is another. The Hawaiian 'Pahu' were originally used at the stone Heiau (temples, or sacred worship sites) to call the islanders to pray, before the old Hawaiian religion was abolished by the Christians. They (the Pahu) had religious significance that went far beyond this single use, however, and at a few of the Heiau used for human sacrifice on Molokai they predominated over the setting with foreboding news of pending sacrificial rites.

When the Hula came into being, somewhat smaller Pahu were used to punctuate the characteristic chanting that always accompanies traditional chanting ('*mele*') Hula. These drums are today known as *'Hula Pahu'* and are chiefly differentiated from the religious Pahu by their slightly smaller dimensions. Traditionally, Pahu were made using the belly skins of the shark and ray for drum-head material, but today, given the sacred nature of the shark to Hawaiians, the increasing scarcity of sharks, as well as over-fishing and human predation, ordinary steer-hide or goat-hide is used almost exclusively.

I bought a nice example of the Hula Pahu carved by Victor Lopez, although I am told that his drums pale in comparison to others that are of the highest quality. A 15-inch-wide Pahu measuring 20 inches in height can cost as much as $1800, depending upon the maker, while larger and more ornate ones (used principally at ceremonies and for formal Hawaiian festivals) may cost as much as $5,000 or more. Mine was priced at $950, but it is still quite a beauty by my limited standards of comparison. I have several others in my collection, but most are somewhat smaller than the one I bought from Victor. Making a Pahu is truly a time-consuming and artful undertaking, since cutting the tree, sectioning it, curing the wood and then carving it may take as long as several years, when done properly. The intricate and painstakingly dedicated nature of this traditional craft is often lost on visiting haole malihinis, who are used to manufactured goods that are high-quality, but mass-produced and machine-made, imported from China. As a result, the often-high prices asked for authentic, hand-crafted Pahu are often something of a shock to tourists looking for cheap souvenirs of their visit. If anything, this shows how detached most people living in a materialistic culture have become from the realities of artfully hand-crafted goods.

A while back on the island, after the sun had sunk very low in the sky, I remained behind up on the foggy promontory where *Pala-au State Park* is now located, having walked down the trail a way to the area where the famed *'Ka Ule o Nanahoa'* phallic rock is sited. This huge volcanic rock, shaped in the form of an erect penis (*'Ka Ule o Nanahoa'* in fact translates to *'Penis of Nanahoa'*) is shrouded all about by the thick tangles of Ironwood forest it lies within and it doesn't take much imagination to visualise small shadowy shapes darting about from tree to tree in the woods that surrounded the site, as the wind gusts in from the sea cliffs that rise 3000+ feet above the *Kalaupapa* peninsula. Before long, the clouds and fog began to obscure the exotic view, with the sun now having submerged itself back into the ocean. The resulting mood was positively spooky--about as spooky as someone who is virtually a born-again atheist can experience.

I should say here that this place was originally a place of great power and mana to the ancient Hawaiians, sitting as it is at the top of the sea cliffs overlooking the former leper colony of Father Damian (lying some 3000 feet straight below, beyond the sheer cliff face). It was also originally as bald as Colonel Klink on *Hogan's Heroes*, having no natural vegetation cover. 'Ka Ule o Nanahoa' was regarded as a site possessed of tremendous fertility power and it is still felt that a woman who spent the night sitting on or at the base of this stone monolith would become pregnant within a very short period. Enough tales and recorded incidents exist today to give some impressive credence to this belief, although whether the power of the human mind to 'will' events into being was behind it or some residual spiritual mana of great strength is a hotly debated subject to this day. Offerings are regularly left at the site by both tourists and locals, often consisting of money, flowers, sacred rocks wrapped in *Ti-leaf* offerings, and prayers for fertility.

My plan was to remain the night myself (not having any fear of an unwanted pregnancy, of course) to take in the spiritual atmosphere on a first-hand basis. Just for shits and giggles, I had brought Victor's Pahu along with me and planned to play the drum exploratively as the night gathered about this ancient and very sacred Hawaiian site. Inherent skeptic that I am, I fully expected to experience nothing more than the rustle of wind in the trees and small night sounds that indicate geckos and other small nocturnal critters coming out to hunt. Besides, it was a casual lark and I have absolutely nothing to lose except a few hours of passing time.

Down the hill from the stone *Ule,* just slightly, is another large rock that is shaped amazingly like the vulva of a woman, with a small trickle of ground water passing down and out of it in a strange and spooky manner. I was located between the two sacred stones, on the sloping trail that connects them, and sat down with my Pahu to eat a candy bar and reflect on the gathering silence, broken only by the sighing of wind and the small animal murmurs mentioned above. There was no one else about for miles, as far as I knew, for the last tourists of the day (a German group visiting from a stay on Maui) had long since packed up and gone back down the hill to K'kai. Tentatively, I pulsed out a few small beats on the drum. In the utterly silent gloom of the trees, the beats sounded magnified and seemed strangely to grow in volume, rather than diminish, in the leafy bowers all about me. Stopping for a few seconds, I listened to the wind in the trees, trying hard to imagine ancient spirits hovering curiously about to see what this strange *haole* drum message was saying. There was, of course, nothing else to hear, but it was fun to give my imagination this safe lead to roam about on...

Until, that is, a few minutes later...after I had self-consciously resumed my rhythmic beating, gaining little confidence in the supposed absurdity of what I was doing. To my immense surprise, the sounds of the forest now seemed to include a faint tapping that I hadn't noticed before. Looking about, I decided that it wasn't as much tapping as it was the muffled beat of another drum. *Kayden, brahs! Latez!* It certainly seemed to be a drum, at any rate, and there was no way to tell where it was, how far away it lay, or who was beating on it. As I listened, the sound of the other drum (for it was definitely a drum) increased noticeably. There was no mistaking the deliberate pattern of the beats, nor the power behind them as I listened incredulously to the sounds.

Telling myself *"This is getting a LOT spookier than you bargained for...",* at that point I decided to remain quite still for a moment, while I considered going back up the trail, which by now was cloaked in gloom. Any card-carrying pagan in the audience would certainly have felt the change in the lightly charged, gathering atmosphere, I'm sure, but I suddenly felt an increasingly strong disinclination to experience any more of this or see where it was leading. Hastily grabbing my Pahu, I rather quickly trundled back up the hill in the darkness, glancing at the dim bulk of Nanahoa's huge erection as I passed it. By the time I had crested the hill and had my car in sight, I could still hear a faint and muffled *thrum-thrum-thrum* coming from somewhere in the darkness behind me.

To this day, I still don't know what to believe. Had I evoked the restless spirits of the ancients, sitting there sacrilegiously pounding out a call to unknown ancient powers in a language I didn't understand? Had some local *kanaka* trickster nearby, also equipped with a Pahu, had similar thoughts and tried to scare the daylights out of *dis one da kine* Haole?

I'll never know for certain, but I still think back on that incident today and wonder mightily about what it may really have meant. I certainly may not be a conventionally religiously inclined person by nature, but I also don't preclude any other possibilities, either. Even if this were mostly the product of an overheated imagination and a gloomy, utterly silent forest, it was genuine enough at the time to give me a distinctly real case of chicken-skin!

THE MARCHERS OF THE NIGHT

Every Hawaiian has heard of the *'Marchers of the Night', 'Ka huaka'i o ka Po'.* More than a few have actually seen and experienced the procession of these ghostly spirits of long-gone ancestors, chiefs, and gods. It is said that such a sight is fatal...unless one has a departed relative among the dead to intercede for him. If a man is found stricken by the roadside, a white doctor may pronounce the cause of death as heart failure, but a Hawaiian will think at once of *the night march*.

The time for the march is between half after seven when the sun has actually set and about two in the morning before the dawn breaks. It may occur on one of the four nights of the gods, on the nights *of Ku, Akua, Lono, Kane*, or on the nights of *Kaloa* (all ancient Hawaiian gods).

Those who took part in the march were purportedly the chiefs and warriors who had died, the *aumakua* (ancestors), and the gods, each of whom had their own march.

If a chief enjoyed silence in this life, his march would be silent save for the creaking of the food calabashes of his servants, suspended from their carrying sticks, or of the royal litter, called *manele*, if he had not been fond of walking. If a chief had been fond of music, the sound of the drum, nose flute, and other instruments were heard as they marched. Sometimes there were no lights borne, at other times there were torches, but not so bright as those for the gods and the demi-gods. A chief whose face had been sacred, had a follower (called an *alo*-kapu) lead the march and no man, beast, or bird could pass before him without being killed; even his own warriors might not precede him, for to have anyone see his face was instant death for the offender. If on the contrary his back had been sacred (*akua-kapu*), he must follow in the rear of the procession. A chief who had been well protected in life, who had no rigid kapu upon his face or back, would march between his warriors.

On the marches of the chief, a few *'aumakua'* would march with them in order to protect their living progeny who might chance to meet them on the path. Sometimes the march would occur when a chief lay dying or just dead. It paused before the door of the departed royalty for a brief time and then passed on. The family might not notice it, but a neighbor might see it pass and know that the chief had gone with his ancestors who had come for him.

In the march of the *'aumakua'* of each district there was music and chanting. The marchers carried candlenut (*Kukui nut*) torches which burned brightly even on a rainy night. They might be seen in broad daylight and were followed by whirlwinds such as come one after another in columns.

They cried *"Kapu-o-moe!"* as a warning to stragglers to keep out of the way or to prostrate themselves with closed eyes until the marchers passed. Like the chiefs, they too sometimes came to a dying descendent and took him away with them.

The march of the gods was much longer, more brilliantly lighted, and more sacred than that of the chiefs or the demi-gods. The torches were brighter and shone red. At the head, at three points within the line, and at the rear were carried larger torches, five being the complete number among Hawaiians, the *"Ku a lima"*. The gods with the torches walked six abreast: three files of males and three of females. According to legend, one of the three at the end of the line was *'Hi'iaka-i-ka-poli-o-Pele'* youngest sister of the volcano goddess. The first torch could be seen burning up at Kahuku when the last of the five torches was at Honu'apo. The only music to be heard on the marches of the gods was the chanting of their names and mighty deeds. The sign that accompanied them was a heavy downpour of rain, with mist, thunder, and lightning, or heavy seas. Their route the next day would be strewn with broken boughs, or leaves, for their heads were sacred and nothing should be suspended above them.

If a living person met these marchers, he had to get out of the way as quickly as possible, otherwise he might be killed unless he had an ancestor or an 'aumakua' in the procession to plead for his life.

If he met a procession of chiefs and had no time to get out of the way, he might take off his clothes and lie face upward, eyes closed, breathing as little as possible. He would hear them cry *"Shame!"* as they passed. One would say "*He is dead!"* Another would cry *"No, he is alive, but what a shame for him to lie uncovered!"* If he had no time to strip he must sit perfectly still, close his eyes, and take his chance.

He was likely to be killed by the guard at the front or at the rear of the line, unless saved by one of his ancestors or by an 'aumakua'. If he met a procession of gods, he must take off all his clothes but his loincloth (known as the *malo*and used to cover one's *alas*) and sit still with his eyes tightly closed, because no man might look upon a god, although he might be permitted to listen to their talk. He would hear the command to strike (by one of the marchers); then, if he were beloved by one of the gods as a favorite child or namesake, he would hear someone (an aumakua) say *"No, he is mine!"* and he would be spared by the guards.

Many Hawaiians living today have seen or heard the ghostly marchers. Ms. Wiggins, Mrs. Pukui's (highly respected Hawaiian historian *Mary Kawena Pukui*) mother, never got in their way, but she has watched them pass from the door of her own mother's house and has heard the Ka'u people tell of the precautions that must be taken to escape death if one chances to be in their path (as in the following).

A young man of Kona tells the following experience:

"One night, just after nightfall, about seven or eight in the evening, he was on his way when of a sudden he saw a long line of marchers coming towards him. He climbed over a stone wall and sat very still. As they drew near he saw that they (the night marchers) walked four abreast and were about 7 feet tall, walking slightly above the ground. One of the marchers stepped out of line and ran back and forth on the other side of the wall behind where he was crouched, as if to protect him from the others. As each file passed, he heard the voices call out "Strike!" and his protector answered "No! No! He is mine!" No other sounds were heard except the call to strike and the creak of a 'manele' (litter). He was not afraid and watched the marchers closely. There were both men and women in the procession. After a long line of marchers four abreast had passed there came the 'manele' bearers, two before and two behind. On the litter sat a very big man whom he guessed at once to be a chief. Following the litter were other marchers walking four abreast. After all had passed, his protector joined his fellows..."

In the old days, these marchers were common in *Ka'u* district, but folk today know little about them. They used to march and play games practically on the same ground as in life. Hence each district and each island had its own parade and playground along which the dead would march and at which they would assemble.

Mrs. Emma Akana Olmstead tells me that when she was told about the marchers of the night as a child, she was afraid, but now that she is older and can actually hear them, she is no longer afraid. She hears beautiful loud chanting of voices, the high notes of the flute, and drumming so loud that it seems to be beaten upon the side of the house beside her bed. Their voices (the marchers) are so distinct that if she could write music, she would, be able to set down the notes they sang.

Or so it is said today.

"I PISS ON YOU FROM A GREAT HEIGHT!"

What great mountaineer uttered these immortal words? If you guessed *Aleister Crowley*, you'd be wrong (but nice try anyway!) and it certainly wasn't recently demised New Zealander and Everest conqueror Ed Hillary! If you guessed *Louis-Ferdinand Destouches* (who used the pseudonymic surname '*Celine*' in his writings--actually the Christian name of his maternal grandmother), you'd still be wrong, but only by virtue of a technicality (since Celine was NOT a mountaineer, although it is indeed his memorable phrase).

The phrase in reference is reputed to have been disparagingly levied at Celine's critics, after he returned to France from exile, and it is (I believe), a testament to Celine's unique individuality that he was able (by virtue of his supremely strong faith in his nihilistic assessments of the human race) to summarily dismiss those who savagely castigated him for his pro-German, anti-Semitic associations, during the German occupation of the Second World War. I was personally somewhat disappointed to learn that a triumphant climb of the *Grandes Jorasse* in the French Alps somewhat ahead of a competing English party of climbers had not inspired this wonderful bit of repartee, but it is still a wonderfully stylish way of saying *"Piss off!"*

Celine was as outrageous as he was unique, and although a physician as well as a writer, his personal view of life was anything but congruent with the Hippocratic Oath. Although perhaps a hypocritical hypochondriac.

Celine may not have been a mountaineer, but it is probably good that he wasn't, since even without assuming the characteristics and traits of uniquely distinctive individualism that an infatuation with high places seems to foster, the schadenfreude nature of his personal *Weltanschaung* placed him well within the league of other supreme egoists (such as Crowley, whom I shall address somewhat later in this discourse) who utterly rejected hope as a faith for fools to embrace.

Celine's transcendent disdain for humanity is palpably felt in the following excerpt from his first novel, 'Voyage au Bout de La Nuit' ('Journey to the End of Night')*: "From up high where I was, you could shout anything that you like at them. I tried. They made me sick, the whole lot of them. I hadn't the nerve to tell them so in the daytime, but up there, in the anonymity of blackest night it was safe. 'Help, help!' I shouted, just to see if it would have any effect on them. None whatsoever. These people were pushing life and night and day in front of them. Life hides everything from people. Their own noise prevents them from hearing anything else. They couldn't care less. The bigger and taller the city, the less they care. Take it from me. I've tried. It's a waste of time."*

His first two books, *'Journey to the End of Night'* (1932) and 'Death on the Installment Plan' (1936) written after he had taken his medical degree and been established in Parisian medical practice for a while, boosted Celine into public prominence. They were thinly disguised autobiographical interpretations of his own early personal life experiences and reflected his nihilistic recoil at the infinitely sad complexities of life that fluctuated insanely between the polar chaos of wildly unstable rational thought and utterly relative emotional objectivism. Celine's later published works, most of which have seen translation from the original French into English, paint a progressively bitterly hopeless, chaotic, nihilistic, and utterly despairing picture of the collective fate of humanity. Descending from tragic pathos into the stygian depths of abject hopelessness by virtue of his inability to actively share his acutely painful outlook with any other person, Celine increasingly painted himself into a mental corner of hateful rage against the perceived sufferings of human kind until he fell

entirely through the false bottom floor of reality.
Another excerpt from '*Voyage au Bout de La Nuit*' follows:

"In this world we spent our time killing or adoring, or both together. 'I hate you! I adore you!' We keep going, we fuel and refuel, we pass on our life to a biped of the next century, with frenzy, o any cost, as if it were the greatest of pleasures to perpetuate ourselves, as if, when all's said and done, it would make us immortal. One way or another, kissing is as indispensable as scratching."

An argument may be made that his experiences in the First World War had profound impact on what followed in his life, since having only received a basic education by the time the war broke out in 1912, at the moment of his enlistment in a French cavalry unit, he was only 18. During the savage, brutally inhuman carnage experienced at the Ypres Salient, he was severely wounded. Injuries received there left him with a left arm handicap, severe headaches, and a lifetime affliction with Tinnitus (ringing and buzzing of the ears).

Infrequent note is made of the immensely internalised emotional trauma incurred by any and all who fought in the WWI trenches and who were subject to the unimaginable horrors of being shelled by artillery that so characterised static trench warfare, but Celine was undoubtedly as greatly traumatized (or more so) by his wartime experience as any modern war victim with *Post-Traumatic Stress Syndrome*. All of this, added to the base quality of post-war France and world affairs set into motion as a result of that war (the Communist Revolution chief among them), contributed immeasurably towards Celine's utter loss of faith in his fellow man.

Another quote from '*Voyage au Bout de La Nuit*': "*Those who talk about the future are scoundrels. It is the present that matters. To evoke one's posterity is to make a speech to maggots."*

When France fell to Germany in 1940, the result of a war as fully provoked by the unsatisfactory termination of the first one as by any other factor, Celine remained in France where he worked in municipal clinics. The development of Celine's strongly anti-Semitic feelings resulted in a series of pacifistic pamphlets in the traditional French manner (hundreds of pages) that delineated these feelings and although these sentiments were pointed to later as primary evidence of collaboration with the Germans, it remains a fact that he was often anti-Communistic in his orientation, and at odd times even anti-German. When the Allies repatriated France, Celine fled to Germany and the devastation of Berlin, eventually settling in Denmark, where he was arrested and imprisoned at the behest of the French Resistance.

In 1951 Celine was eventually cleared by a court in France and exonerated, although his post-World War 2 life was forever haunted by the lingering accusations of anti-Semitism and German collaboration. Black-listed by the French literati (even by *Sarte* and others whom he had originally inspired and whom he had greatly lionised), his works were ignored and rejected. In 1961, he suffered an aneurysm and died on the outskirts of Paris.

In recent years, his brilliantly tragic awareness of the absurdity of all human life and the senselessness that humanity endures has been rehabilitated to a great degree and in more recent years an increasing number of his later works have been translated into English.

It has always been to me most interesting that Celine's works were all more or less based on his own life and his personal experiences. This has traditionally been a prime dictum for any aspiring author—write about what you know—and quotes most often attributed to him today are invariably pithy, scathingly pessimistic and futilely antiheroic in the essence of that hopelessness they convey about human life.

I have a feeling that had Celine not been so powerfully affected by his wartime experiences and instead found refuge in the vastly beautiful French mountains, the world would be the worse off for having not been so profoundly impacted by his usefully antagonistic rejection of religious hope, faith, and the (fanciful) promises of figurative human redemption offered as a sop to dreadful reality by most conventional deities (God, Allah, or whomever).

Having related all of the foregoing history, I am reminded that Celine's famously disdainful *declamation "I piss on you from a great height!"* was well recalled by Yosemite Valley rock climbers of the late 50s and early 60s (Yosemite Valley 'Golden Age' rock climber Steve Roper references this in his book, *'Camp 4: Recollections of a Yosemite Climber'*), since their original artificially aided ascents involved prolonged bivvies, perched precariously over the abyss of that awesome infinity that stretches thousands of feet above the Valley floor. Taking dumps and loosing a whiz or two from those 'great heights' were physically real and genuinely necessary counterparts to Celine's more figurative and allegorical act, a fact that was not for a moment lost on the irreverent (and also mildly nihilistic) Yosemite 'Golden Age' Camp 4 rock-rats who pioneered the first free climbs of those sheer granite walls.

At an opposite corner of the radically nihilistic portion of the mountaineering envelope was another of the *'Fin de siècle'* notables, *Aleister Crowley*. Crowley, arguably one of the simultaneously most interesting and repellently bizarre personalities of the late 1800s and early 1900s, garnered a reputation throughout his life as 'the wickedest man on Earth' for his interest in the occult.

Crowley, destined to become notorious as (among many other things) a supreme egoist (in an age that produced many), was born on 12 October 1875, some 18 years after the founding of the English Alpine Club and only 10 years after early Alpinist Edward Whymper's first successful ascent of the Matterhorn.

The son of a man who had inherited his wealth from a well-to-do English producer of ales (The Crowley Brewery) was involuntarily immersed at birth in an ultra-religious Christian evangelical environment, since his parents belonged to an extreme sect of the '*Plymouth Brethren*' known as the '*Exclusive Brethren'*. Long story short, Crowley was 'lifestyle-enabled' by virtue of his family's wealth and probably largely the result of being a strong-willed, rebellious, and highly intelligent young man, was propelled towards the opposite extreme of Christian convention after the early death of his father left the family's rather substantial fortune to him. Entering Cambridge, subsequent to having studied in several public schools in the UK, Crowley read English literature (after having switched from the moral sciences). At the age of 21, for reasons still not fully understood, he veered off on a course that found him increasingly drawn up in a study of the occult and 'black magic'.

He was also involved, while at Cambridge, in homoerotic associations with several others, although it should be noted that *Oscar Wilde* was first arrested and imprisoned for 'the love that dares not speak its name' during the first year Crowley was at Cambridge. [it should also be mentioned that the late 1800s and early 1900s also found much homosexual 'admiration' in common currency among young men. This fact doubtless had much to do with the nature of the English 'public school' system and it figures in literature of the period to a substantial degree (viz. D.H. Lawrence's works, etc.). Even legendary *Everester* George-Leigh Mallory (lost with Irvine on the tragic

1924 British Everest Expedition) was subject to innuendos of this sort, due to the celebration of masculinity that commonly pervaded male ethics of that era, and in fact there is enough evidence to suggest that homoerotic passions certainly circulated around Mallory among his close friends, even though there appears to be no direct evidence to show that he was ever willingly a homosexual, to the best of my knowledge].

It was while at Cambridge that Crowley became interested in mountaineering and after learning the basics at Cumberland Fells and Beachy Head, he spent a great number of holidays in Europe climbing frequently in the *Benese Oberland* region (Eiger, etc) of Switzerland. With his fanatical personal conviction and supreme self-confidence, he soon established a reputation as an excellent climber, being credited many solo climbs and also with several first ascents of various Alpine routes in the Swiss Alps. This is not too hard to understand, for in the early 1900s, mountaineering was widely regarded in the same manner as was Arctic exploration--a very masculine and uniquely English undertaking, combining elements of adventure, heroism, egoism, and the very stuff of classic late Victorian English eclecticism. This was also a period in which lectures and public speaking events focused upon the early Alpine ascents were proving very popular in London and other major population centers in England, since the pioneering Victorian preoccupation with climbing mountains for sport had caught the public's fascination in a spectacular manner.

Crowley's participation in mountaineering found him involved in 1902 with the first attempt to climb K2, the so-called 'killer mountain', situated in the Karakorum Range between Pakistan and China. Although unsuccessful, that expedition was a highly contentious undertaking for a number of reasons. Among these was the arrest of the expedition leader (Oscar Eckenstein) in Pakistan, a circumstance that reportedly involved the then-president of the English Alpine Club, one William Conway (who was apparently Eckenstein's nemesis). Shortly after being interned for a three-week period of detention in Kashmir, owing to his arrest, Eckenstein then returned to the K2 basecamp only to find himself immersed in a raging disagreement over which route to take up the formidable mountain. Despite a consensus among the climbers that favored taking the Northeast crest route, Crowley (described in accounts of the affair as 'bizarre and irreverent') held out for an ascent of the Southeast ridge. Crowley, as events turned out, was correct, and the first climbing attempt had to turn back at only 6000 meters. In base camp, there was talk of ending the expedition at that time, but Crowley is reported to have pulled out a revolver and threatened several of the other climbers to make his point that the Southwest ridge would 'go'; whatever the circumstances of the decision to press on, a second attempt was subsequently made up his suggested Southeast ridge route.

This route, taking the climbers into the saddle between K2 (at 8611 meters, the world's second highest mountain after Everest) and *Skyang Kangri* (a peak of 7544 meters), promised to allow the possibility of success, but when a fellow climber showed evidence of developing pulmonary edema, Crowley supposedly recognised the man's peril and insisted on evacuating the man off the mountain. While his actions apparently saved the man's life, it also ruined any slim chance of the team's successful ascent.

Simply a further enigmatic episode from a continuing subsequent series of enigmatic events in Crowley's life, perhaps, but it is highly interesting to speculate that K2, still to this day widely regarded as one of (if not the) most dangerous mountains in the entire world, might have fallen to a successful summit team led by Crowley as early as 1902 (K2, 'The Killer Mountain', finally fell in 1954 to two

Italian climbers, some 52 years later!). Of course, one of the things that makes K2 especially dangerous is its notoriously unstable weather, a subjective hazard created by its isolated location in the midst of an otherwise sheltered geographic location, that has repeatedly frustrated attempts on it throughout the years. In much the same manner that an isolated peak, such as California's Mount Shasta that also stands alone, K2 can and usually does create its own unique meteorological micro-clime that makes it an especially hazardous climb (when factored into its other liabilities of extreme height and vertical nature).

After the return from K2, Crowley's mountaineering interests continued at least sporadically until in 1905, when at the age of 30 he was approached to join a team that was proposing to climb Kangchenjunga in Nepal (the world's third highest mountain, at 8586 meters). This expedition, also highly embroiled in conflict and unfavorable circumstances, found Crowley involved in a climbing accident in which 3 sherpas and a fellow climber were caught in an avalanche at high altitude and buried under the snow. Various accounts speculate on the circumstances, but accusations were made that Crowley failed to help the others try to recover the buried climbers and essentially turned his back on the attempts. Whatever the true circumstances of that particularly contentious event, this expedition also failed to summit the peak after reaching about 22,000 feet (Crowley claims he personally reached over 25,000 feet) and shortly thereafter returned to England.

Upon his return, Crowley became even further involved in the pursuit of *'magick* (his unique term) and the more extreme limits of the pursuit of the occult. At any rate, this pivotal vector off the mainstream of conventional occult belief led to an intensely sensational cult-following attendant to Crowley's supreme egotism and interest in what he deliberately termed *'Black Magick'* (to differentiate between it and traditional preoccupations with traditional 'magic'). Crowley became actively involved with a number of prominent occult organizations and as a highly literate individual, poet, and writer, published a number of papers on this arcane area of activity. This, combined with the always strong demands of his sexual drive, resulted in his literally taking over several occult groups of the era and establishing himself as the supremely notorious and outrageous figure he is today regarded as.

Another influence on Crowley's life that is worth mentioning here is an increasing addiction to *heroin* (actually a German pharmaceutical invention), a narcotic that was in those days commonly prescribed for relief of bronchial asthma (!). It is interesting to speculate on the fact that Crowley was an asthmatic, I think, since asthma is a symptom indicative, in all too many cases, of an extremely high level of emotional volatility.

As Crowley's heroin use and his experimentation with a wide range of drugs continued over the following decades, he became increasingly more and more bizarre in both his behavior and beliefs. At one point he believed his second wife was a bat and had her tied up and forced to sleep upside down at night in a closet (hard to believe, but apparently true). His several wives were either driven mad by his behavior or otherwise perished, and to say that Aleister Crowley was one of the most unique and distinctively different anti-social characters to emerge from the early 1900s is considerably understating things. He died in 1947, at the age of 72, of a respiratory infection—a rather long life for someone who had religiously violated just about every tenet of good health and prudent living anyone could imagine. At the time of his death he was addicted to a daily amount of heroin in general described as '5 times the dose' that would be terminally deadly to an ordinary individual.

Among the characteristics Crowley is today noted for, in addition to his arcane occult predilections, his profuse literature, his sexual aestheticism, and his reputation as a seeker after moral 'wickedness', Aleister Crowley was also an outspoken racist, an extremely chauvinistic sexist, and a heavy substance abuser. It is safe to say that Crowley was the product of an era that set the stage for such an exaggeratedly extreme lifestyle (the end of the morally repressive Victorian age), but he was certainly decades ahead of his times in pursuit of vices that even today would be considered shocking and highly controversial.

Despite those excesses for which he is best known, his reputation for being a considerably talented and driven mountaineer early in his life (before he started abusing substances) should not be dismissed or otherwise buried in the avalanche of notoriety that surrounded his always outrageous life. He was arguably brilliant in terms of setting himself apart from others of his era, no matter what you may think of his morals.

For an excellent summary of information surrounding the many events of Aleister Crowley's controversial life, dial up: http://en.wikipedia.org/wiki/Aleister_Crowley .

Kalikiano Kalei

AN OCEAN RAN THROUGH IT

It is Christmas Day. As I sit here, looking out on the cold winter breaks that are rolling in along the coast, my thoughts are not out there floating in the pungent kelp beds but reaching back to a dry, desert time earlier in my life, some 24 years ago and 11,000 kilometers distant from these pacific shores.

My black porcelain coffee mug sits close at hand, its contents already cold despite having been just poured. On the counter, the despised Starbucks press-pot I have begrudgingly adopted in which to brew my coal-dark decoction of caffeinated *joe* seems to mock me silently, as I momentarily reflect on my intense dislike for green corporate mermaids of the Starbucks persuasion. I am also ruefully reminded that as I get older, the coffee becomes an increasingly more important part of my daily ritual.

Searching through the dusty attic of my mind, I remember that the Arabian word for coffee is *Gahwah* and that coffee, whether dispersed by a capitalist monopolistic outfit like Starbucks or not, came to us originally from that fabled region of desert harshness we are presently wasting human lives and trillions of dollars in.

Back in the early 80s, while I was resident in Berkeley, a particularly painful romance had just come to its conclusion and I was filled with a sense of intense personal grief and anger. I have learned that at times like that, when the pain of emotional hurt still has a bitter, salty sting to it, that I tend to do things that I would perhaps not otherwise even remotely consider. That was just such a moment.

I had been recently reading T.E. Lawrence's precursor to his immortal *'Seven Pillars of Wisdom'* (titled *'Revolt in the Desert'*) and had Arabs on the brain, I suppose, but knowing my tendencies to alter course 180 degrees in moments of duress, I was already thinking vaguely of the French Foreign Legion. Wasn't that where the lovelorn suitor retreated for solace in the great classic adventure tales of the early 1900s? I knew myself well enough to recognise a greater than usual sense of the romantic idealist in my makeup (a confluent result of being too widely read at an early age, I suppose), but I had no idea at that point that within a year I would be living right smack out there among the Arabs in the storied Western Escarpment of the Hijazi mountains that loom over Saudi Arabia's Red Sea shores. Momentarily relishing the mental picture of myself fitted out with a French kepi and carrying a rifle on some doomed frontier border trek near Marrakesh, I set about regaining some sense of domestic continuity, hoping that the pain of losing the love of my life (to a *law student!* Even *more* galling!) would diminish into a mere background throb of dulled hurtful self-indulgence.

Fate has a way of dictating a course other than what one fancies is the proper resolution for moments of significant personal unpleasantness, however, and less than 8 months later I was disembarking from a jam-packed *Saudia* (Saudi Arabia's national airline) 747SP jumbo-jet at the Red Sea port of Jiddah. My first distinct and still ineradicable memory of that moment is the instant formation of dense fog *within* the aircraft's interior when the super-chilled and dry cabin air hit the hyper-humid heated air of Jiddah's sere frying-pan of an airport at the instant the aircraft cabin door was opened. It was somewhat like passing from a vividly clear patch of sky directly into a cloudbank in an aircraft. One minute everything was clear and distinct and the next, you couldn't see you hand in front of your face. To say it was mildly startling is understating things, since airliner cabin air is extremely dry (humidity of about 15%) and cool, while the ambient ground temperature along the Red Sea is usually above 100 degrees, with a humidity of 75%. When two weather precursor catalysts like this confront each other, an instant artificial fogbank is the result.

Several hours and a Graham Greene type *'Mr. Toad's Wild Taxi Ride'* later, our taxi had crossed the that bleak and wretchedly hot (140 degrees in the sun) stretch of dry coastal desert known as the *Tihama* and we found ourselves facing an impossibly steep and towering wall of sheer mountain precipice that rose abruptly from the desert into the sky to a summit, some 7,000 feet or so above us. Clearly marked upon its rocky face was a zig-zag pattern traced in white against its reddish sandy hues. This, I was told in broken English by our driver (a Saudi *Bedu* with a gaunt, semi-crazed look in his eyes), was the switch-backed, Italian built roadway up which we would have to travel in order to reach our destination: *At Taif*, the summer residence of the Saudi Royal family and seat of government during the hot months. It had been laboriously hacked out of the living rock by a combined assault force of over-compensated Italian engineers and under-paid Yemeni ditch-diggers, back in the 60s, with a total loss of only 300 lives (not including goats, camels, and many sheep).

Long story short, we did indeed make it up that perilous road intact and safe, despite the obvious burnt-out remains of numerous cars and taxis that lay in plain sight at the bottom of cliffs below each turn. To this day I can only determine that somehow or other, fate decreed that my companions and I live so that we could fulfill greater destinies than that of ignominious roadkill attributable to Bedu driving ineptness. The sight of several absolutely crushed automobiles along the way with dead camels on their collapsed roofs did very little to reassure us that Allah was on *our* side during our dangerous traverse, but we finally managed to reach the top of the Hijazi precipice alive and arrived safely at our destination (*Al Hada Military Hospital*), if still scared stiff by numerous near-death moments. I then recall reflecting briefly on whether or not the Arab Bedu had at some time, in the past centuries mated with Japanese warriors of the *'Divine Wind'* persuasion, since these wild-spirited Bedu would have made fine *Kamikaze* pilots, indeed.

At any rate, in the succeeding months I settled into my new accommodations at the hospital, perched as it was on the edge of the Hijazi escarpment. Across the small plateau sat HRH Prince Abdullah's massive summer residence, looking more like a small city with a replica of the Taj Mahal situated at its center than a private home for royal summer residence only. I would later find out exactly what that compound was like inside its fortress-like gates, as an invited guest to some of the wild debaucheries held there, even though I *wasn't* a cute western nurse with a nice tight ass and big *bazoongas* (they had to allow a few token men to those affairs, if only to preserve the cordial niceties of diplomacy and despite the fact that all they *REALLY* wanted were over-sexed western women to seduce—but more about that at some other time).

For my part, this was all new to me and my mind was filled to overflowing with hopelessly romantic notions of the former noble Arab civilization, with all its fabulous culture and history concurrent with the ignorance of our western 'Middle Ages'. I soon came to understand that the era of *Ibn Kaldun* (in Arabic, ابو زيد عبد الرحمن بن محمد بن خلدون) and his flowering culture had long since passed into the shades of history and that the 1932 discovery of oil in the Kingdom of Saudi Arabia had brought with it a plague of the worst aspects of western excess. The fact that Prince Abdullah, then the Crown Prince under King Fahad, would shortly ascend to the throne of the Kingdom was not something I focused on, since King Fahad had only recently assumed the crown from his elder brother, Mohammed.

Interestingly enough, elderly King Mohammed had been in residence in Taif the summer I arrived and had had a massive coronary infarct (read: heart attack), from which he failed to recover on our cardiac surgery operating table, despite our best state-of-the-art interventions. Given the extremely high-fat, high cholesterol diet the 'new' Saudis (as opposed to the old and vigorously austere and healthy, desert-dwelling Bedus) were used to, enabled by all of that oil revenue, it should come as no surprise to anyone to learn that coronary occlusions were the number one cause of death in the Kingdom and were in fact almost as common as head colds are in the West (the second most common cause of death: car crashes and frequently with camels, who loved to rest on the nice warm desert roadways at night, in the dark).

At the risk of sounding like some sort of ghoul, it was a great place for any cardiac specialist to set up shop, consequently, so there I was, daily putting Band-Aids on aortas and ligatures on femoral arteries. I could have composed a song titled *"Let's just say I sorta, stomped on your aorta"* to accompany my occasional lackluster off-time guitar strumming, but I failed to avail that opportunity with MCA. Still, it isn't every day that a King who controls a third of the world's entire liquid wealth passes on to the next world under your very nose. I remained uncertain whether or not he found the promised Islamic paradise teeming with beautiful virgins and spring water fountains, or Saint Peter's Pearly Gates of Christendom waiting for him on the *Other Side*... I suppose I'll have to wait a bit before resolving that particular question to my own satisfaction (hopefully!).

So, there I was, a recently arrived *'Amriki'* in this ancient land of Bedouins and endless sand. There was much to learn about this new home away from home (for it would be, over the next 10 years or so of my life) and learn QUICKLY, before some small and inadvertent violation of public morality resulted in my having my tender young Western ass thrown into a dirt-floored, boiling hot Saudi slammer full of depraved Bedu sodomites.

Fortunately, despite the severely strict Islamic morals that we Western infidels were expected to practice and observe, things were pretty relaxed on the Al Hada residential compound that lay adjacent to the hospital facility, some 12 klicks up the escarpment from town. We had a large swimming pool, a spacious gymnasium, lots of workout gear, weights, and what have you to occupy our spare time. It was in that gymnasium one afternoon, after a long day probing coronary arteries and ballooning blockages, that I just about dropped my jaw on the floor (along with my cool).

I think I had just finished up several sets of bench presses with 150 pounds of weights and turned around to take a look at the gym area near the locker rooms. Right there, to my immense surprise and less than 25 feet from me, was one of the most beautiful women I have ever been favored to lay eyes upon!

Now those of you who know me will recall that I am extremely partial to darker hued women from the Far East or the Pacific Islands, with their long and lustrous black hair, almond-shaped eyes, and lithe, feminine figures. It is therefore somewhat rare that I ever pay much attention to *honky broads* (white Anglo-Saxon women), or as we would call them in the islands, *haole malihini wahines*.

Ever since my earliest days in the Air Force (during Vietnam), I have found that women of Asian extraction (especially when mixed with the blood of native islanders, such as are found in Hawaii) typically offer the best possible combination of feminine assets under the sun. I speak here of not just slender, lovely figures and gorgeous long dark hair, but sensually spirited, if reticently modest personalities, curiously mixed with a measure of significant physical strength and an animated depth that could have come directly from *Pele's* (the Hawaiian Goddess of Fire, under the tenets of the ancient island religion) sister.

Rarely have I encountered white Anglo-Saxon women who compare favorably with these languorous alluring maidens of Asian and Asian-Pacific ancestry, since for the most part, Western women too often wear their armor on the outside like a shield (whereas Asian women and Asian-Pacific women wear it just beneath that soft, velvety exterior with all the pleasing bumps on it…I call it the *'iron fist in the velvet glove'* effect). The formidable personality is still there, but that arrangement of *appearing* to defer to men allows us poor benighted males at least to pretend that we have a *small* vestige of our self-imagined superior prowess in all things intact. All in all, a very satisfactory accommodation by my reckoning and FAR superior to the typical Western woman's tendency to emasculate men with a withering first glance.

Be all that as it may, this creature facing me in that gym was spectacular, despite the fact she was clearly and obviously a Westerner. Clad in a sports-bra and Lycra tights, she was doing some gymnastics on the parallel bars that virtually left me breathless. The definition of her lithe, but well-toned arms (I am an acknowledged sucker for superbly toned upper arms on women) exactly matched all the rest of her gazelle-like body, and I was shortly to find out exactly how appropriate the use of the term 'gazelle' was in describing this…my initial response to the sight of her there. Gazing open-mouthed and no doubt stupidly at her medium shade of short brown hair and deeply tanned skin, I felt like I was caught up in some sort of *Star Trek* type 'Tractor Beam' that drew me towards her as surely as the sun draws everything into it with its immense and irresistible gravitational pull. She was *stunning!*

This, I quickly came to learn, was *Daniella*, a South African expatriate critical care nurse who actually worked adjacent to our cardiac surgery suites. She had come over from '*Joberg*' with several other nurses of South African Boer extraction and had just recently arrived on contract herself.

Since I had absolutely lost every bit of cool I normally possessed and was reduced to a staring, gawking, puddle of lava as I continued to gaze at her with a stupefied mien, all I could do was turn back to my weights, pile on a few more hunks of pig iron, and reflect on all that spectacular femaleness that was spinning on those wooden bars with the agility of a natural athlete. There were only a few others in the gym with us at the time, since there had not been that many patients on the heart center's schedule for that day and most of the staff had already gone back to their residences.

Despite my being in what I consider the best physical shape of my life at that particular time, my previous luckless experience with the fair sex had led me to habitually regard myself as some sort of congenital *Quasimodo*. Hence, all I could do was glance at her occasionally, try to smile a bit without looking like a certified looney, and overall try to feign an air of disinterested nonchalance. Imagine my disbelief and shock when after completing several of her routines, she toweled off a bit and then directly came over to me and introduced herself. I can't remember exactly how tongue-tied I was at that moment, but I can imagine my eyes were as big as pie-plates, although I sincerely hope I had not yet been reduced to drooling stupidly like some sort Mongoloid idiot.

Although a bit defensive by habit and feeling as if I owed her some sort of apology for staring at her so transparently, it took me only a few minutes to recover my wits and relax, for she herself was about as perfectly at ease and friendly as anyone I can ever recall having met, anywhere.

Daniella (that wasn't really her name, of course), had the most delightful South African English accent I had heard—either before that moment or after. As someone who has always had an inordinate regard for elocution, language, and verbal eloquence, I think I was already half in love with her by the time she had her second word out. That lilting accent, combined with the perfectly toned outline of her drop-dead beautiful body, flat stomach, tight ass, perfectly molded breasts and all was simply too much for this poor old *'Amriki'* expat in King Fahad's Court to handle. I'm afraid all my vaunted Irish bravado and verbally adept bullshittery must have failed me completely, so much of an impact did she make on me (and I'm not exaggerating any of this here—on my scale of 1-to-10, she was easily a 12).

By the end of that workout session, Daniella was barely breaking a sweat, but the sheen of her perspiration was apparently scentless. Ether that, or the pheomones produced by her unique biochemistry were such as by my reckoning, she had a bodily aroma equal to the sweetest perfume imaginable. As if all this weren't enough, when we were both through working out, she came over and boldly reached out to pull my head close while *she planted a big wet smooch directly on my lips!*

I just about died right then and there, I can assure you. Talk about a completely unanticipated turn of affairs! I mean, meeting someone for the first time calls for a handshake and *perhaps* penetrating looks. NOT, by most reckoning, for a wet, full-frontal lip-lock that spoke of unimaginable potentials to come. I barely made it back to my flat!

As the days passed after that initial shock of an encounter, I quickly learned more about this unusual and animated wonder of a woman. She was a runner, among other things, and had run several of those ultra-marathon type races from Joberg to Durban in her native South Africa before coming to Saudi Arabia. She was also a climber who enjoyed rock work and had studied classical ballet back at home for many years. Now I know that this is starting to take on the nature of what sounds like a fairy tale, but believe me, it almost was, given my own past track record of dismal near-failure to attract anything more than the romantic attentions of a female she-goat. Daniella became more and more the perfect human form of a female creature I had largely constructed only in my mind over all those years. And yet, here she was, right there in real flesh and blood, and clearly (so it certainly seemed) interested in me (for reasons that were *WAY* beyond my understanding).

Although at first it was a bit startling to learn she was an *exertional asthmatic* (someone who experiences the vasoconstrictive effects of asthmatic dyspnea upon exercising) when she brought out her inhaler to take an occasional puff or two, it wasn't long before this didn't seem odd at all. She also had a curious habit of briefly staring deep into one's eyes in an intensely concentrated manner, framed by the most beautiful auburn eyebrows, as if she could read thoughts and uncover secrets otherwise hidden away in one's thoughts. I still think about that now and then and wonder if she had some sort of extrasensory ability most of us lack. She would tilt her lovely head, with its mass of short brown hair, to the side and search your eyes so deeply it seemed as if she was trying to suck unutterable feelings right out of your brain!

But this was only scratching the surface of Daniella's pleasing, but perplexingly mysterious nature. I would later find out exactly how pleasing that nature actually was from direct experience, of course, but at the outset all I could do was wonder at what family background and what early life circumstances had managed to produce such as exotic creature as she obviously was.

As the weeks passed and then the months, we became running partners, coursing over the dirt trails and paths at the 7800-foot elevation that Taif occupies. Throughout that time, we remained very close, with a bond of closeness developing somewhat along the lines of that which a brother and sister would have, yet suggestive there was far more to it than that. It was a sort of closeness mingling fraternal affection with an unconsummated, underlying stream of suggested passion that puzzled me and defied my understanding.

Even something as perfectly 'ordinary' and healthful as running, in those parts of the Arabian 'outback', was still fraught with an adventure-tinged component of risk, since just about anything we expatriates accepted as perfectly normal public behavior back home was looked upon as egregious sinfulness by the stringent standards of Taif's Islamic culture. There were times when we had taken a brief stretch of roadway to run on that locals in their little white Toyota pickups would seem to suddenly veer crazily and deliberately towards us on the road's shoulder, as they passed by. I later learned that this was one way of expressing local disapprobation over our exposed legs and arms. For Daniella's part, her short brown hair probably helped disguise her female identity (especially under a shapeless loose T-shirt), but even if the locals thought we were just two male expats running bare-legged, it was still looked down upon as *'harram'*(forbidden), since under strict *Wahabbist* interpretations of the Islamic faith, ANY exposure of bodily flesh is forbidden.

There were less vigorous moments to share as well, particularly long, thoughtful strolls together atop the Taif plateau under the backdrop of vast, starry nighttime skies, and particularly memorable walks beneath the thin crescent of the moon, that together with Mars ascendant nearby reminded one literally of the symbol of Islam around the world—the crescent moon and star. To say it was poetic is understating things considerably. To walk quietly, with no words needed, arm in arm with this beautiful creature provided a sense of fulfillment that I have never achieved ever again with another woman. It was as if we were each the complement of the other, two hearts and one beat as the old saying has it. It was serenely meaningful, this shared time spent with Daniella, and my recollections of those moonlit walks under the luminous spirals of the Milky Way are among the most memorable of my entire life, even today.

As the months passed, I was in no hurry to bring that ultimate, furthest physical measure of closeness into actuality, for I was already as much a part of Daniella's whole matrix as either of us felt anyone could or should be. For our part, neither did we feel the need to rush this delicious and to me amazing sense of singularity of spirit to any possibly higher level of physical union, although it did ultimately come to that not long after. I meanwhile wrote prodigiously of this feeling, producing the usual volumes of poems and prosaic expressions of heightened feeling and emotional sensation that such closeness invariably inspires in me. I still have almost all of that mass of emotion-laden word-mongering in my files, but it is all so exquisitely personal that few would doubtless appreciate it half as much as do I each time read those words.

Finally, on a climbing trip down the escarpment, things happened of their own accord and I at last entered that final and most intimate aspect of Daniella's great infinity of allure that had hitherto remained unaccessed. I had brought all my Class 6 climbing gear (artificial aids) and we had planned a day's outing only, with a lunch and everything packed into our knapsacks. The wall to be climbed was a somewhat hidden prominence a bit up slope of the hospital, but far enough out of the way so that the only creatures within viewing would be the large birds that soared in the thermal updrafts that spilled over the escarpment's edge. It wasn't a difficult hike and the climbing itself was limited to several pitches of what I would call 'exciting Class 5' stuff, so by the time we had regained the top of the plateau, it was late afternoon, with the sun already draped into lengthening shadows as it neared the horizon, across the desert *Tihama* below.

Near the edge of the escarpment was a small recessed area that is hidden from the sight of anyone standing atop it. It was grassy and smooth and a delightfully private and secluded niche carved out of the living rock of that great escarpment. Depositing all the gear there, we sat back to drink in both water and the spectacular view of a hundred miles of desolated openness that characterised the vista only those with our outlook could appreciate. Despite the sun and warmth, we were both refreshed by the unusually gentle breeze that drifted up towards us and the resulting mood of serene beauty and spiritual emotion was most ethereal, yet also quite palpable.

Daniella sat down beside me and we drank the cool water we had brought with us for a few quiet moments. And then, in that peculiar manner she affected, she placed herself directly between me and the breath-taking view and searched my eyes briefly with that deep, soul-sucking gaze of hers. Then, taking my head in her hands, she kissed me lightly on the lips. It was as much of an invitation to cross that final barrier as an electric signal can be. I needed no further inducements and slowly and gently removed her bra as she pulled her pants down with the grace of a dancer. After removing my T-shirt and shorts, we melted into one another with an intensity of pure physical passion that I doubt seriously will ever come my way again.

Daniella became at one both a savage animal and the most delicately sensitive lover imaginable. Amazingly, neither of us had much of an odor, since our chemistries were so closely attuned that even the sour stink of our sweat merged and mixed with perfect chemically aromatic congruence. Daniella quickly pulled me into her with the same level of hunger that shined out of her carnivorous eyes when she gazed deeply into my own and I could feel myself losing all control, as I penetrated to that molten core of her innermost physical recesses, plunging into the heated warmth of her taut body. Rutting there, fused together like a single creature, poised on the edge of all eternity (yawning 7000 feet below) and almost entirely mindless of an immortal sense of timelessness that permeated the unreal visual setting, we became totally lost in each other's fantasy. Before either of us was aware of it, the sun had disappeared and we were now lying naked and spent, still fused together under the moon's first rays. It was a full moon, fortunately, or I would have been a bit ashamed to think of flaunting my host country's moral conventions under the very symbol of its religion.

Daniella remained at Taif after my contract ended and although we remained in touch, she ultimately disappeared into my past, leaving no trace except our letters and a disclosure that I had no clue of when we were together.

As it happened, I somewhat later learned (to my shock) that Daniella preferred *women* for sexual partners and was apparently what is known crudely as a *'lipstick dyke'* (a lesbian who affected a glamorous and 'normal' female appearance and who could be mistaken for an exceptionally beautiful *heterosexual* woman, if it weren't for the fact that she preferred women for sexual partners).

Thinking about this today, I still marvel that what I consider that perhaps the peak experience of my life—both spiritually and sexually—came at the exquisite ministrations of an amazing woman, who normally preferred to love other women. Why we had such an intensely close relationship despite the apparent status quo of her sexuality is a perplexing question I shall never have an adequate answer for…nor have I *ever* cared to provide a logical explanation for it. After all, it is well known that some individuals are *bisexual.*

All I know is that I experienced all the delights of heaven and earth in her embrace and in her company and *nothing* can ever be as profound an experience as that was. This remains the result of an extremely paradoxical encounter I experienced in the Kingdom of Saudi Arabia, these 24 years ago.

T'WAS A DARK AND STORMY NIGHT

"It was a dark and stormy night; the rain fell in torrents--except at occasional intervals, when it was checked by a violent gust of wind which swept up the streets (for it is in London that our scene lies), rattling along the housetops, and fiercely agitating the scanty flame of the lamps that struggled against the darkness."

So starts the epic, timeless prose of Edward George Bulwer-Lytton's archetypal 1830 paragon of bad writing to which we are all indebted for inspiring innumerable annual contests (the purpose of which is to encourage us mortal word-hacks to aspire to similarly stunted parody opening paragraphs). The most well-known of these competitions is, of course, the original *Bulwer-Lytton Fiction Contest*. Immediately below appears another such classic specimen offered to the world by internet guru Dave Taylor.

"The hair flew in Prudence Truebottom's eyes as the wind kicked up, blowing the curtains in a ghostly waltz, tipping the paintings ever-so-slightly a-kilter, forcing the clouds outside even thinner, and ensuring that however she turned herself, she'd have to face the reality that Alex, her beloved Alex, wasn't coming back and that Daddy was right yet again: hot air ballooning without a control valve is a sport for fools, not adventurers."

Here are two further gems possessed of high amusement quotient:

"The Insect Keeper General, sitting astride his giant hovering aphid, surveyed the battlefield which reeked with the stench of decay and resonated with the low drone of the tattered and dying mutant swarms as their legs kicked forlornly at the sky before turning to his master and saying, 'My Lord, your flies are undone.'" (Andrew Vincent).

"The ancient Peruvian Airlines DC-3 lumbered slowly over the snow-capped peaks far below as Gunderson turned to Ricketts and marveled at how their avian import business "Incahoots" had led them once again to the far reaches of South America in search of the elusive gray-spotted owl."

Naturally the level of intensely word-wrenching blitherance only gets worse with each succeeding year. For those of you dead keen on overdosing on more such specimens of *terrible tomery*, visit the official website of the Bulwer-Lytton Fiction Contest, which is found at www.bulwer-lytton.com/ .

One could spend a whole day there, immersed in the sort of immensely entertaining literary effluvia old Bulwar-Lytton's efforts inspired, way back in the mid-1800s, but unless you have a strong constitution and an inversely weak modicum of respect for your own wretched writing abilities, it is perhaps better to limit the visits to a short dive on each immersion. I should say here for possibly the zillionth time that I am not unmindful of the abysmal nature of my own writing, since it is generally known that in order to fully appreciate something, one must have intensely resonant sympathetic affinities (sort of along the lines of the cause/effect result of successfully applied homeopathic medical therapy). Having declaimed that little airburst of alliterative ebullience, it shouldn't be surprising to hear that whenever I plough through the Bulwar-Lytton competition entries, my whole being absolutely quivers with sympathetic vibrations. *QED.*

December 7th. "Pearl Harbor Day". Outside, the storm that was predicted earlier had finally blown out of the Pacific in full force and right onto the doorstep. Before I rose in the AM, the sound of the surf outside seemed louder in tenor to my ears as I lay bundled up in multiple layers of warmth in front of the hearth. Having elected to eschew the sleeping loft for a smaller futon in the main room the night before, things were quite cozy enough with the combined body heat of two huskies and a human, and I had no real desire to arise. Raki and Laika, still engaged in their endless turf war for dominant claim to my attentions even as they sleep, were arrayed on either side of me, providing furry bolsters of active warmth to enhance the duvet's warmth. The air inside the cabin was crisp with the residual chill of the passing night, but offset as it was by the wonderful womb-like comfort of my tight little knot of bedding, the sensation of sticking one's nose outside the covers was not uninvigorating and not all that unappealing. There's something deliciously synergistic about chill air and the strong scent of still fresh pine logs with their oozing sap rivulets that positively stimulates the olfactory organs. The distinctive aroma assaults the nose not unlike the undeniably sour scent of stale, unwashed underclothes, but in a diametrically opposite and highly pleasing manner (that's a Bulwer-Lyttonism, heh-heh! You see how easy it is?).

As I listened for a few more moments to the thunderous roar of the pounding surf, my full appreciation of the moment was only interrupted by two other intrusive elements: a chorus of sporadic husky snorts of the sort that doggy-dreams produce, and the occasional banshee howl of wind gusts as they cut across the corners of the cabin's windward façade like a sneeze from Betty-Jo Biolosky's protuberant nose. The overall enticement of the combined effect was too great to resist and despite the coziness of my *gow-dow* (that's Cantonese for 'dog house') cocoon, it was time to rise and briefly perform the obligatory morning high mass offerings at the high alter of the Chief God *Caffeineus Strongus*.

My struggles to remove myself from the confining unconscious embrace of two somnolent furry forms was finally successful and we all got up together, tails wagging (theirs, not mine) and tongues hanging out (all of us, as they anticipated the first treat of the day and I salivated over the thought of ingesting my first decoction of French Roast and Sumatran Arabica beans of the day).

After the water had reached a tentative boil on the propane stove I reached for the press, having already used the creaky old hand grinder to produce a perfect coarse grind suitable for the press-pot coffee technique. After letting the just boiled water cool for a minute, I carefully cascaded the water into the pot, glancing out the window at the now turgid, now swirling waters stretching out beyond to the horizon. The ocean, which the day before had had the consistency of smooth glass, was now filled with rank after rank of white-topped waves steaming relentlessly toward the land at a slightly northwest angle to the shore.

At each windward blast of salt-laden air, clouds of saline spray and sea-spume whipped off each of these monsters as they collectively approached the land with the inertial determination of an army of horny Viking raiders. The clouds over them hung low and gray, blending into the gray bulk of the sea so perfectly that it was almost hard to tell where the sky began and the sea left off. It appeared to have the making of a perfectly wonderful storm (note: there is a difference between 'a perfect storm' and *'a perfectly wonderful storm'*, since the *former* is not necessarily agreeable to the human sense of aesthetics and implies cold, wet, directly sensate misery, whereas the *latter* suggests a warm, cozy vantage from which to witness the stormy effects in perfect comfort).

I have found that it is exactly on such days, at such times as this that the creative juices run around wildly rampaging in my noggin, supersaturating my cranial sap, and it is a certain bet that during such sensorially stimulating moments, the words literally flow off my finger-tips in an effusively irresistible emulation of talentlessness that surely must mimic the best output Bulwer-Lytton was ever capable of at his most supreme moments of literary inspiration! Such stormy conditions as this have always been moments of creatively catalytic impetus for me and I cannot think of anything more suitable for filling up endless pages of virtual paper with non-relevant drivel that these climatically chaotic moments that all tumble forth at the merest bidding.

Think of writing for those of us who are definitely at the bottom of the literary barrel as a form of journalistic masturbation, if it helps to visualise the process. Falling somewhere in between GB Shaw at the top of the Periodic Chart of brilliant linguistic gibberish and Bulwer-Lytton's younger and incoherent half-wit brother at the nether extremity, my own musings probably fall somewhere at or about the lowest 2-percentile. While GB Shaw may figuratively whack off with the supreme clarity and creative imagination of a mythical *Onan*, old Bulwer-Lytton and I must be content with the obligatory and dysfunctional rote hand motions of a cerebral palsy afflicted person suffering from the latent effects of a C-3 fracture. It is about as pretty a process, by any stretch of the muse's imagination.

At any rate, and with grotesquely misapplied and inappropriate figurative metaphorical anomalies mercifully overlooked, stormy days for me are stimulating days that get the convolutions of the old cerebrum positively buzzing with tangential thoughts that have little or no connectivity to any larger body of meaningful or useful reflection. One such thought that popped up as I lasciviously enjoyed the morning's first steaming cup of joe was the fact that it was December 7th, the anniversary of that fateful day in 1941 that FDR alluded would forever live in infamy. The great clouds of billowing gray storminess and the chaotic agitation of the spectacular waves that crashed into the land outside *The Bunker* were certainly an appropriate accompanying backdrop for a thought like this about the actual event, since that event is best characterised in the mind's eye by successive spectacular explosions and unending, roiling towers of thick, black diesel-fired smoke over Pearl Harbor, on 7 December of 1941.

Of the fact that 2000+ soldiers, sailors, and civilians died on that day there is no argument, but of the event's relevance as a never-to-be-forgotten moment in history there is considerable difference of opinion that to this day creates a curious and highly emotion-laden dialogue between individual Americans. As the survivors of the Japanese attack on the Pearl base drop away, the contentiousness is nonetheless heated, since the human condition unanimously predisposes to a fondness for conspiracies just as surely as it does toward a regard for trashy gossip about public celebrities whose last names end in *Hilton*. Invariably on this annual remembrance of that day, interviews with the American (and most recently Japanese) survivors are trotted out and faithfully aired on both local and national television. The Pearl harbor interviewees repeat the same stories, and bring forth carefully recollected and congruently similar personal experiences incurred on that moment in early December when waves of Japanese warplanes swept over the island. You can literally see in their faces the intensity of the memories forever burned into their brains at that time, as if left by some great, white-hot cattle brand of fate.

As fascinating history, these accounts of personal ordeal and reflexive response to the very real imminent peril each of these men faced are edifying and instructive...up to a point...since story-telling is invariably great fun when properly accomplished, and always instructive in some manner or another. It's when the old geezers begin moralizing and trying to make ethical sense out of their experiences that the value of these unavoidably annual excursions into the vault of American memory becomes tedious, irritating, and aesthetically repellant. The principal reason for this is because any discussion of war, killing, violent national struggles, and/or catastrophic contexts of international sociopolitical will by nature presuppose the establishment of some sort of absolute moral hierarchy in consequent association.

There are several uniform characteristics to this process of remembering war experiences that bear focusing upon, whenever an old war vet purges his vault of wartime memories. Most characteristically, at least to me, the ascendant sentiment that surfaces from every single account of extremely personal association with war that has been undergone is that there is an unconsciously irrepressible need to establish one warring side as 'the good guys' and the other as the 'bad'. Thus, a sort of moral struggle to pin the blame on one's enemies immediately takes the advance guard position in these reminiscences, as inevitably as vaginal dryness chronically occurs in post-menopausal women. In those vets who are not intellectually endowed, that's where the ruminative process is forever halted, frozen in the mind and soul like a fly forever sealed in petrified amber resin. For those old war-horses with a bit more gray matter still left to play around with, however, sooner or later an awareness dawns that those yellow-skinned *boogeymen* (substitute 'enemy of choice' here, whether turban-topped, slant-eyed, or as much of a pasty-white honky as am I) who were trying so hard to kill you are, after all is said and done, *also* human beings, the universally shared commonality of whom (each with basically similar human hopes, thoughts, desires, outlooks, and needs) inevitably comes into sharper focus *later* in their lives.

The next phase of the process mandates contacting old surviving enemies and getting together in an atmosphere of amicable co-acceptance of what fate has handed them to together commemorate those youthful days of nationalistic antagonism in rites of somber celebration. This is the classic 'shared experience' dynamic of human life that serves to eventually bond others who may have once been violently polarized by political hatreds (so perfectly exemplified by emotion-charged war propaganda) earlier in their lives. Pearl Harbor Day remembrances are today accordingly increasingly characterised by such gatherings of aged, former American and Japanese soldiers who in the twilight of their many year spent trying to puzzle out the whole mess of their involvement, typically succumb to the geriatric effects of diminished Testosterone *titers* and *FINALLY* are able to see beyond the belligerent purple haze created in their minds, by that always contentious biochemical component of the human body, to grasp whatever truth may (or may not) lie beyond.

At first glance and without any deeper thoughts on this curious process, it is easy to become indignant and impatient with the obvious futility of such a highly predictable and cyclically recurrent aspect of human of affairs. Why, after all, charge off to battle, mindlessly slaughter as many of the opposing army as possible in the most deviously clever and merciless manner possible, and then later come to the awareness that these are *actually* future potential good buddies with whom you might greatly enjoy quaffing a few root beers and sharing stories with some day?

In a word, *hormones*. Once the basic biochemistry of the causative process behind Pearl Harbor day (and any other collective or personal human conflict you can think of) is better understood, and a broader awareness of how this status quo has affected the entire history of the human race since Day One is grasped, one is tempted to think that perhaps the mythical Amazons of ancient Greek legend had it right after all: get rid of all the male babies at birth and just keep a few specially selected studs around for breeding purposes (preferably well hung, I would imagine, and not especially endowed with IQ).

The sad fact is and always has been that all wars are the product of a fatal admixture of two elements (virtually exclusively male in origin), one of environmentally formative substance and the other hormonal in nature. These are: 1) the clever tool-using ability of us opposed-thumb higher primates, and 2) a severe imbalance between estrogen and testosterone (with the bias being towards the latter) in the genders. As regards the latter influence, it is well known that the balance of these gender-specific hormones changes over the term of the human life span, diminishing remarkably towards the end of the cycle. Thus, women become progressively aggressive and may altogether lose that softly feminine nature (that is so fatally attractive to us XY types) as they age; men, for their part, become mellower, less aggressive, and more compliant as the male/female temperament characteristics tend to reverse poles.

When you take the deplorable male condition in early life of being mentally immature, whilst charged to the eyebrows with testosterone, the question of why humanity is constantly at war over the usual trivial differences of economic or political opinion is no longer the enigmatic riddle, wrapped in mystery that it might at first appear. Young guys are prepared by nature to be thoughtless physical fighting machines...a condition that obtains with some constancy throughout their lives until shortly before the end of their days (assuming they don't end up as premature cannon fodder, rotting away on some remote battlefield). At that time, they are finally released to a substantial degree from their hormonal captivity and may perhaps reconsider their world through the more unclouded hormonal lenses (e.g. the present state of the *Pearl Harbor Remembrance Day* events) that age confers. Thus also an explanation of the fact that former Imperial Army Sergeant Yukio Fukutume and US Navy Chief Petty Officer Rock Bawls are now to be found at the Pearl Harbor O-Club enjoying a beer together as mutually convivial drinking companions on 7 December every year (a circumstance that predictably ends up being used to great personal advantage on the evening news by some drop-dead gorgeous split-tail news-anchor to pad out her nightly agenda of inanely stupid examples of inanely stupid human behavior).

It's certainly a waste of my time (and I hope yours as well) having to be subjected to more absolutely boring dullness of this sort on the national news media at this time of the year (and thank goodness there's no television here in *The Bunker*).

Meanwhile, outside the rising storm has grown in increasing fury as wave after wave of black clouds comes roaring in from the sea, and the heightened fury of the gray ocean threatens to pulverize that part of the coastline left over from Mother Gaia's last sea-borne attack on our cretinously sedate human misapprehensions of our Universe. The pups have grown restless and my butt has long since gone to sleep, perched on the edge of this flat and thinly padded chair that I use. The long-promised rain has finally begun to thunder down and things are getting, as Bertie Wooster (of P.G. Wodehouse's *Jeeves and Wooster*) would put it, *"dashedly wet and all".*

I'm going to give my somnolent and sore nether extremity an ambulatory break to re-enervate itself, and take the pups outside for a quick leg-lift or two, leaving this annual remembrance of the Pearl Harbor Day nonsense to torpedo itself and sink back into the miasma of eternal human befuddlement that typifies human life on this lovely planet (that most of us don't appreciate anywhere as much as we should).

Since I've already reached the exalted heights of the 10,000 worst bad writers level in Bulwers-Lytton competition, the next objective on my literary list of aspirations is the most challenging yet: *The "Best Bad Sex Writing Contest".* [Someone pointed out to me recently that I should have a fairly good advantage in this particular endeavor, given the previous products along these lines that have already sprung forth from the dried-up little coconut of my fecund imagination...].

Remember Pearl Pureheart! Woof!

IF DOGS DON'T GO TO HEAVEN...

In 2004, one of our beloved huskies (a huge russet colored male Siberian named Deejay) crossed the rainbow bridge after a brief and rather unexpected illness, leaving us once again a single-dog pack. Our other huskie, a female Siberian named Laika (whose namesake was the famed Soviet space dog that traveled into Earth orbit on Sputnik II, 3 Nov, 1957) and an alpha dog, clearly showed signs of being somewhat disconcerted by Deejay's sudden absence. Although we had raised Laika from puppyhood, Deejay had joined us about two years after we got her and she had gotten used to sharing the home with the big gentle giant. While she did not fully understand what had changed, she clearly sensed that something was different: the other dog she shared our home with was suddenly gone.

Accordingly, we began to think about getting a companion for her. A careful analysis of all the options left us with the conclusion that it would be a good idea to adopt a rescue dog, after the breeder we had adopted Deejay from suggested this alternative to getting another puppy. It sounded like good advice, so we soon found and got in touch with NorSled (*Northern California Sled Dog Rescue group*) and were amazed at all the wonderful 'rescue' huskies in their charge that needed forever homes.

Although my experience with Siberians was still somewhat limited at that time (2003), I was passionate about the breed, given their common ancestry with *Canis Lupus* (wolves). In my earlier undergraduate days, I had been quite interested in animal behavior, being particularly fascinated with wolves; especially with the work done by famed Austrian Conrad Lorenz on wolf imprinting. That study had first directed my attention to wolf-descended Spitz type dogs (Siberians, Malamutes, Samoyeds and

American Eskimo dogs, et al). Having had had a few Alaskan Malamutes earlier in my life, Laika was my first experience with the Siberian breed and I was soon sold on the breed.

Shortly after contacting NorSled my attention was drawn to a six-year-old B&W Siberian male named *'Cherokee'*. Cherokee was glowingly described by NorSled as *'a 60-pound boy who was both playful and controlled'*, got along well with other dogs, understood the word 'no', was affectionate but not possessive, and walked well on a lead. An outdoor dog all of his 6 years of life, Cherokee had ended up at a Yuba County shelter three times (for reasons unknown, since he was not a fence jumper or a digger, according to NorSled's description), but apparently his previous owner had decided that he wasn't worth the impound retrieval fees after his third such adventure and surrendered him to the shelter!

"Unbelievable!" I thought, as I read more about Cherokee, who seemed to be a wonderful dog by all accounts. Little did I know his glowing description was a *gross* understatement, although I was shortly due to experience even more disbelief!

And so it was that one particularly hot & dusty summer afternoon I drove up to Yuba City (from Sacramento) to meet Cherokee. Somewhat mysteriously I had been warned not to be put off by his appearance, but when his foster mom opened the door, I immediately saw why! Cherokee's former owner had *shaved all his hair off* and Cherokee looked at with me with what can only be described as a wistfully perplexed doggy expression that clearly said *"This is sooooo embarrassing!"*

Apparently, the previous owner knew absolutely *nothing* about the breed and since the Sacramento Valley is typically extremely hot during the summer she must have thought that she was doing Cherokee a favor by giving him a whole-body buzz-cut to stay cool! I admit it was quite startling to see a nearly *bald* Siberian, but the Yuba County area is full of eccentrics and 'colorful characters' (many of them descended from Steinbeck's 'Dust Bowl' immigrants of the 30s), so anything's possible up there! Even 'scalped' Siberian huskies with Native American names.

What really struck me about Cherokee was the fact that I sensed a strong chemistry between us almost at first sight. Somehow his 'naked' aspect didn't really bother me and while we gazed at each other I felt a palpable intensity in his look. For my part, my instincts immediately informed me that here was a dog that had inner depths of character and great potential as a loving, loyal companion. Cherokee was, needless to say, as good as adopted at that first early moment in our association.

Not particularly enthused with the name 'Cherokee', my wife and I decided to rename him 'Raki' (although 'Raki' is a strong anise flavored Turkish liquor, it is also has Japanese connotations). My study of Lupus dogs had convinced me that the best canine names are short and simple, with no more than two syllables; hence Raki was perfect not just for that reason, but also because it included the last strong sounding syllable of his former name. I was amazed by how Raki took to his new name so quickly, just as he did to nearly everything he was introduced to. [By a somewhat whimsical coincidence, if you search for 'Raki' in GOOGLE, the third entry for this word that comes up shows no less than five images of our own 'Raki!]

Raki stayed with us for four years before departing due to a combination of ailments that included brittle *ketoacidosis* (a particularly complex form of type-1 diabetes), a stroke, and severe cataracts, but in those four years he established a place for himself in my affections that no dog will ever equal. I readily admit that I'm a very sentimental individual, but having consciously decided to have no human children, our Siberians are our family and to say I still miss wonderful Raki, eight years after he passed is the utter truth. I can't even write about him now without tearing up a little at the memory of what a loyal, loving and utterly trusting guy Raki was!

After the diagnosis of his severely advanced diabetes was made we began insulin therapy, which required twice daily injections...not something most dogs would readily accommodate...but Raki tolerated the regimen stoically and endured his suffering nobly, without protest. When he later developed a large non-cancerous lesion on his leg that had to be surgically removed, he let me change his dressings patiently and trustingly, without any attempt to guard the wound. Although he was also losing his sight due to intractable bilateral cataracts, it was only when Raki suffered a seizure, leaving him immobile, that we felt the only humane recourse was to let wonderful Raki depart over the rainbow bridge to end his suffering.

I spent Raki's entire last day at his side, silently saying goodbye with my hand stroking his fur until it was time. [The picture on GOOGLE images entry 'Raki' at the extreme left shows Raki as he was just hours before his departure, still smiling broadly as if to say *"Not to worry, boss. I love you too!"*]

Finally, we left for the Vet's office and our veterinarian, a wonderful woman with true affection for dogs, administered the IV injection that would send Raki on his final journey. As I sat there, holding his big head in my hands, he gave me a final lick as our Vet listened to his heart. Very soon his eyes closed gently and Dr. G affirmed his passing. It was incredibly poignant and sad.

I'll *never* forget the exquisite eloquence of her words as she finally left his side, faced us, and described the gradually slowing heartbeat she had been listening to: *"It was as if he just quietly and peacefully got up and padded away from us..."*

* * *

"If dogs don't go to Heaven, I want to go where they go when I die." -Samuel Clemens

LE CERVIN, WHERE IT ALL BEGAN

> *"It is not the fortune of everyone to live in the sight of the mountains, nor is it the habit off all who dwell amidst their folding arms to seek inspiration on their topmost pinnacles. Many, indeed, who have only read of mountain climbing, consider it a waste of energy. But for all who are willing to receive their message, the glorious eternal mountains extend a silent invitation. To stroll up a hill or toil to the summit of a mountain is often to find at its uppermost vantage a new vision of life and all its possibilities. In mountaineering, one enters into intimate relations with the greatest heights and depths our planet has to offer."*
> -Leroy Jeffers (1878-1926)

Think of a mountain. Any mountain. Chances are excellent that your imaginary mountain will stand out tall and forbidding in your mind's eye: immense and ponderous, reaching up to the roof of heaven and shrouded by perpetual snow plumes borne on a relentless wind, it will be hard to visualise without feeling an attendant chill of forbidding excitement.

Mountains are the stuff of legends, the raw material of countless romantic stories about fearless adventurers who seek to know the solitary secrets of the earth's highest places. For most of us, mountains will always remain thus, merely geological phenomenon of captivating interest of which we have no greater personal experience or knowledge. But for the luckier ones among us, these majestic upper reaches of the planet's crust have a unique and singular appeal. As Leroy Jeffers noted in his lifetime of mountaineering, the expanded appreciation of life which familiarity with the high places gives us is more valuable than all the gold on earth and more precious than the rarest diamond. As a mountaineer who has maintained a lifelong love for these lofty heights, I almost pity the poor earth-bound individual who has never experienced their uniqueness and beauty in an up-close and personal way.

I recall exactly the first time I ever entertained a thought about the possibilities of attaining such things as the summits of mountains. I was an undergraduate student in Berkeley, California, and it was the late 1960s, a time when the post Bohemian awareness of San Francisco's 'beat' movement was having its effect on the new generation who were seeking renewed personal enlightenment and understanding. I was an avid reader then, as I am now. One day I picked up a copy of *Jack Kerouac's* book, *The Dharma Bums*, and started reading it. The Dharma Bums is not a book about mountains, per se; rather, it is more of a narrative of personal discovery in America of the 60s and 70s: a time of social uncertainty, war, and political upheaval.

In the book, Kerouac describes how he and poet Gary Snyder (Japhy Ryder) trek back into the Sierra Nevada Mountains of California and ascend a peak known as the Matterhorn. The Sierra Matterhorn's only resemblance to the more famous one found in Zermatt, Switzerland, is in its profile seen from directly below the Matterhorn Glacier, on its east side. From that angle, it does indeed resemble its namesake, with a pyramidal peak rising distinctly from the Sawtooth Ridge it occupies with several other summits, all in the 12,000-foot range.

I was immediately hooked by the image I conjured in my mind of this stairway to heaven's verge. It wasn't long before I was reading everything I could get my hands on that might indicate where precisely this mysterious peak was located in the Sierras' vast spine. After a bit of study, I finally found it on a topographic map, and before long I had my gear loaded up in my old VW *kaeffer* and drove 5 hours till I was at what I suspected was the starting point for the approach hike.

That first trip was unsuccessful, largely owing to my lack of ability to use topographic maps well enough to recognize which of the many peaks in the area was the right one. The next 3 trips were similarly futile, but only in the sense that I still hadn't discovered the right peak to climb. Despite my setbacks, in the course of several months of that summer I had gained a great deal of experience with ice axe and crampons, the basic tools of the mountaineer's trade. Little did I suspect that I was on my way to becoming a die-hard mountaineer.

Finally, I succeeded in getting to the top of the right mountain. I had climbed my first mountain and it had the distinction of being the Matterhorn of the Sierras. That was the start of my life-long love of the mountains and ironically, I owed it to a love of bohemian philosophy and literature. From that point on, the Matterhorn was my special mountain, just as it still is today, some 25 years later. In fact, I claimed the first ascent record for climbing the Sierra Matterhorn with a horn (a real *Matter-horn*, as it were); the horn was a trombone, actually, and I wish I could have seen some of the doubtless startled faces in Yosemite's Tuolumne Meadows when they heard the strains of music wafting down from the summit one summer day). I also made the first ascent with life raft for a glissade down the Matterhorn glacier, but that's another story altogether.

In 1983, while working in the Kingdom of Saudi Arabia on my first of what were to be many contracts as a medical worker there, I planned a pilgrimage to Zermatt, Switzerland, site of not just the archetypal European Matterhorn itself but the birthplace of the modern sport of mountaineering. Somehow, as a mountaineer in those heady Berkeley student days, I just couldn't escape the image of that magnificent pyramid of Swiss granite that my own Sierra Matterhorn was named after. Even in the student coffee house I habituated, the *Heidelberg* on Telegraph

Avenue, a large framed poster of the Swiss Matterhorn dominated the paintings on its walls. By this time my mountaineering library was literally bursting with information about the famous peak, as well as volumes on those early pioneers of the Golden Age of climbing in the mid-1800s. I had resolved to scale its forbidding flanks if ever I had the chance, and in 1984 that chance finally came.

If ever there were the practical equivalent for myself of what the obligatory Haj (religious pilgrimage) to Mecca is for the Islamic devout, this was it. Instead of a *Kaaba*, my holy site consisted of about 4478 vertical meters of solid Swiss granite, and instead of circling endlessly around it chanting, I was going to scale its prodigious heights and meditate silently upon its summit in my own version of communing with whatever spiritual deities may exist.

The little Vallaisian town of Zermatt is a place absolutely steeped in mountaineering history, for it was here that the earliest Victorian English hill walkers came on holiday in the mid-1850s to marvel at the hitherto unscaled Swiss Alps. Perhaps it is something intrinsic in the English blood that their nation has historically figured prominently in the annals of mountaineering; perhaps it may be attributed to the 'madness' that Victorian gentlemen tended towards in their adventurous outings. Whatever it was, the English were the first to climb some of the lesser Alps in the Canton of Valais. The picturesque little alpine village of Zermatt soon attracted legions of English tourists in those early days, all eager to relax in the small town and admire the majesty of the 14,685-foot Matterhorn which loomed above--almost in the back yard of the mountain hamlet. It wasn't long before some of these gentlemen adventurers began to try to find a way up this most magnificent of the alpine peaks, but none were successful until a fellow named Edward Whymper--a lithographic artist and illustrator by profession--came along and showed everyone how to do it.

By this time (the early 1960s), the English expatriates in Zermatt had gotten together and formed the world's first mountaineering association, the English Alpine Club. Most, if not all of its members were spellbound by this daunting pyramid of stone which seemed to be unclimbable; some were of the opinion that it was foolhardy to even attempt such a climb. Nevertheless, Whymper was undeterred and began a series of reconnaissances, trying various routes on the Matterhorn's flanks. His objectives were partly to capture the beautiful scenery in a series of lithographic engravings, but always there remained his unspoken goal: to find a way to the top of the mountain's seemingly impregnable ramparts.

After many unsuccessful attempts, in June of 1865 Whymper finally succeeded, leading a group of seven persons (three other Englishmen, himself and three guides) up what is now known as the *Standard Swiss Route*--following the northeast ridge known as the *Hörnli.* The ascent was successful, attaining the top of the vaunted citadel of granite. Everything went well until the group started to descend. In one disastrous moment, just below the summit roof known as the *Dachel,* one of the party slipped, pulling all of the roped party towards a seemingly fatal fall over the edge and down the stark, steep 4000-foot sheer face of the Matterhorn's North Face. At the last instant, Whymper and his guides were able to arrest their slide and attempted to take the strain of the entire party.

The rope in use was not a single rope but was in fact two ropes--one a slightly smaller and weaker one joining the four others to Whymper and two guides, who were secured by the thicker, stronger one. At the moment when the full strain was taken by the rope, the section between

Whymper's three and the other four parted and all save Whymper and his two guides where swept over the escarpment's lip, where they fell 4,000 feet to the glacier below.

It was a monumental tragedy, by the reckoning of those in Zermatt at that time, and it would soon become a singular source of speculation and conjecture the world over for decades to come. Thus, began the enduring legend of the first successful ascent of the Matterhorn. Even today, in a time when hundreds of people of all ages, sizes and fitness regularly ascend and descend this famous mountain, the tragedy of Whymper's first ascent in 1865 inspires wonder and bemusement. Of course, mountaineering has subsequently grown into a popular world-wide phenomenon since those early days of the Victorian gentlemen explorers; but most mountaineers will still recall the fact that it all began here in Zermatt, on the Swiss Matterhorn, in 1965. Today, such early ascents pale into virtual insignificance in the shadow of such modern, almost superhuman feats of climbing accomplishment as Rheinhold Meissner's oxygen-less alpine style solo climb of Everest; but to many of us, the Matterhorn is still the Godfather of all mountains.

My own ascent of the Swiss Matterhorn began in late 1983, with preparations and travel plans being made to visit Zermatt in the early summer of 1984. As an American member of the European *Naturefreunde Touristenverein*, an outdoor group dedicated to the love of the mountains (originated in the late 1800s to provide recreational opportunities for German factory workers) I knew of the existence of a NF/TVN chapter in Zermatt. However, owing to the fact that the earliest tourist hotel in Zermatt--the *Seiler Hotel Monte Rosa*--was also the historical "headquarters" of the English Alpine Club, I decided to book a stay there for purely nostalgic reasons. The NF/TVN rates, as a private club, were quite modest compared to the princely sums demanded by the Seiler hotel, but I was determined to savor the ambiance of this 'watering hole' of the earliest climbers. The hotel preserves much of the original character and flavor of its late 1800s notoriety and anyone interested in the past 'Golden Age' of mountaineering history ought to plan a stay at the Monte Rosa at least once on their visits to Zermatt. Although a relatively average individual possessed of ordinary means and an average income, my contract in Saudi Arabia, coming as it did at the height of the US Dollar's favorable overseas exchange rate in '84, was enabling me to do things I had never thought I'd be able to afford. Consequently, as I felt was befitting my newfound status as a *wealthy* expatriate, I made arrangements to stay in the historic Monte Rosa for a week in early June of 1984.

Came June and I caught a flight to *Genève* (or *Genf*, as it is known in German) on Swissair from Riyadh. After a delightful overnight stay in a quaint old hotel in Geneva's Vieux Ville (Old City), I took the Schweitzer eisenbahn east, following the shores of *Lac Lemán*, through *Montreaux* and finally up the Rhône Valley to the small town of Brig/Visp, where a narrow-gauge railway continues up the *Zermattertal* (gorge) to picturesque Zermatt. The somewhat lengthy train ride is absolutely beautiful and travels through some of the most scenic vistas in all Switzerland; it is a joy in and of itself.

Finally, after a stunning ride on the cog-railway's narrow-gauge train up the gorge, we pulled into Zermatt's Bahnhof, which is protected from avalanche by sturdy sheds. There, in the chill mountain air which is blessedly free of noisy motor vehicles and their noxious fumes (cars must be left lower down the mountain at a small village called *Randa*--the only way into Zermatt is either by helicopter, by foot, or by railway), one of the dozens of small electric shuttles picked me up and took me to the Hotel Monte Rosa. Tourism is the lifeblood of tiny Zermatt, the hamlet having no other economic means of supporting itself, and the *Burgemeinde* jealously preserve the natural beauty which is their birthright as well as their proverbial Golden Goose.

The next day, after spending the evening wandering about, visiting the discos, and breathing in all the quaint surroundings that constitute Zermatt, I visited the local Swiss Alpine Mountain Guides office to inquire about climbing fees and arrangements. Although anyone in reasonably good condition may aspire to hire a guide and attempt the 4,000-foot climb, the Zermatt guides are very careful to ascertain whether or not one has the ability and stamina to undertake the ascent before agreeing to take anyone aloft. Outside the window of the guide office, the frosty cathedral-like bulk of the Matterhorn's citadel looms almost unbelievably, dominating everything in the vicinity and standing starkly alone and supremely elevated above everything else around it. Just the sight of it at dawn, haunting the skyline like a mysterious specter of stone, makes the heart beat faster. The Zermatt guide office itself is a simple, unpretentious place on appearance. In the window are notices about rates and recreational outings offered.

Inside, at the counter, a coffee pot brews black liquid and an office assistant sizes-up prospective clients with studied disinterest. Near the counter, conversing in low tones, are some of the local men, who although they don't wear apparel identifying them as guides, surely must be. The initial feeling one has is that here one is an interloper, an unknown quantity. That feeling quickly dissipates, however, as the questions begin and the answers start to come forth. One can hardly blame the native Zermatters for being a bit stand-offish by nature--after all, the places is crawling with tourists of every caliber and quality, many of whom have no place on *any* mountain!

In the early morning at this time of the year there are usually few if any clouds circling the mountain, and it simply sits there, commanding respect and awe by its very august presence alone. Inside the guide office, the guides will quickly but completely go over the pertinent considerations of an ascent of the 4478-meter mountain with their prospective clients, and inordinate stress is usually put on what one must regard as the objective and subjective dangers of such a climb.

While the ascent itself (roughly 4000 feet of 45-degree angle climbing) is not especially technically difficult, there are two factors which require some sober thinking. First, and most obvious as you look up at the expanse of the East and North Faces which lie on either side of the Hörnli Ridge, is the severe exposure involved in the climb. Each of the two faces drop steeply away to the glacial apron below without interruption. While unlikely, a fall on either side would be a long, but terminal drop to infinity. Second, the fact that the Matterhorn thrusts itself up in a solitary manner, standing alone as it does on the Matterhorn plateau, creates some subjective dangers having to do with climatic conditions.

The standard ascent of the mountain (1218 meters from the hut, via the Hörnli Ridge) takes about 4-5 hours (depending on the fitness of the climbers), starting from the Swiss Alpine Club's Hörnlihutte. Characteristically, although the summit remains cloud-free in the early morning, by about 11 or 12 o'clock the thermal effects peculiar to the peak's mass interact with the weather to start creating a wreath of cloud around the upper third of the mountain. During the normal climbing season, this means that by noon the whole upper half of the peak is frequently completely obscured. For this reason, the ascent usually begins at 4AM, so that by about 9AM the summit has been reached and descent has begun in cloud-free, high visibility conditions. The unique Alpine meteorological patterns set in motion by the Matterhorn's immense granite bulk thus create one of the most subjective potential hazards that one may encounter on the mountain.

Not surprisingly, thousands of individuals have made the ascent of the Matterhorn since that first success by Whymper in 1865. Children have done it, people in their 60s and even a few in their 70s, handicapped persons have made the climb--it is no longer the preserve of those brave elite of the mountaineering fraternity. However, due to its popularity and the fact that on any given weekend during the climbing season there may be as many as several hundred people in various stages of going up or down the Matterhorn at one time, the third most significant hazard associated with a modern ascent is *rock fall.* A review of the mortality statistics for the Matterhorn will reveal that *rocks inadvertently dislodged by climbers have killed more people on the Matterhorn than any other cause.* The fact that many people making the climb are not experienced mountaineers makes this hazard far more likely to occur, and a sturdy helmet is virtually *de rigueur* for everyone going up this most famous of Alpine peaks.

Lest it seem too easy, I ought to hasten to add that the ascent is physically arduous owing to the high altitude involved and the vertical elevation of the Matterhorn (14,685 feet / 4478 meters). Only individuals in very good condition ought to make the climb. This fact notwithstanding, many people make the climb that are not especially fit or well-toned. Still, for those who wish to experience this unique bit of mountaineering history, the spectacular scenery and the views from the summit of the Swiss Matterhorn are all worth the effort, many times over. And there is that singularly special feeling of spiritual identification and integration with this mountaineering 'holy place' that one feels after having scaled its imposing heights.

My chat with the guides provided all this information and much more, for they are admirably serious about wanting to assure the safety of their clients. Furthermore, no mountain guide genuinely enjoys being stuck high up on a mountain such as this with an incapacitated or otherwise hors de combat client, whom he must safely get down again. In the event of the need for such a rescue effort, there is a unique organisation based in Zermatt called *Air Zermatt*. Owned by certain members of the Zermatt Burgemeinde, Air Zermatt is a high-altitude helicopter service which provides, in addition to high altitude mountain rescue, other things such as helicopter rides above and around the famous mountain and ski access to some of the higher ski areas in the region. So skilled are the pilots of Air Zermatt that injured climbers have been plucked off the very summit itself, provided the weather is tolerable. For their work, they use specially adapted high-altitude French *Alouette III* helicopters that are designed to fly more efficiently in the thinner than usual air. Their collective rescue exploits make for some exciting reading.

Former Air Zermatt Chief Pilot Siegfried Stangier's account of his own career as a rescue helicopter pilot (*Retter, Die von Himmel Kommt!*) is highly recommended, although it is not available in English. As an aviation person, I had ample opportunity to interview author Sigi during the course of my climbing visit in 84, and managed to overfly the Matterhorn's summit several times with him to get a feel for the nature of his risky work in the treacherous air currents that are created by the Matterhorn. Working with the Swiss Alpine Club and REGA, the Swiss national helicopter rescue service, Air Zermatt has saved the lives of countless climbers over the past 40 years. Hopefully, you won't have to observe their professional expertise at work from close proximity, but it certainly is a nice feeling knowing that such last-ditch measures are available, should the unthinkable occur high up on the Matterhorn's granite flanks!

After meeting with the guides and inquiring as to prices and logistics, they were satisfied by my own background and experience in mountain climbing techniques and a date was made to go up. The cost, at the time, was about SFr 500 for guide and services (10 years later, the cost is more like *SFr 900* for the same experience--inflation!). In the event of someone wanting to go up who has never climbed before, but who is otherwise in excellent condition, a practice climb or two is usually arranged first on a nearby peak such as the *Breithorn* or the *Rifflehorn*. Once the guides are satisfied as to the ability of the prospective climber (lacking evidence of previous experience in the mountains), an ascent is scheduled for the Matterhorn itself, weather permitting, although conditions are invariably good most of the time during the standard climbing season.

Several days later, the time for my date with this peak of my childhood dreams was at hand. We left in the evening of the day immediately preceding the ascent, taking the *Luftseilbahn* (cable car) from Zermatt to the upper terminal at the Schwartzsee; from there, carrying climbing packs and ropes we hiked the final thousand feet to the Swiss Alpine Club hut known as the Hörnlihutte (situated at 3260 meters). There we spent the night after enjoying a hearty meal and some camaraderie with others and their guides, also *en route* the next day.

At 4 AM sharp my guide was up, getting his gear together. I had no trouble awakening since I hadn't slept a wink the entire night--a combination of excitement and the usual difficulty I have getting any sleep at high altitude the first day or so of any mountain trip. We had a quick breakfast of müesli and instant oatmeal and were soon out on the ridge above the hut, trying to get ahead of the other groups who were a bit slower or larger than ours, so as to free ourselves of the exaggerated but realistic concern over rock fall.

The views by now were stunning, as they are in fact even from the Hörnlihutte itself. The air was cold and crisp and the skies were absolutely crystal clear, despite the early hour. We made good time up the 45-degree ridge, since hand and foot holds are excellent and both of us were in top shape. Within several hours we had made it all the way up to the Solvayhutte, a high-altitude mountain refuge at 13,210 feet which is small but provides excellent emergency accommodations for anyone unfortunate enough to need them.

After a rest there for food, water and some sober gazing at the seemingly sheer drop on all sides of the Solvayhutte's doorway, we were back up at it again; it occurred to me that one had to be careful about taking a trip out of the hut to relieve one's self at night, since the doorstep of the hut is about the size of a large postage stamp! Heading up once more, the route veered briefly out onto the East Face as the route zagged higher to the permanent snowfield that covers the *Dachel*, or roof. Below us, the others were still struggling up and having no one ahead of us conveyed a great sense of satisfaction that whatever rock fall occurred would be minimal and not man-instigated.

Finally, the skies were starting to get quite light. Unclipping from a section of fixed rope attached to one of the more spectacular sections of exposed rock, we tracked up the Dachel's icy snowfield using crampons and ice axes to the final summit ridge. The sense one has at this point of being perched absurdly high up in the sky, with the ground falling away on all sides, is quite breath-taking. I paused, just short of what is known as the South Summit (slightly lower than the North Summit) to reflect on the drama which eternally embroiled Whymper and his fellow Victorian climbers in historic climbing speculation on that day in June, back in 1865. Having read a great deal about all this some years before, I could vividly imagine what it must have felt like for them. It left me with a chilled sense of awe and wonder, as I mused on what they had accomplished with little more than their determination, and the primitive gear and clothing of that time.

Then it was on to the North, or 'true' Summit, which is at the far end of a rocky spine with icy patches in the perpetually frozen crannies of the summit rocks. The true high point of the Matterhorn is adorned with a filigreed iron summit cross, in the style of all the well frequented Alpine summits. The cross commemorates the lives of all those who have been killed attempting to do what we had successfully done and is a product of the deeply devout beliefs of the very Catholic people who live in the high alpine hamlets of this region.

It took a few minutes to realise what I had done. I had made it to the top of the Matterhorn, finally. I had made it to the summit of my life-long goal: *Angels 146*, as an air traffic controller would term the altitude in aviation parlance--Angels 146 on the doorstep of Heaven. It was indeed 'heaven' to me, and as the first party to make the ascent that beautiful day, we had a bit more peace and quiet in which to appreciate the singular beauty that this high and historic vantage offers than those following would have. It was amusing to think about how frequently I had routinely been this high in an aircraft; but what a different feeling it was to be way up there with both feet firmly planted on the earth! Soon, the summit would be crowded and noisy as all the dozens who were now struggling up the route finally reached their objective. I was alone with my thoughts for a while, but then it was time to grab a few photographs of my guide and myself and head back down before the gaggle of tyro climbers burst upon us and shattered the rare and beautiful mood of the legendary place

The descent was just as demanding as the ascent, owing to the fact that different muscle groups are used going down. Further, according to statistics, it is on the descent that most mountaineering accidents occur, due to fatigue and a somewhat lessened state of focus (this was the case on Whymper's successful first ascent!). Now the concern for rock fall was again fresh, as we passed group after group following the track towards the top of the mountain. Finally, however, we reached the Solvayhutte where we paused again, and then continued on down to the Hörnihutte, where we had lunch on the hut's deck. Above us climbers were visible all along the ridge, and it made one pause to ponder just how routine the ascent of this once impregnable mountain fortress had become. Finally, I folded up my tiny Zeiss Trinovid binoculars and we trudged back down the path to the Schwartzsee leftseilbahn terminal for the ride down to Zermatt, which was waiting for us at an elevation of 5315 feet AMSL below the Matterhorn massif.

It had been--if I can be excused the pun--one of the peak experiences of my life, and certainly a memorable one. One of the great goals of my life had been attained. To paraphrase Neil Armstrong's immortal words as he set foot for the first time on the moon*, "It may be a small step for mankind, but it's a giant step for this man."*

What had started many years ago, with a book written by Jack Kerouac about the self-discovery of the post-Beat generation, had culminated in my finally fulfilling a personally enriching dream that had been an important part of my whole life up to this point. A figurative milestone had been reached. An accomplishment of no small personal meaning.

The rest of my stay in Zermatt was less arduous and no less enriching (since the nightclub life there really rocks!), but there is so much to see in this historic little Alpine recreation area that the remaining days passed quickly. Such sights as the *Alpine Museum*, the *English (Anglican) Church*, the interesting graveyard in which many famous (and not so famous) climbers have been laid to rest over the years, and the frenetic night-life with underground discos and tourist watering-holes--all were enjoyable and memorable experiences. The spirited sense of good feeling and pleasure that the area inspires is unique and invigorating--even if you don't aspire to scale the peaks.

But nothing...nothing...can compare with the silent glory of standing up there on the roof of the world, listening to the chill wind keen with stories of climbers long gone, relishing that moment of personal triumph, which for me shall remain long in my memory...standing there on the doorstep of heaven at *Angels 146*.

THE FABULOUS FURRY FLYING FUZZ BROTHERS

For the past 25 years, my wife and I have been blessed by the patter of tiny feet (well, huge paws really, since they're actually not so tiny!) around our home. After deciding that human kids simply cost too much in today's chaotic American culture (according to statisticians, it can vary from about US$ 125,000 to more than US$ 350,000 to raise a child from birth to age 18 in America), and given the severely deleterious effects of modern 'pop-culture' on their complex growth and maturity processes (not to mention the odds against being able to bring them up properly, adversely influenced as they are by all their deadbeat peers), we elected instead to dedicate ourselves to four-footed canine 'kids'. While it still isn't cheap to care for and maintain doggie companions, at least one can be assured that they won't grow up to become surly, ungrateful and resentful little paragons of social dysfunction who hate their parents!

But I digress. When our previous two Siberians crossed the Rainbow Bridge, one right after the other, we suddenly found our lives profoundly empty and turned once again to NorSled (the Husky rescue group) to help us replenish the family pack. It wasn't long before NorSled notified us that a pair of male Siberians (named *Walter* and *Shiloh*), actual littermates and about 7 years of age, were in dire jeopardy of being euthanised in the LA Animal Shelter simply because they were deemed too old and the pound was overcrowded; the pound had decided that they were 'unadoptable' simply because they were 'middle-aged'! This horrific precariousness of their pronounced status was compounded by the fact that they had just been *'red tagged'* and were therefore already on the LA Pound's schedule for *'imminent disposal'* (within several hours).

For my wife and I, the timing couldn't have been better and we quickly volunteered to take them both in as fosters through NorSled, with adoption pending satisfactory socialisation and bonding with them. I am pleased to say that they both turned out to be delightful *boyz*, each with a distinctly endearing and unique personality, and their place with us was assured. They soon became known to us as *'The Fabulous Furry Flying Fuzz Brothers'* (or just *'the boyz'*, for short) owing to their sibling status, their fuzzy features, and their incredible good fortune in having escaped a tragic and totally unjustified end.

Sadly, after about a year with us, Walter developed a fatal, fast acting cerebral lymphosarcoma that took him from us in a few short weeks, but Shiloh remained and has proven himself to be the sweetest, most loving guy you could ever imagine. In order to provide Shiloh with necessary doggie companionship at home (since dogs need peers to relate to, as well as humans), we shortly thereafter acquired another NorSled charge, a 6-year-old male 'Malberian' cross named Peary, who also turned out to be an irresistibly loveable goof, and who fitted into our family pack beautifully.

Words are insufficient to adequately express our appreciation for and gratitude to NorSled for their continued dedication and commitment to saving wonderful guys like Walter, Shiloh and Peary from the accidental fate of having ended up in unsuitable homes with irresponsible owners. It is safe to say that we ourselves can't conceive of existing without several of these big furry Siberian companions around us to bring both unbounded happiness and fulfilling perspective into our lives, every single day! We can do well enough *without* problematic, expensive, and more often than not uncontrollable *human progeny*, thank you very much, and found that we are quite happy to settle for our wonderful and eternally loving doggie kids instead.

[As Sam Clemens once brilliantly observed: *"If you pick up a starving dog and make him prosperous, he will not bite you; this is the principal difference between a dog and a man."* How true!

Another famous individual, Sigmund Freud, was noted for having once opined: *"Dogs love their friends and bite their enemies, quite unlike people, who are incapable of pure love and always have to mix love and hate in their object-relations".*]

* * *

(The melancholy final chapter: Everything comes to an end.)

Sadly, about 10 years back, wonderful Peary tragically expired one morning from a sudden cardiac event. One second he was on the couch and the next Irene heard two short 'yips' from his direction and went over to him to find that he had suddenly *expired*. It was a real shock, since we had no warning whatsoever that he had a potentially fatal heart condition. Laika, our other remaining girl (our very first, as a puppie), also soon passed on due to a fast growing cerebral lymphosarcoma, allowing us to adopt Shiloh and Walter.

After 'Walter' (one of the two brothers) passed on, due to another aggressive cancer, we were left with *'Shiloh'*, now fondly known to us as *Sooka*, who continued to be our faithful companion for the ensuing 10 years. Meanwhile, in order to give Sooka a doggie buddy, we acquired Nala, a 3-year-old female Siberian. Thus, up until this week, we've had these two remaining doggie members of our pack sharing our lives.

Regrettably, age takes its toll on all living critters, dogs included. In the past 6 months, Sooka gradually lost his hearing and his left eye mysteriously ceased to function, leaving him with limited (party obscured) vision. Additionally, Sooka went on Tramadol, a powerful pain reliever for hip & hindquarter arthritis. In the most recent weeks, Sooka, now quite gray but still looking pretty good for his age, got progressively more limited in his activities at the ripe old canine age of 16+ years (actually, that's truly remarkable for a Siberian). For the past month, he's been limited to low-energy, quiet and very slow walks twice a day, but retained his appetite and general awareness, despite loss of the vision; it was also apparent that he was in the grip of 'doggie dementia' that, combined with his vision, hearing and ambulation problems, were quickly rendering him markedly disabled. Very recently, despite being on strong pain meds for his hip/hindquarter difficulties, he had lost most of his ability to get out and around without extreme difficulty. Over the past week that status has continued to deteriorate to the point where he can't really get to his feet without some help.

After much soul-searching and reflection on this, we felt that the very best thing for him would be to send him on his way across the *Rainbow Bridge* to join all the other lovely Sibes over there that we have shared our lives with. It is truly an end to a life-long saga, since having reached the 70s, we've decided that we can no longer take care of further pups, let alone a severely disabled boy like SOOKA. When 'Nala', who is now a spritely & energetic 12-year-old 'senior', finally departs some years hence (hopefully), we will likely no longer have a family pack as we have always had in past. It saddens me to think that we are finally losing Sooka, but take some comfort in the fact that he has had as good a life as any fondly regarded member of our rescue-pack could have hoped to enjoy; he has given us many, many moments of endearing companionship while with us and we love him fiercely. [His affectionate nickname is *'the Flop Dog'*, but don't even ask why…it just has always been my 'pet' name for him.]

Sookadog embarked upon the final journey of his life this morning, at about 11:45 AM (Thursday, 4 May 17, just a month short of his 17th birthday), with us at his side and his beloved squeak toy (which we had given him on Walter's demise; he passionately attached himself to it when his brother 'Walter' passed away and wouldn't leave the room without it in his mouth) in his paws (see pictures).

Bravely, he was able to walk from the car to the Muller Veterinary Medicine Center where we've always sought cared for our Sibes, and was trusting and gentle when they inserted an intercath in his vein to administer the two-part lethal injection. That first injected med put him into a deep sleep, keeping him from feeling any pain when the second med dose, an anaesthetic 'overdose', stopped his heart from beating. It was all over within minutes and Sooka underwent this final procedure with the same trust, affection and gentle demeanor he has always shown us.

To say it was tragic for us is a considerable understatement and although Sooka is our 6th Siberian companion lost, it *never* gets any easier.

Sooka will be fondly remembered, along with his pre-deceased brother Walter and all our previous doggie companions every Equinox and Solstice, when custom requires that we light a small candle for each one. Personally, I can't imagine a life spent without the companionship and unqualified, pure affection that our domesticated 'wolf-dogs' have blessed us with.

We'll sorely miss you, Sooka!

OUTDOOR BOB AND THE LEAF BLOWER FROM HELL

We have this neighbor, see? I call him 'Outdoor Bob' because he's ALWAYS outdoors. Bob frequently gives indications of being a real-life *Tim 'Tool-Time' Taylor* clone, since he appears obsessed with powerful, noxious and noisy mechanically operated garden tools.

Bob, so wifie learned some time ago from Bob's better half, is a serious insomniac and since he has serious difficulties going to sleep at night, gets up at all hours and prowls around the neighborhood, ostensibly keeping an eye on things (Bob's a one-time retired ex-prison guard). He's also a retiree, doubtless with lots of time on his hands.

That's fine, since 'Outdoor Bob' is by rights a good fellow, communally spirited and a fine neighbor...except for his one truly aggravating idiosyncrasy and that's an obsessive-compulsive relationship with his 200 HP, *Dual-Hydramatic*, fuel-injected, fully suspended and supercharged gasoline leaf blower.

Bob is so involved with this garden tool-on-steroids of his that he's turned into a regular Leaf Cop in our section of the 'hood. He obviously sees himself as being a Good Samaritan when he prowls about his front lawn (and that of his immediate neighbor, a wonderful, old retired Chinese-American fellow we all respect & love), eradicating tree waste products and making the world safe from rotting vegetation with public-spirited dedication.

Regardless of his obvious motivational myopia, Bob clearly hasn't a clue that some of us in this neck of the woods *hate* noisy, dirty leaf blowers so intensely that it occasionally drives us to fantasise about homicidal schemes involving firing-squads, pock-marked concrete walls, blind-folds, last cigarettes and short-lists of culpable neighborly urban miscreants who disrupt domestic tranquility.

Outdoor Bob, I have theorized, turned into the semi-crazed leaf bounty hunter that he is partly due to his OTHER immediate neighbor, an older fellow who has this HUGE deciduous tree in his backyard that grows right on the border between their two homes. The tree's owner (let's call him 'Martin') is a recovered multiple cardiac by-pass patient, who strives to lead a stress-free and relaxed life, tending his roses and minding his own business. You see, Bob has a backyard swimming pool on his side of the fence separating his and Martin's property and this tree, which is unusually large and overgrown, regularly deposits half its shed leaves on Bob's pool. This, of course, drives Outdoor Bob mad with insane frenzy, since he is having to constantly clean up all the debris from this particularly messy tree of Martin's. Admittedly, in his defense, it's an annoying and irresolvable dilemma with no obvious resolution possible.

This bad experience with trees doing their natural 'job' (copiously shedding leaves) seems to have set Bob on the path towards becoming what I call a *'Leafopath'* (not quite a *leaf psycho*path, but I'm sure you know what I mean). Bob has become indeed that and he has accordingly armed himself with one of the world's most powerful leaf blowers available in the Western world to take on lawless leaf droppers.

Since Martin (Bob's neighborly nemesis) could care less about what *his* tree drops into *Bob's* yard, they have reached an impasse whereby they can barely be cordial with each other and I'm sure Bob has become such an irritating complainer about Martin's tree that Martin likely takes secret *Schadenfreude* delight every time a gust of wind makes a leafy new deposit in Bob's pool.

Given that their dispute stands about as much chance of resolution as a Neo-Nazi Skinhead's chances of becoming a member of the Jewish faith, Bob seems to have (perhaps subconsciously) taken on a new role in life as the scourge of all leaves, everywhere. All of that is fine and good, except that Outdoor Bob also fancies himself a sort of 'good-neighbor leaf vigilante' and makes his rounds with the leaf blower every single day of the week. Not only that, but his leaf-blowing pathology has moved him out from the boundaries of his own property onto the neighboring lawns, where he takes it upon himself to rearrange THEIR leaves as well as his. He also ventures out into the street and again, acting somewhat like the Wyatt Earp of our block, blows the leaves in the street this way and that, mostly away from his own lawn. In this he persists even on the windiest days, when 'rearranging' leaves makes as much sense as undergoing a frontal lobotomy to get relief from headaches.

Now, I personally have a distaste for ANY unnecessary neighborhood noise and most especially for machine-created disturbances of all kinds. Anything that clanks, buzzes, whines or moans excessively that is powered by a mechanical motor serves to irritate the hell out of me, since I am of the opinion that 'noise pollution' is an execrable and largely inexcusable intrusion into the needs of people in congested residential neighborhoods for peace, quietude and domestic reflectivity.

Unfortunately, the concept of 'noise pollution' as an increasingly serious environmental problem (i.e. quality of life) seems to be beyond the remotest awarenesses of far too many people, most having been socialized by our technologically enslaved American culture to equate noise, power and goodness with anything that rises above 68 or so decibels.

As for myself, I have been an environmentalist all of my life, starting off back in undergrad school days in Berkeley (CA), and have also been an ardent outdoorsman, mountaineer and champion of natural things. That sort of outlook clearly makes an instant enemy (to me) out of anything made by man that is artificial, noisy, polluting and/or aesthetically deleterious. In today's highly mechanized society, that makes leaf blowers one of the prime offenders against otherwise peaceful domesticity...especially when one's urban neighbors are typically only a few feet distant from you.

Leaf blowers, surely one of the nastiest and most annoying inventions since the snowmobile and the chainsaw, are not just excessively noisy (why? Because engineering effective mufflers & sound deadening devices for small gasoline engines requires more R&D money than manufacturers want to invest in their machines), they are also smelly and create clouds of pollen saturated dust that fill the streets with spores and other hay-fever-causing materials to create major havoc for the majority of people who suffer from seasonal allergies (probably about 85% of us, at least).

Ask any runner or bicyclist who has had to run by or through such a cloud of leaf-blower-created, dust-laden effluent on his/her daily jaunt and he/she will affirm the fact that leaf-blower use should at the very least, be carefully regulated like firearms, pet owning and/or human procreation (read: 'baby-making', for those who are not imaginatively adept at drawing inferences). That is, given their potential for creating untoward effects and sparking ill-will between aesthetically sensitive people and less broadly aware individuals, the use of leaf blowers ought to be at the very least restricted to specific times or days and perhaps even decibel *'do-not-exceed'* limits. Personally, I'm a believer in the quiet & highly therapeutic value of good old fashion manual leaf control devices (rakes) and would love nothing better than to see leaf blowers banned outright.

Aside from powered outdoor tool freaks (like Outdoor Bob), the present industry of garden & lawn maintenance service providers argues that the leaf blower has enabled them to adopt an extremely cost-effective 'blitzkrieg' approach to performing lawn services. What used to be quite labor-intensive (lawn mowing & leaf raking, for example) is now a relatively quick, precise and simple procedure, enabling them to exponentially expand their customer base, thereby increasing income and simultaneously decreasing man-hours of effort. One result is that mechanised garden service providers now maraud through domestic neighborhoods like small Panzer divisions!

My reply to that argument? *Tough patooties!* The way leaf blowers are used these days results not so much in leaf containment & disposal but in what I call 'leaf rearranging'. This is a particular specialty of Outdoor Bob and his megamonster leaf blower, since he doesn't seem to understand that leaf-blowing when there's ANY kind of a breeze is not just ineffectual but absolutely stupid. 'Rearranging' leaves that will in the next gust be right back where they were before takes a unique and special kind of brain-cell failure, in my opinion.

Yesterday Outdoor Bob unlimbered his trusty blower and persisted in battling leaves despite the fact that the local wind was *blowing steadily at 30 MPH*. That's not an exaggeration, either, since the pert little, big breasted female weather person on the local media channel confirmed what was all too evident to anyone standing outside and nearly being blow sideways by the gusts (*"Steady at 30, gusting to 45"* was how she phrased it).

And that's fully part of the problem regarding Outdoor Bob. He just doesn't seem to either understand or care about 'leaf-to-wind speed' considerations. Further, his manic leaf blowing has begun to resemble a sort of OCD therapy that he is compelled to engage in every day (he's already been out there *TWICE* today, *fer gawd's sake*!).

But wait…there's more! Yesterday Outdoor Bob mounted a particularly massive offensive against errant leaves and not just tried to clear his (Chinese-American) neighbor's lawn, but that of the neighbor on the far side of the Chinese gentleman's lawn, since the wind was blowing his leaves merrily down the street onto everyone's lawn that lay downwind. Um…*hello? What don't we understand about the effects of WIND?*

Finally, in a massive final assault on his hated leafy enemy, Outdoor Bob turned towards our home (located across the street from him, sort of catty-corner) and started to blow leaves that had come from our beautiful, big camphor tree back onto our lawn. He even came into the driveway and walked on our front lawn, trying to corral and contain OUR leaves on OUR lawn.

Well, that was definitely *waaaay* overstepping the limits of both proprieties and common sense, since camphor trees shed several times a year and my wife and I (who have no problem with falling leaves naturally doing their 'gravitational thing') have a lawn service person over every Wednesday to take care of our front lawn maintenance (unfortunately they too use a leaf blower, but at least it's only once a week).

Living in Sacramento (CA), a small hinckty cow-town that coincidentally is also the State Capitol and whose motto is *'The City of Trees'*, there's little quarter either given or taken on the issue of leaf blowers by the city council (a group that exercises about as much in the way of municipal wisdom as all *Three Stooges* combined). Thus, those of us who suffer interminably from the noisy thoughtlessness of our fellow citizens seem perpetually doomed to suffer through this epidemic of leaf-blowers without respite.

As would be reasonable, given my mightily suppressed urge to castrate Outdoor Bob for his outrageous leafy excesses (and thereby help prevent future iterations of his spawn), I turned to the internet to see if others have been tempted to take the law into their own hands in dealing with domestic harmony disrupters like him. Naturally GOOGLE immediately turned up at least a dozen or more recent instances in which some outraged and temporarily driven-over-the-edge citizen beat the living *pahootie* out of such an idiot, typically resulting in a legal ruling of unjustified homicide (without intent to kill...perhaps just *maim* a little?). It was a sobering reminder that it's never easy living anywhere among other *humming beans*, whether in a community or in an even tighter residential context.

Basically, there's no convenient option to deal with the noisy intrusion of these infernal devices (at least here in the...*groan*...'City of Trees') other than the fermented grape juice that God presented humanity, thousands of years ago, as a sort of natural handy 'local anaesthetic' to treat grosser violations of normative human behavioral conduct in a community.

Since I knew that any protest directly to Outdoor Bob delivered in person by myself would likely result in a rapidly hormone-charged escalation of mutual antagonisms, I wisely let my sweet little 5-foot-tall wife take her rake out there and 'shame' Bob into retreating back onto his own lawn. It seems to have worked, as she innocuously buttonholed him (he's a fairly reasonable fellow, after all) and subtly suggested (with a friendly smile) that his blowing the leaves back onto our lawn (mind you, this conversation conducted in the midst of a howling 30 mph wind) merely complicated the pending job our own lawn service people faced. The ole female guilt trip works every time (on ANY man, for any reason).

Worked like a charm (at least to get Bob to realise to a sufficient extent that he was way overstepping the bounds in his leaf-destroying, evangelical enthusiasms). Amusingly, it reminded me of an old Student Leftist tactic we had employed, back in my 70s Berkeley student protest days, of getting all the women and children 'up front' between us & the pigs. After all, if you can't deal with them directly, hit 'em up with some inherently instinctive normative, Christian logic (i.e. women and child abuses are definitely NOT acceptable to good, God-fearing Christian LEO people, no matter who you are or how far along your personal psychotherapy program is progressing!).

Sigh. Speaking of that, I wonder how Bob's insomnia is doing. At least he's not prowling the neighborhood streets at night with his infernal leaf machine!

Postscript

A last word on Outdoor Bob: Did I mention that Outdoor Bob also has two evil little Cocker Spaniels that bark their heads off all day long at the slightest provocation? Well, he does. And they are among the most neurotic little sorry-excuses for yapping canines I have ever seen. My Uncle had one and his was just as bad.

One of the reasons I am a Siberian Husky fan is that they are NOT prone to barking. That isn't to say that they NEVER do, but they are NOT maddening little yap-yap-yappers like most American Cockers tend to be. Siberians are normally very quiet by contrast and, naturally enough, given that trait, make terrible guard dogs (but I don't keep dogs for that purpose; I value loyal companionship above all else, which Siberians are noted for).

It's been observed by several on-line dog authorities that if not carefully selected from a concerned and reputable dog breeder, Cockers can be among the most neurotic breeds found (right up there with *Jack Russells* and...ugh!...*Chihuahuas*.

At any rate, I suppose it's fitting that Outdoor Bob be burdened with hyperactive, hypersensitive and hypernoisy pets. Let them drive *HIM* crazy!

"WHAT DID YOU DO IN THE WAR, DADDY?"

Note: When I was in the Air Force and facing the possible consequences of being a uniformed active duty war-protestor, I found myself idly wondering what I'd tell my (future) kids about my involvement in the Vietnam War. Of course, my wife and I elected not to have any kids, having met somewhat late in life, so the question is now moot. While most of my peers eventually went over to Vietnam and became heroes of a sort, I managed to stay entirely in the US ZI (Zone of the Interior) throughout my service and became a faceless non-entity in the military snake-oil biz. This retrospective narrative details of some of my military experience as a *'Hawkeye Pierce'* clone in the US Air Force medical service (with SAC) in the mid-60s. [Note: No citizens of North Dakota were hurt or injured in the creation of this memoir about the making of SAC's 'Cold War' in the cold north! This story is also very likely the exception that gives the lie to Strategic Air Command's tag-line that *'Only the best go north!'*

As these stories go to press (2017), American Historian Ken Burns has just released his epic 18 hour history of that awful and unnecessary war. To see it all now and to reflect back upon it is sobering. I am forced to confront my youthful idealism squarely and acknowledge that youth is a time of immature aspirations that time may and often does change.

1) Don' wanna make war no more, no more

When I was still a tender-hearted, rather sheltered young adolescent, someone in Washington DC decided to start a war. *Again.* It was 1966 and this time it was once more the Chinese Communists who were responsible for getting the American beehive all stirred up all over again (Korea was an earlier and related hive-shaking event, of course).

Actually, that's not quite correct, since 'the war' didn't start in 1966; it actually began back in 1917, when the Bolsheviks succeeded in overthrowing the last Russian (Romanov) Tsar. By 1966, however, 49 years of worldwide political foment and economic change had brought the Communist Chinese nation into being, along with all greater Communism's smaller geopolitical 'sputniks', and the specter of Communism's continuing appeal to the down-trodden masses cast a giant and rather unwelcome shadow on America's cozy little materialist, capitalistic tea party. [*Note*: it may or may not be of passing interest to explain here that the Russian word '*sputnik*', in actual fact the first Soviet earth satellite that was launched in 1957, translates roughly to *'fellow traveler'*. Thus, both terms (*Sputnik* and *'fellow traveler'*) have some bearing on this subject.]

Although rabid congressional Commie hater Joseph McCarthy had been deposed not long after having created a national witch-hunt in the 1950s for the purpose of seeking out and eradicating *suspected* (emphasis, emphasis) Communist sympathizers in America, many politically well-connected Sons of Freedom continued to fear anything that suggested America's happy little socio-economic paradigm of democratic capitalism might not be as free from Commie taint as it was cracked up to be. In terms of political philosophy, the right-wing 'domino theory' still held ascendance, reasoning that America must intervene wherever possible in the world to prevent unaligned nations from falling over, domino style, to the threat of Communism's avowedly expansionist aspirations. To far too many patriotic Americans, 'John Birch' was still a national hero and the sight of an American flag (*any* American flag) had a Pavlovian effect on those who fancied themselves as potential defenders of the Christian 'free world' in its fight against the dastardly Bolshevik atheists. Sigh!

Just my luck, then, to be in my sophomore year at the local college, an emotionally insecure, somewhat sheltered, and academically uninspired undergrad with no well-defined career aspirations of any sort. The French had recently bailed out of their *Anamese* colonial territories in SEA after being soundly thrashed by the Viet-Cong's precursors, the Viet Minh, and by 1966 America had already long-since passed the 'MAAG' phase ('Military Assistance Advisory Group') of US involvement (wherein US military advisors were sent to work with the Vietnamese military forces in a strictly non-combatant instruction and training role). I was rather distractedly barely keeping my head above C-level in my studies at the time and my weekends were committed to passionately hedonistic wave-sets on the California coast, which my dilapidated old 1940 Chevy Deluxe Coupe could barely get me to without its radiator running dry. I fancied myself a surfer, despite persistent and hard to ignore evidence to the contrary. In fact, not only was I a complete 'wipe-out' at trying to stay balanced on a 10 foot longboard (for 10 seconds on a three foot curl), despite my wearing all the regulation gear (shades, baggies, a fake 'Iron Cross', Mexican huarache sandals, Woolrich shirts, and anything Madras-patterned I could get my hands on), regardless of my using all the then-hip surfing terms *('bitchin', far-out, 'dude', wahine, cowabunga, skag, gremmie, hodad*, etc.), the chicks were absolutely, completely and categorically disinterested in me.

It was therefore quite easy for me to retreat emotionally to embrace the cherished 'lonely surfer' (remember that wonderful old Jack Nitzsche song?) posture that the surfing stereotype hewed to in those days, since there was simply no reasonable alternative to my being the very personification of that image I had already spent an adolescent lifetime (a few years) cultivating...a romantic loner. *Ah!* Misunderstood, ignored, but secretly semi-heroic in my own mind, I fancied myself a sort of oceanside rebel in the James Dean mold, since we both loved Porsches and disdained the proletarian *hoi-polloi* (the main difference between us being as I saw it, aside from his being handsome and a movie star, was that Dean had been able to actually *own* Porches and it was all I could do to buy my $50 asthmatic 26-year-old '40 Chevy Coupe).

2) Me and my buddy James Dean

Of course, my frequent weekend trips to the coast in that old Chevy took me west along State Route 46 (originally known as US Route 466), since I preferentially hung out at Pismo, Avila, and Cayucos beaches. Each time I passed the Highway 46/Highway 41 intersection (near *Cholame*, a small bump in the road surrounded by nothing for miles except dry fields) where James Dean had died in his Porsche 550 Spyder (in 1955, some thirteen years earlier) I would absently reflect on that incident, while keeping one eye on the Chevy's temperature gauge. Dean's fatal accident with *Donald Turnipseed* (the other driver's real name, I swear it) was about as avoidable as my pending decision was about the war and it always made me a bit spooky, driving past that infamous site late in the day with the sun low on the horizon and full in my eyes, to think about it. Maybe Dean was my hero, and perhaps the good *did* die young as the old saying has it, but was I *really* willing to die prematurely because of someone else's paranoiac sense of patriotic obligation? My youthful career as inept surfer dude and failed chick-magnet notwithstanding, the future might *still* hold better things in store for me and I was in no hurry to turn in my transit pass just yet for a 6-foot-deep hole in the ground!

So, there I was...failed surfer and self-styled misunderstood rebel. It was yet a comfortable fantasy with which to dress and bandage all my juvenile psychic wounds, however, and death (whether seated in a silver Porsche or slogging through a tropical rice paddy) is just so, well...*final!* One weekend, I actually stopped at the Dean crash site on the way to Avila and got out to drink a coke after filling the nearly empty radiator from the last three-gallon plastic jug I had in the rumble seat. As I tossed the fizzy liquid down, the radio newscaster was saying something about how the Selective Service had just decided to start yanking *ALL* student draft deferments, making *every-one* prime draft bait! Mulling that unhappy news over under the hot sun, I spent a few minutes distractedly searching the ground for any overlooked small slivers of silver aluminum that might have been missed from the crash, but in the thirteen years since Dean had died, Dean's legions of fans had long-since clean-combed the area for crash souvenirs of their iconic hero and all I found were a few cow pies and a dead bird. More death to think about. Hmm.

Shortly after this news about the change in draft deferments had been released, I found myself sitting in a political science class on campus when a vision of the possible personal consequences of what had just transpired hit me right between the eyes with the impact of an imaginary AK-47 bullet. Looking out the classroom window of my mind, I fancied I could see my holographic self slumped-over quite dead in a flooded rice paddy, with a ragged edged red hole in my forehead. It was a scary and sobering flash to be sure, since I am by nature a pretty cowardly and timorous creature who hates to even step on an ant, let alone engage in fierce battles with some unseen enemy in a tropical outback region, eight thousand miles from home. A little more thought about all this prompted me to formulate two possible alternative options. The first involved a daunting and somewhat longish trip to the Canadian border to seek asylum and the second called for a much shorter one to the local US Air Force recruiter's office, since I reasoned that I could more *safely* safeguard my brain in *that* branch of the service than I would be able to as point man in a Marine platoon, dodging *pungi*-stakes, frag-grenades, AK-fire and mines in Vietnam.

3) Decisions, decisions!

The first option posed several complex logistical problems in that 1), I was still enrolled in college and my family wouldn't approve of my suddenly bailing out without a very good reason, and 2) my poor old Chevy would surely give up the ghost entirely if I attempted an 800-mile run to the border in it. That pared the options down considerably, so shortly after that I opted to visit the local Air Force recruiter and took a hard look at the options open to me there. One thought remained upper-most in my mind and that was that Momma hadn't raised her precious little fair-haired boy to rot away in some lonely rice paddy on the far side of nowhere.

For as many years as I could remember, I had abstractly dreamed of becoming an Air Force pilot and had in fact decided that once I finished my lower division work in college I'd join that service under the auspices of what was then called the Air Force Pilot Training Program. With my usual luck, I learned from the recruiter that this program had just been terminated and that in future all pilot applicants would have to furnish proof of a completed four-year baccalaureate for acceptance into flight training. Modern aircraft technology state-of-the-art had apparently progressed to the point where they figured you needed a college degree to fully understand how to fly military airplanes. Looking back on things, it was probably just as well (given my already admitted gentle nature), since flying 30,000-pound warplanes off into a hazardous hail of hostile anti-aircraft fire is not a task well-suited to ruminative, bucolic and highly reflective personalities like mine (I mean...what if *I died* doing something I fancied I loved, only to realise at that last gasping second that I'd much rather have been peacefully sniffing daisies somewhere?!). And that's not even taking into consideration the very real possibility of having my nether aspect explosively resculpted by a well targeted SAM-2 and having to eject, perhaps seriously wounded, into a swarm of angry Vietnamese peasants below who would just as soon kill *'Yankee Air Pirate'* foreign devils on the spot as allow the VC to cart them away into captivity. Nope, no implacably stoic John McCain was I, not even a Don Knotts younger-and-smarter-brother clone!

At any rate, since the officer corps option was closed off to me, I listened to what the Air Force had to offer its enlisted recruits. Although the Army was still letting recruits have their choice of specialties, there were so many Vietnam 'escapees' like myself clamoring to gain entrance to the Air Force that no promises could be made. It was clearly a buyer's market, enlistment-wise. You signs on the dotted line and you takes your chances. That was it. At least the recruiter was honest about that unhappy fact, contrary to the usual vituperous practice (it's still the norm today, by the way) of promising the moon and then pulling the rug out from under enlistees the moment they had been sworn in (*"Sorry sucker, your sweet ass belongs to Uncle Sammie now...mwah-hahahaha!"*).

Having given everything considerable thought after that initial encounter with the recruiter, I agreed to enlist and was scheduled for what the military calls the AFQT (Armed Forces Qualification Test), which was a sort of functionally dumbed down SAT exam. Varying slightly from service to service, its purpose was to determine what specialty one was best qualified for and yielded aptitude data in four primary skills and knowledge subtest categories that included 1) General, 2) Mechanical, 3) Administrative, and 4) Electrical. I recall having qualified highest in 'electrical' and 'administrative', but followed closely by the remaining two. However, that was a long, long time ago and the only thing that really remains electrifyingly fresh about the exam experience is that based upon my test results and subject to Air Force career skill areas open at that time, I was offered the choice of three specialties: 1) Medical Service, 2) Food Service, or 3) Air Police! As a person who has never ranked gastronomy high on my personal list of interests and as someone who has forever distrusted the integrity of law enforcement agencies, the choice of becoming an Air Force medic was therefore the only logical and reasonable option to avail myself of.

4) Off to Girl Scout Camp with the US Air Force

Once my entry medical exam had been completed at the Los Angeles physical processing center, it wasn't long before I was shunted off to begin four weeks of basic training at Lackland Air Force Base in hot, humid and thoroughly uncomfortable Amarillo, Texas. As a California coastal resident used to cool Pacific Ocean breezes, the interior of Texas, with its swelteringly hot and humid Gulf Coast climate, was definitely not to my taste. However, the four weeks went by fairly quickly and about all I recall from the experience, some 44 years later, is an unending frustration with having to keep toilets clean enough to eat out of. It really seemed senseless to me at the time, but is was all part of the indoctrination process designed to cut the rough corners off a wildly diverse group of immature youngsters and reshape them into a new and useful uniformity of thought and action.

In the Air Force boot camp our physical conditioning was called 'physical training' or PT for short. Instead of hard-as-nails USMC-like DIs (Drill Instructors), we had somewhat more gentle TIs (Training Instructors) and our flight of post-adolescent enlistees were handed over to a certain Technical Sergeant Dawson. Although we lived in awe of Sgt. Dawson, he was actually more like an endlessly patient mother to us than a mean-hearted source of perpetual torment. I was actually quite surprised to find out how mild Air Force boot camp training was (compared to the Marine Corps version), but that's just as well, since we were all just a bunch of little lost kids trying to get our rather puerile minds around this slice of the entirely new experience we had all signed up for.

Of course, some of our group were more 'lost' than others, since the individuals making up our flight came from all over the country. Two in particular I well recall as being particularly intellect-challenged. They frequently transgressed the limits of the Dawson's concept of the acceptable and after one memorable breech of egregious behavior, Sgt. Dawson called them both into his office at the end of the barracks and said something on the order of *"OK. From now on you two will report to me as 'Dipshit #1' and 'Dipshit #2' Do you understand?"* They both yelled out *"Yes SIR!"*, while standing at attention and for the ensuing several weeks the rest of us were regularly entertained by the sight of them hitting a brace in front of a scowling Sgt. Dawson, using those names. This loses something in the telling, naturally. Suffice it to say you had to have been there to appreciate the full hilarity of the recurring spectacle.

At the end of the four weeks, during which we studied all the basics of citizen soldiers, and prancing around the exercise track in garishly yellow T-shirts and AF blue nylon shorts (yuk), I ended up considering two of our full complement of 60 'students' as worthy peers. One, a heavy-set, pink-jowled Pole from Ohio named Dumbrowski, and the other, a lanky and laconic string-bean from Oklahoma named Robert Acton, were pretty decent guys by my reckoning, but I shuddered to think what terrible things the others might do to the carefully oiled machinery of the US Air Force, once they were turned loose in their subsequent specialties after a few scant weeks of training.

Looking back, several very important bits of knowledge acquired at Basic Training have remained with me through the years and proven quite valuable again and again.

They are 1) never let anyone in a position of responsibility learn your name; 2) never volunteer for *anything*; 3) never try to substitute muscle power for brain power, and 4) adopt the simple tactic of keeping your mouth shut (since it makes one appear to be far more intelligent that one might *actually* be; the *reverse* is also true).

5) Learning how to put Band-Aids on baby *booies*

From Lackland, that great stamp-mill processor of fresh Air Force enlisted fodder, I was next sent to Sheppard AFB outside Wichita Falls (TX) for the next phase of my training: three months of intensive medical specialization that would qualify me to do everything from applying Band-Aids to slashed carotid arteries to sewing traumatically severed limbs back on with little more than barbed wire and spit. The medical course instructors were colorfully named Sgt. Mapp, Sgt. Rosebud, and Sgt. Levenson, each a fairly engaging individual (and all blessed with a great sense of humor, thank God, since one of my secret talents was that of cartooning and I skewered them all mercilessly in my multi-panel sketches).

Not having a car, I spent all my time on the base, although Amarillo was reported to have quite a scenic ambience, with its vine-entwined and flower-strewn canals and many lovely settings for tourists. My main pastime was reading and I haunted the base library while most others were off getting howling drunk downtown on their off-hours. Another of my recreational activities consisted of prowling around the base, seeing what there was to see, since Sheppard was also the Air Force's primary A&P specialty training base and more than half of it was devoted to rows and rows of interesting older parked aircraft that student powerplant and airframe mechanics used to perfect their skills. For me walking around those areas was like dying and going to heaven, since there were at least a couple of examples of most of the airplanes in recent use (1966) by the Air Force to be found there. This included whole rows of older North American F-100A Super Sabres, ANG KC-97 Stratotankers (the military version of the Boeing 377 Stratocruiser airliner), A Boeing B-52D or two, T-6 Texans, NAA B-25 Mitchells, and even a few Martin B-26 Invaders among many others. One sight I recall very clearly was the nearby fire and crash training area, where old airframes no longer useable would be doused in JP-4 jet fuel (essentially kerosene) and set on fire so that crash-rescue trainees could practice putting the fires out (and rescuing personnel). It was quite a show (and an unwitting taste of many similar future sights I would experience in future) but I remember feeling a bit sad to learn that classic old airplanes were frequently destroyed in this manner. I guess even at that early age, the 'aviation historian' in me was making itself known!

When we had time to talk in the odd off-moments, my classmates and I would occasional speculate on the present course of the war we were all being trained to participate in, wondering where we'd eventually end up once the training had been completed. The best guess of most, given our specialty as 'medics' was that we'd be sent off to the front line medical areas near the big US air bases in Vietnam (like *Cam Ranh* and *Tan Son Nhut*). Incoming hostile motor fire was the biggest concern there, although there were also occasional VC saboteurs to worry about. At least that sort of danger wasn't in the same league as walking point with the grunts out near *Khe Sanh* or dangling out an open Huey door over a troop drop-zone!

6) Why not Minot?

Came late September with our courses having been completed, all of us eagerly awaited our orders that would assign us to both our new commands and to our first duty assignments. Up to that time I had never even heard of *'Strategic Air Command'*, but that is the command I had been handed over to. My first duty station...a very far cry from the hot, sweaty environs of Southeast Asia...was at a base in North Dakota near some prairiedog city named 'Minot' that hosted a strategic bomber wing: *Minot AFB*. It had a strange sound rolling off the tongue. Little did I suspect that once arrived at that remote northern base, given the typical fourteen below winters the name of the base would promptly freeze on your tongue if you kept your mouth open longer than a split second to utter it!

Very soon after graduating ceremonies had been completed and belongings packed up in the OD duffels everyone had been issued, we were all on our way out of quaint, humid old Wichita Falls (TX) and off to new adventures we were at that point incapable of even *dreaming* about. My flight out found me crowded onto an asthmatic old TWA Convair 540 airliner that connected with another flight out of Bismarck (ND) which would eventually deposit me at Minot. The airliner ferrying me on the last leg of the trip from Bismarck to Minot was an equally elderly *Frontier Air* Convair 440 that shook, rattled and rolled more loosely than Elvis himself (so it seemed), but after a while we began our descent to Minot International Airport (formerly a grass landing strip for Piper and Cessna puddle jumpers...at least before the arrival of the US Air Force and their shiny new base, some 12 miles from town). Outside visibility was totally obscured by a driving snowstorm as dusk approached, but the pilot was apparently able to use a combination of VFR, IFR and an especially powerful lucky rabbit's foot to find the field and set us down on solid ground with a resounding thump before the engines froze over. Once the door had been opened by the blonde stew, a frosty gust came howling through the doorway to remind me that this was truly another part of the world totally apart from my own cozy coastal clime. Looking out the door, my first actual glimpse of Minot was a large sign that said two things: *'Only the best go North!'* and somewhat lower down, *'Why not Minot?'* Why not Minot indeed? It didn't take long to come up with a number of excellent arguments to counter that cock-eyed bit of Chamber of Commerce PR optimism (my personal favorite was *"The freezin's the reason"*).

Minot, North Dakota, is presently a city of about 37,000 people and the 4th largest in the state. At the time I first arrived there, back in late 1966, it was home to about 33,000 people, the 40% white segment of which being comprised of mostly of Germanic and Scandinavian (primarily Norwegian) descended people. Minot sprang into existence back in 1886 when the Great Northern Railway pushed its part of the transcontinental railroad through the state and has since been supported by largely agricultural industries such as daily, cattle, and crop farming. In 1955-56 the US Air Force decided to build a huge new air base near Minot, eventually using it to host a *Strategic Air Command* bomb wing (the 450th, later the 5th) of B-52 intercontinental bombers and a tenant 5th Fighter Interceptor Squadron (Air Defense Command) flying Convair F-106A Delta Darts. Somewhat later a missile wing (the 91st SMW) was also established there consisting of several squadrons of thermonuclear warhead tipped Minuteman ICBMs. The base, with its many personnel and large positive impact on the Minot economy, has been a welcome and stabilizing influence on the region for many decades. At a mean elevation of about one and a half thousand feet, and located nearer the Canadian than lower state borders, the summers in Minot can be swelteringly hot, while the winters are severely cold.

Thus it was, that I stepped out of that rickety old Convair 440 and found myself staring absently down at my snow-covered GI shoes, probably not unlike Dorothy in the *Wizard of Oz* when it finally sank in that she and Toto weren't in Kansas anymore, and wondering what the immediate future had in store for me. Whatever it turned out to be, I reminded myself, it wouldn't involve getting picked off by a Viet Cong sniper hiding in the paddies just off Provincial Route 1.

7) I am introduced to 'Gomer Central'

One of the interesting sidelights about the US Air Force's presence in Minot is that although the main base is 12 miles to the north of the city, the Air Force agreed to take over and share an existing eight-story VA facility in downtown Minot named the *'John Moses Veterans Hospital'*. The VA hospital had originally been built back in the early 1950s to take care of the large number of disabled and injured vets hailing from the state, but having the Air Force agree to share operational responsibilities worked to the advantage of both the VA administration and the Air Force, which could use it as a large hospital complex to support the base. Technically, the vets benefitted from having access to the Air Force specialists and medical teams, but the John Moses facility also helped train new Air Force personnel (such as myself and our '90-day wonder' medical officers).

Out on the base, the 862nd Medical Squadron (which I belonged to) additionally maintained a large multipurpose clinic facility, with attached flight surgeon's office for aviation medicine concerns, but the base's dependents (and severely ill military personnel) could be accommodated and cared for in the extensive VA facility in town.

Since I had just arrived at the base and in view of my very junior status in the greater scheme of things at the field, it was a natural move to assign me to the John Moses Hospital initially. After I had been checked in at the medical squadron's orderly room, I was taken to my new quarters in a large modern dormitory next to the hospital that was used to house enlisted medical personnel.

In contrast to the airmen's barracks on base, the hospital's dormitory was a luxury assignment, since it was divided into separate rooms, each holding from two to four airmen. Perhaps the best part of the deal was that because winter conditions would frequently isolate the base from the city (due to heavy snowfall and frequent blizzard conditions), those of us at the hospital in town had the place all to ourselves at such times and we were located only a few blocks from the Minot State Teacher's College (now Minot State University). The first thing I learned about my new duty assignment from my roommates was that MSTC was just bursting at the seams (like a well-stuffed bra) with hundreds of gorgeous young women of Scandinavian ancestry! My notorious chick-repellant qualities notwithstanding, that still sounded pretty *good* to me!

8) Some SAGE reflections

Before I was able to settle in to the John Moses Airmen's dorm, however, I was whisked off to the base to complete routine in-processing. This took place in a huge, multi-storied, squat beige monster of a concrete blockhouse (measuring several hundred feet on all sides, as well as vertically) that sat somewhat out by itself near the flightline. This, I was told, was the *SAGE Building*, but no one offered any more information about exactly what the '*SAGE*' in 'SAGE building' was all about. All I knew at the time was that the SAGE Building's ground floor served a number of administrative purposes, including in-processing for newly arrived troops. It was only much later that I learned that the SAGE Building was the semi-hardened facility that housed what passed for the guts of two of the world's most advanced (as of 1966) digital computers, together comprising a system designed to control and direct (via up links) our Air Defense Command fighters against airspace intruders. [Note: SAGE stood for *'Semi-Activated Ground Environment'* and it has been dealt with in a separate article.] The many yellow and black framed security warning signs in the SAGE Building impressed me with the knowledge that *whatever* lurked unseen on the building's upper floors, it *must* be something worth dying for, since *'Use of Deadly Force has been authorised'* cautions were plastered all over the various elevators and stairways. Compared to security restrictions on other parts of the base where armed Air Police *(*known as *'Apes'*) with beady eyes and itchy trigger fingers roamed about with live rounds loaded in their M-16s, the SAGE signs were merely a teaser indication of the seriousness of the nuclear combat mission that Minot was tasked with. Serious or not, it definitely caught my attention, as an FOB newbie!

Once I'd been checked in as a new arrival for the 862nd Medical Group, my first duty assignment, and received my bulky N-3B arctic parka (and the rest of my cold-weather 'bunny suit', as we called them), I was returned to the city of Minot and John Moses Hospital in one of the base crash ambulances. The strange smell that permeated it was caused, I was told by a cheerful fellow medic who drove it, by a load of embalmed cadavers that had just been hauled in from the base's small morgue. Then without skipping a beat, he asked me if I'd had lunch yet? "*Um? Uh, no...thanks!*"

John Moses Air Force Hospital is today no longer to be found in Minot, having been finally demolished (in the mid-80s) after decades of caring for crusty old *Norskahoovian* WWI vets in its salad days, but in 1966 it still presented a rather imposing sight to us new arrivals. Some eight stories tall, it held several hundred acute and long-term care beds, as well as all the usual hospital departments, specialties, surgeries, clinics, etc. On the typically clear, bitterly cold North Dakota winter mornings the smoke from its adjacent electrical power generating plant would send up a single vertical plume of smoke from its tall chimney several thousand feet above the small caldera the complex was sited within, before mild surface gusts began playing with it. The sight of that white plume, seeming to rise right up into the cold lower heights of the stratosphere in the frosty chill of early morning, never failed to arrest my thoughts as yet another winter day in Minot dawned.

Outlying buildings on the campus accommodated the hospital's complement of female nurses, the powerplant, the airmen's dorm and the Hospital Commander's residence. Situated near the powerplant was a *medevac* heli-pad where one would usually find a parked Air Force blue and white Huey UH-1 helicopter on standby. One additional small building housed administrative officers and the two male nurses we had on staff, and a large morgue occupied still another.

My own digs, located on the second floor of the airmen's dorm, had space for four corpsmen and there were two already assigned to that room when I got there. One was a compact, dark-haired fellow of Greek ancestry named Michael Zaharakis and the other, a smaller Airman named Francis Bouchard, was of French Canadian descent. His nickname, Mike explained to me, was 'Frenchy'. These two would be my roommates in the coming months ahead and soon became my close friends, as well.

This late in the season, the snow would fall regularly in the Minot area and from inside the dorm you could easily discern the unceasing keening of the wind as it moaned around the sharp corners and sills of the main building. It was a curiously plaintive sound, not unlike the sinister sound effects version of wind in horror movies and it didn't take much imagination to conjure departed souls hovering outside, perhaps those of old veterans who had died at the facility and were reluctant to depart. Considering a few stories I heard later about some of the old vets who had passed on at John Moses, it wasn't that hard to imagine at all.

9) Life on the frozen plains

As I settled into this new life on the North Dakota prairie, I began to find much of it almost enjoyable, since unlike the poor stiffs isolated out on the base, those of us at the hospital felt more like a regular part of the Minot civilian community. There were some parts of the daily hospital routine that definitely were *not* enjoyable (such as emptying bed pans, placing and emptying urinals, inserting urinary catheters, and...that most unpleasant task of *digitally removing* impacted *faeces* from crusty old vets who were in various states of advanced end-stage disease), but much of it wasn't all that demanding. Since this 'on-the-job' training was the follow-up part of my clinical school studies, I was kept fairly busy learning proper medical and clinical procedures and there wasn't much time to mope about.

The vets the Air Force had inherited in taking over the facility from VA consisted of about 180 individuals among the 300-bed population. Many were in terminal stages of various malignancies, most were quite elderly, and more than a fair number were crotchety, cantankerous and short-tempered old fellows, principally of Norwegian extraction. Given their extreme illnesses and hopeless status I can't really say they weren't entitled to their nasty, ill-natured outlooks, but it certainly didn't gain them much sympathy from the young and relatively naïve young corpsmen charged with taking care of them. Many of the old vets had been ignored or poorly cared for at home before being admitted and many had toenails that had remained untrimmed for so long that they curled over on each other in a sort of Goat's horn appearance. It was quite a sobering experience to encounter this grotesquery for the first time. Severe bed sores, of course, were almost a given.

10) A particularly sad incident

One old vet in particular remains fixed in my mind, an extreme case among the many others. His name was Roald Pahl and at the time he was suffering from severely advanced (terminal) CA of the GI tract and throat. The CA in his throat had eaten away his larynx and upper respiratory tract to the point where he was left with only a tracheostomy stoma (an opening directly into his trachea through which he breathed) and no voice at all. Of course, trying to understand his needs and intentions was substantially complicated by his inability to speak, and his usual nasty mood didn't help the process along, either. Such was the severity of his condition that his stoma had to be repeatedly suctioned throughout the day and night to remove the accumulation of tenacious fluids that secreted into his airway, threatening to choke him.

Without meaning to be unkind to poor Mr. Pahl, such was his unfortunate overall appearance that he looked startlingly like the Lord of the Rings character *Golum* at first glance. It was clear to most of us that he was just barely hanging on to life, but tenaciously and with no perceptible intent to go unresistingly that last inch of the way towards drawing his final breath. It was disturbing to have to witness his progressive decline each day, let alone take care of him, but that was part of our duty, so we all coped with this unhappy vision of misery as best we could and did our best for him. I had to regularly remind myself that he was, like all of us, some loving mother's son...

One morning that I will never forget I came on the AM shift to find Mr. Pahl under my team's care. After taking care of all the necessary shift-change tasks, I went into Mr. Pahl's room to assess his condition, but found him strangely quiet and serenely reposed, as if sleeping: a most unusual status for him. Taking a closer look, it suddenly dawned on me that Mr. Pahl wasn't breathing at all, but since he wasn't red in the face or any evidencing signs of apparent dyspnea (difficulty breathing), I quickly guessed that he had somehow passed on in the night. Leaning over to inspect his trach stoma, I found to my dismay that it was stuffed full of small white puffy cotton balls!

Someone (one of the corpsmen?) had apparently taken it upon himself to end Mr. Pahl's unhappy, painful life in the dead of night by suffocating him. I never found out who did this, nor had I wanted to at the time, since to me this was clearly and obviously an act of murder no matter how you looked at it and it was all simply too much to accept. At that early date in my life I hadn't even heard of the phrase 'mercy killing' either, so I was simply shocked into numb silence. Removing the cotton balls seemed to be a logical thing to do at the time, however, so I did so, not thinking about any possible ethical questions arising from my attempt to determine whether or not he might still be alive, and nothing further was mentioned about this by anyone.

As far as I know, Mr. Pahl was officially determined to have died in his sleep from 'natural' causes arising from his terminal illness, but I still occasionally look back on that moment with disquieting reflection. *Fortunately*, there were no further incidents like that while I was at John Moses Air Force Hospital.

11) Getting to know my new fellow-inmates

My new roommates in the dorm seemed to be nice enough, but Mike, the dark haired Greek fellow had a most unusual and curious sort of charismatic affect about him that was as palpable as the static shock one might get from touching a brass doorknob. You might describe him as a sort of synthesis between the mad Tsarist-era Russian monk *Rasputin* and *Mr. Rogers*, since although Mike's personality had a penetrating unworldliness about it, he also was as genuinely and believably well-intended as the Cardigan-sweatered children's matinee host. I soon learned that Mike was a science fiction fan and given to deeply esoteric religious spirituality of the Eastern Orthodox kind. 'Frenchy' Bouchard, the other roommate, was a bit more amorphously engendered than Mike in terms of personality and can best be described as Mike's devoted *side-kick*, his experiential mentor: a sort of comic relief *Pat Buttram* to Mike's *Roy Rogers*, or *Pancho* to the *Cisco Kid*. Both were good people, fortunately, and being a bit of a precocious little nerd myself, we immediately hit things off perfectly. Not quite *'the Three Amigos'*, but close enough within the context of US Air Force 'blue uniformity'.

That my new roommate Mike was a good natured and interesting person was quite fortunate for me, since as an only child I had always had difficulty making friends and usually ended up with only one or two truly close buddies with whom I could relax and interact. Mike and I seemed to share many similar affinities, but as science fiction fans who had both read the genre extensively (and also been involved in what we called 'fandom', which was what the organized sci-fi culture of sci-fi enthusiasts was known as), we got along famously from the first day. [Note: Science fiction *fandom*, for those who may not be aware of it, are what comic fans are to comic book art. 'Fans' *("fen"* is the more popular plural) attend conventions, write their own sci-fi stories, publish fanzines (amateur magazines about sci-fi and sci-fi fan activities), and so forth. They were the original publishers of today's popular amateur 'fanzines', long before comic fans and the youth mainstream discovered that form of self-expression, and have existed as a popular sub-culture from the earliest days of science fiction as a legitimate literary form since back in the 1920s.]

Mike was, as I already mentioned, quite an interesting person. He came from a family of Greek-Americans, had a younger sister, and had suffered a bit from the extremes of an alcoholic father as a child. Still, he had what can only be described as an angelic *personae*, if a man can ever be convincingly characterised by that term. In this, he shared the same sort of beatific affect enjoyed by bohemian hipster Jack Kerouac, who was frequently described by those who knew him as having an innocent, angelic *aura* about him. Mike was also a very sincere, entirely honest person who hated deception, deceits, and dissembling of any sort. As I shortly also came to understand, Mike was furthermore an ardent pacifist and war protestor. He had joined the Air Force for almost the same reason I had, as an alternative to getting caught up in what was to him a most unjustifiable and insupportable war he did not believe in. As a *true* pacifist of genuine conviction, Mike was against war in any way, shape or form.

One day, after all of us had been released from duty at the end of our respective medical shifts on the wards, Mike and Frenchy took me downtown and introduced me to the Minot USO, which was installed in the basement of a downtown Minot former bank building, located near where highway 83 through Minot crosses over the railroad tracks. It was to be quite a catalytic introduction for me.

Likely due to the outlying location of the base (12 miles north of town), very few airmen came down to the USO. In fact, as events turned out, we literally had it all to ourselves most of the time. It was a pretty bare-bones affair, actually, with a pool table, a few chairs, some magazines (*The Lutheran Standard*, *Modern Scandinavia Digest*, etc.), and occasionally some doughnuts to accompany the perpetually boiling coffee on hand that could keep you awake all night without half trying. There was an old mimeograph machine in one corner donated by the local

Lutheran Church and a decrepit (but still functioning) type-writer that looked as if it had been used to help prepare Lincoln's Gettysburg Address. Little did the USO realise that they had just helped establish another 'underground GI coffeehouse' in the growing covert movement to resist the Vietnam war!

12) The anti-war movement gains momentum in a bank vault

Mike had already taken a whack at publishing an anti-war mimeographed magazine that he produced in small numbers and circulated around the hospital. Although a few copies made their way to the base, it really had very little success in reaching most of the troops out on the sprawling confines of MAFB. Still, it was a modestly well-prepared magazine, full of innocuous content, his usually trenchant (and cogent) editorial opinion, an occasional cartoon (by Mike, who used the *nom de plume* of 'RAKI'), a few poems here and there, and less remarkable content. The USO 'advisor' who was appointed to oversee things at the Minot USO in a nominal way was the pastor of the nearby Lutheran church and LSA advisor (*Lutheran Services of America*), Pastor Bergans. Of course, the *American Lutheran Church* (back in 1966 this Lutheran body had not yet merged with the *Lutheran Church in America*—a union that occurred in 1988) was opposed to the war in Vietnam, so there was an added and substantially reinforcing reflection of our already restive and resistive anti-war mood to be found therein.

That winter, and throughout the entire succeeding winter, when the streets were piled high with snowdrifts so large that cars were unable to travel on them, we would gather together in the USO's 'bunker' and huddle over ways to get the anti-war message out. For all the really substantial effect we had on the war's progress (it was negligible), it was still a great place to get away from the military mentality and uniformity of thought we were otherwise exposed to at the hospital and on base. It was also a very evocative setting for late night flights of poetic expression, fits of writing activity, and lots of daydreaming about how a world without war would be...if the US would just *bail out* of that god-forsaken patch of SEA turf America insisted on defending with such stubbornly dogmatic determination.

13) Christmas is only what you make of it

At Christmas, not really much into the obligatory holiday mood that pervaded the corridors of the hospital, we had a Christmas dinner of pizza from the local pizzeria, tossed down with near-beer. Outside the former bank basement the city had erected a large if somewhat *Charlie Brown-ish* municipal Christmas tree that was bedecked with strings of short circuit prone lights, clumps of dingy tinsel, and a *woebegone* tinfoil angel awkwardly impaled upon the uppermost top of the tree. Finishing up the pizza, Mike grabbed a cheap Pakistani-made sword he had purchased at the nearby surplus store and struck a suitable Han Solo 'Star Wars' pose in from of it (*Star Wars* the epic sci-fi movie was still about 20 years off in the future, at that time), which I managed to capture on film (one of the few pictures I still have of Mike).

The snow was falling lightly and it was cold as day-old s**t as we goofed around near the tree and of course there was no traffic nearby, so the sight of three figures dressed in green Air Force arctic parkas chuffing madly about in the snow drew no attention whatsoever in the absolute dead of that dark night. To us it was just another unremarkable celebration of the erstwhile birth of the son of someone's god (but a god that no one among us but Mike devoutly believed in) and *any* excuse to goof about and blow off steam was always welcome. The mood and atmosphere of that timeless moment recollected these 44 years later is still fresh. There was something enduring and eternal about it, even if we had we been aware of anything other than the fact that at the age of 20 one has no useful concept whatsoever of the fact that, ultimately and inevitably, eternal, youthful, exuberant life finally comes to an unspectacular end! Given the late hour and no Christmas celebrations to go to, after a while we ended up at a local all-night café for coffee. Three tough looking local NoDaks were sitting at the far end of the cafe and fortunately the fact there were three of us posed enough of a deterrent to forestall any inclination they may have had to do more than glower at us, conspicuous in our Air Force issue parkas as being some of those hated GIs from the base.

Interestingly, the N-3B 'arctic' parka we all wore were made distinctive in that each of our parkas had circles of reflective tape on the arms and a reflective cross (a target?) stitched to the rear. Although some of the *townies* wore these N-3B parkas as well (available at the nearby surplus store) due to their excellent suitability for Minot's cold winters, the civilian versions lacked those reflective crosses (this had been mandated for all base personnel use, so that airmen would be visible on the flight-line and not get sucked into jet intakes by accident). As it was, any person possessed of a reflective cross on their parka might as well have been wearing a red bulls-eye on their back for the benefit of town folk who felt the need to express their irritation over some aspect or abnother of the base's presence.

14) Saint Benedict's Holy willie

As we sucked hot java, staring out the frosted window at the late-night snowfall, Mike was launching into a reflection on the fact that the town's primary Roman Catholic Church had recently acquired a small relic of some saint or another that it was currently displaying. The thought of some macabre body part of a reputed 'saint' being proudly shown off in its little glass *reliquarial* box to the yokels made me shiver, but I volunteered the observation of how neat it would be if they managed to find the saint's mummified *willie* and build a De Molay *'Follow Holy Father's example: abstain from sex'* youth program around it. After all, the mental picture of sex-starved monks and nuns feverishly debouching each other in the dark corners of monastery basements had always held a certain grotesque fascination for me during my studies of Western Civilisation, since the discovery of the remains of dozens of infant remains buried deep under those monastic havens is a proven archeological and historical fact.

Looking across the table at Mike, I could see his eyes glazing over in that now familiar way as he got further and further afield in his esoteric musings. Mike clearly missed his calling, since he had always seemed to me to have had the makings of a good Eastern Orthodox Priest in his make-up. Rasputin with a tender and loving heart? But that bit of déjà-vu speculation come true would occur much later, after he left the Air Force. I was meanwhile wondering what *Oswanna Bergdahl* was doing that evening, out on her family's snowbound farm and celebrating Christmas Eve in true old fashioned Norwegian family style.

15) A fine post-puberty howdy-do!

Oswanna had come to my attention not long after I had arrived at the hospital, since she was attending the nearby teacher's college and there were several extra-curricular student social organisations on the campus, one (LSA) operated under the aegis of the Lutheran Church our USO advisor belonged to. Since most of the student teachers were women, the local male-female ratio was—seen from the viewpoint of a horny GI—absolutely mind-boggling. And since the base would frequently be cut off from town by recurrent snowstorms, during those protracted winter periods we airmen practically had the attention of all those young women entirely to ourselves. The only real problem I could see was that they were all from good Christian (Lutheran) families and I (along with most of my airman cohorts) was most un-Christian in both intent and purpose! How to lure these clean living, sweetly virginal young ladies off the path of filial righteousness and onto the path to eternal perdition was the chief challenge of our off-duty lives, of course. The official SAC motto may have been *'Peace is our profession'*, but it became *'Peace may be our profession, but pu*sy is our passion!'* to us.

Aside from a couple of high school crushes I'd had that never amounted to much, I couldn't claim the experience of having had a real girlfriend before and Oswanna quickly attracted my attention. With short bobbed brown hair, a cute little snub nose, nice hooters and a well-proportioned shape, Oswanna had all the requisite physical attributes, but she also seemed to possess a substantial intellect as well...*always* a plus on my score-sheet. One other airman at the hospital named Russ also had his eyes on Oswanna, however, and through our mutual interest in her we became good friends. Russ was from New York City and played jazz saxophone; he also tended towards depression, as I later found out. Russ and I initially became the best of enemies as we pursued lovely Oswanna in our off-time, but with neither of us gaining the clear upper hand. Given the prominence of strong rural Christian beliefs that prevailed at this time, augmented by the strict teachings of the Lutheran Church (Missouri Synod), neither of us ever got to first base in our intent to bed lovely Oswanna (which was probably just as well, since getting hitched and having to settle down in North Dakota that early in our lives even then had seemed an awful prospect to both of us).

Nevertheless, Oswanna remained high on my list as I also met a few others among the teachers-to-be and gingerly trolled the local waters. There were three others, actually, who caught my attention at the LSA meetings. One, named Robin, was a bit too angular and ectomorphic; a blonde, her manner was rather hyper-staccato and her affect slightly nervous. Another, a short-haired blonde named Lynn, was a bit too well padded and had these deep brown ‘cow-eyes’ that perhaps communicated too much to her already more than ‘willing’ nature; when I finally had the chance to drill for oil on Lynn’s plot, I just couldn’t bring myself to take advantage of her (probably more so because I didn’t relish the thought of getting married and hitched to Lynn forever). Then there was Carole-Anne Johnson, a vivacious blonde who had a sharp sense of humor and a set of perfect hips that promised absolutely no complications with future child-birthing whatsoever! Regrettably, Carole-Ann was a dedicated Lutheran vestal virgin who was ‘saving her body’ for her future husband and, as already emphasised, nothing could have been more off-putting than the thought of marriage to *anyone* at that early point in my earthly learning curve.

Mike, Frenchy and I finally finished our coffee at about 1AM, grinned annoyingly at the tough locals in the cockroach café as we departed, and took our leave to return to the airmen’s dorm after slogging through the deep snow piled up on the Souris River (French for 'Mouse' River) that meandered back to the hospital from downtown. Actually, this was a pursuit I regularly delighted in, crunching along in the snow on that river’s frozen surface. Since North Dakota’s cold dry snow was so much different from California’s moist and heavy Sierra Nevada snow, walking in it late at night when the temperature was fourteen below was an exotic and personally delightful experience. To my reckoning, nothing could beat getting totally encapsulated in our full arctic paraphernalia and going out for a stroll at midnight, during those dark winter nights. The stars were so bright and clear it almost seemed as if they might hurt your eyes looking at them too long, and the sharp dry cold enhanced the scent of everything with a unique piquancy that made even the creosote on telephone poles seem like a sublimely exotic perfume. Quite often, when the solar wind from sunspot outbursts of radiation was strong, the *Aurora Borealis* danced across the sky like a procession of fitful insomniac ghosts. Moments like those remain as fresh in my mind today as any over the entire course of my six and a half decades of life, and I still love the scent of creosote on cold days.

Thinking back on those singularly unique nocturnal winter walks, all I lacked was a faithful sled dog by my side to imagine I was somewhere up in the Arctic Circle wasteland, captured by the ancient Native American spirits' magic in those timeless frozen nights. Unfortunately, my reveries quickly came crashing down to reality once I was at the hospital dorm's door again and the exotic natural perfume of frosty North Dakota nights was quenched by the stink of stale heated air that rushed out through the doorway as I entered.

16) M*A*S*H was closer to the truth than you'll ever know

Still, life in town wasn't half bad compared to life on the base. Back in the 60s most military medical people were notoriously casual about such trifles as rank and military protocol, a custom that the television and movie productions of *M*A*S*H* rather accurately reflected. In the hospital and around its grounds us medics routinely went around without caps, although the regulations strictly specified that all personnel would be 'covered' at all times when outside of a building. Salutes routinely went by the board, especially if the officer encountered was a FOB '90 day wonder' butter-bar nurse, a habit even more ingrained by the fact that many of the nurses (all commissioned officers and 2nd lieutenants at the very least) regularly slept around with the hunkier enlisted men at the hospital. Thus, the *fraternization* that is so severely condemned among the officer corps was, in our instance, conjugal fraternization of the most flagrant sort. One can image how difficult it was to even consider saluting a nurse with your hand when just the night before you had enthusiastically saluted her charms with your *willy*, standing erect and ramrod straight in its own right!

This habit of treating officers casually often got us into hot water when we 'town-troops' were out on the base, since we'd walk around by habit without our caps until some eager young fighter pilot would round the corner and heatedly call us on our failure to render appropriate military courtesies (the rumor that these junior grade Tom Cruise clones all went around with an aircraft pitot tube stuffed straight up their collective *arses* is untrue , but they *were* a bit undeservedly over-awed by the self-exaggerated importance of their very junior officer status). Typically, if we were within a 100-yard radius of the base medical clinic, instead of saluting we'd simply grin and dart around the corner to vanish in the radiography film vault (if the officer decided to give hot pursuit). It became a game we medics played with increasing finesse.

17) Don't ask, don't tell...don't even speculate!

If the female nurses favored sleeping around with the male enlisted men at the hospital, the two male nurses we had at John Moses apparently preferred to just as eagerly keep each *other's* intimate company. Our two male nurses, both FOB butter-bars, were Lt. Gringo and Lt. Dilbert, the former being somewhat short, dark and rotund, with slicked back Hispanic hair, and the latter being more closely approximating a sort of blonde version of Washington Irving's *Ichabod Crane* character. Despite their extreme differences, they were clearly an *item*. Gringo drove a late model Chevy Corvair convertible of which he was inordinately fond, despite its abysmal (and dangerous) handling characteristics, and one would occasionally see them dashing off together during warmer weather, top down, with Dilbert riding shotgun as the Corvair's rear end sagged perilously askew around the corners. They weren't bad guys, really, and just seemed to be a tad more...um, shall we say *sensitive?*...than the other male medics. Nothing wrong with that, of course, since both were very conscientious and thoroughly dedicated to their patients (and probably damn happy to find each other in this very austere and religiously conservative northern region, also). In those days of the 60s, Oscar Wilde's *'love whose name may not be spoken'* was still pretty much buried away in the nearest closet and even the present military *'don't ask, don't tell'* policy was several decades off in the future. Besides, even if they had been flagrant about their relationship, the military needed nurses now that the Vietnam War was in full reheat, so Gringo and Dilbert were safe enough tucked away in provincial little Minot. In fact, most NoDak townies probably weren't even aware that such homo-erogenous pairings even existed (f you exclude Bible lessons about Sodom & Gomorrah, that is)!

Strangely, for someone who hailed from sunny California coastal beaches, I found the dire NoDak winters to be somehow sublime and enjoyable. If the climate was so severe that it found even some of the dire-hard Norwegian-Americans grumbling about finally quitting the farming business and moving to *my* state, I was clearly a bizarre anomaly beyond understanding to them. Such was the unhappy reputation of Minot AFB throughout the Air Force as a 'hard duty' assignment that the mere mention of Minot anywhere on a base around the world brought immediate smirks and nudges. As if the hot prairie summers and icy-cold, sub-zero winters weren't enough of a misery for most, Minot AFB also had the dubious distinction of being hosted by SAC, just a short time earlier under the lightning bolt clutching mailed fist of General Curtis Lemay himself (we called him *'the Cigar Grinder'* behind his back), the non-nonsense father of modern nuclear strategic bombing operations theory and practice.

18) SAC introduces us to the 'ORI' (Operation Readiness Inspection')

While that might not have been enough in itself to inspire markedly indifferent enthusiasms among those assigned to Minot, the frequent SAC 'Operational Readiness' inspections (known as ORIs) *were*. These unannounced inspections of a given SAC base by the top SAC brass occurred unpredictably and fairly frequently, the earliest notice coming from the base control tower upon being notified of an unidentified KC-135 approaching the base on final and requesting permission to land. As soon as word flashed out about the pending inspection, the base would suddenly become a beehive of activity with every single person on it frantically preparing for a white glove examination of the base's erstwhile 'combat readiness'. This typically ranged from microscopic examinations of the dozens of ceramic toilet bowls for slight blemishes, all the way up to an assessment of the polished sheen on Minuteman I missile warhead nosecones and throttle movement lubricity in the nuclear alert BUFFs that were poised for takeoff on the alert pad.

For those of us at the hospital (and at the base clinic), this most often meant wearily searching for dust bunnies and *woolie-boogers* under the beds of our crusty old vets, dust on bedrails, and an inspection of the gleam on our sterilized stainless-steel bedpans and 'ducks' (urinals) under the direct observation of a stern-faced bird colonel from SAC higher headquarters. The dorms also had to be spit-shined to perfection, as well, and any stray evidence of lost nurse lingerie under airmen beds had to be well hidden. However, given a little luck, an ability to roll with the punches and some smooth public relations work by the Hospital Commander (usually a formal 'dining-in' for hospital officers and the higher HQ command staff in the John Moses cafeteria), we usually managed to get through the worst of the ORI fun & games without losing our collective cool. Still, it was usually the closest we would have to get to being reminded of our real military status, in our otherwise *M*A*S*H*-like little medical slice of the uniformed services world.

19) We find out about the SAC 'North/South Policy'

In the summer months Minot would often sizzle and fry under the hot NoDak plains sun and the frequent droughts were not much fun, either, as semi-permanent features of the plains farming region along the Canadian border. NoDak winters, by contrast, were notorious for having severe sub-zero weather for weeks at a time, often just as ferocious and almost as miserable as the worst northern located bases in Alaska. Life at MAFB was hardest for good ole boys from the American south, of course, since they didn't particularly take a likin' to havin' their hominy grits freeze up, but SAC had what was termed the 'North/South' Policy, an official protocol that would routinely assign personnel to alternate and highly contrasting temperature zones. This meant that once assigned to SAC, an airman could rely on being sent to at least one severe cold area, followed by a subsequent duty station in an extremely warm area (Arctic/Tropics). This was intended to temper the experience of all SAC personnel so as to enable them to contend with climatic extremes and function seamlessly in the complete range of global weather possibilities. Keeping sophisticated weapons systems in a top state of immediate readiness for instant nuclear deployment in either type of weather was a daunting and arduous undertaking at best, as most soon found out, but to my reckoning, having to work on the guts of a balky turbojet engine and make it operate properly at 20 degrees below zero HAD to be among the worst of the challenges anyone in SAC faced. By contrast, putting cartoon-character Band-Aids on *baby booies* at the base clinic was a pure lark (if not very adventurous)!

Of course, not all medical duties were as mild and pacific as that. Every now and then we'd have to respond in our big blue crash ambulances to aircraft crashes, some in (and often partly due to) the worst winter weather imaginable. Most were not catastrophic, usually resulting only in bent landing gear, aircraft sliding off the icy runways, and engine failures (on multi-engined aircraft this was not often very serious) that were either approaching the base or taking off from it. In these instances, there were usually few if any casualties, since they were what we call 'survivable' (non-catastrophic) emergencies.

The one major incident that was a total catastrophe involved a KC-135A jet tanker that had been fitted for passengers and that was used by SAC headquarters for inspection visits to various SAC wings. The incident in question occurred in January of 1968, just before I left for a new assignment in Arizona (DMAFB in Tucson), and since I have already written about it in another article, I won't recap the details here. Suffice it to say that all 13 individuals on board (seven crew and six higher headquarters staff, including SAC's Vice-Commander, Major General Charles Eisenhart) died when the 300,000-pound aircraft experienced a failed take-off and impacted the ground about two-thirds of the way down the main runway in a snowstorm. That was the single most destructive crash I have ever been involved with, needless to say, and one can't even begin to imagine the incredible forces involved that can break a human body into such tiny fragments that you literally have to comb the ground to find any identifiable human remains. Although there were only 13 people aboard, multiply that scene by a passenger factor of x 42 and you come close to a fairly accurate sense of what a *non-survivable* modern commercial airliner crash is like. Personally, I usually preferred pediatric clinic baby Band-Aid duty, myself.

20) A really mixed bag of characters

As the winter stretched on, the USO downtown gathered a few more hard-core war protestors under its wing, including one memorable character named Dave Estridge. Dave was an engine mechanic in the base's Air Defense Command detachment, the 5th Fighter Interceptor Squadron and he played a mean folk guitar. Like most of us anti-war protestors, Dave would rather make love than war, as the old saying had it, and he would occasionally play the latest folk tunes for us whenever LSA was hosting a social gathering for the Minot State Teacher's College students. With wild Irish red hair, a gritty Dave van Ronk style voice, and extensive repertoire of *Phil Ochs* songs, Dave could outshine Leon Redbone in his better moments. You'd have thought he was still in the Village (Greenwich Village, in NYC) to hear him play and it made the rest of us (Mike, Frenchy and myself included) rue his natural 4-string talent. So compellingly unforced was Dave's performing ability that he even affected a sort of 'celebrity depression' problem that made him shirk the limelight when he wasn't in the mood to sing (shades of James Dean!). I never found out what ultimately happened to good old Dave, but hopefully he didn't end up across the pond and stretched out on a cold *Da Nang* slab somewhere. Since he was in ADC (based only within the continental US), it is likely he was spared that less than happy experience.

Also mentioned earlier was my old buddy Russell Kelly, who in additional to coping with occasional mild depressions had a sort of Woody Allen complex, complete with small nervous tics and minor neuroses. Russ was my main competition for Oswanna, our mutual heart-throb, but he was always fearing rejection by her so his life was usually inconsolable. That left a bit of breathing-space for me to squeeze into Oswanna's awareness, but one day I blew what fragile relationship I had with her to pieces, thanks to my too-clever sense of humor.

I had noticed that there was a company back east that would print sweatshirts with whatever a customer wanted emblazoned on it, so on a sudden inspiration I ordered a powder blue sweatshirt with the words *SIGMA EPSILON XI* on the front. Since the teachers' college had sororities, it was a natural to see some of the students walking about in similarly decorated sweatshirts. Oswanna was actually quite pleased when I presented it to her, giving her some sort of line about her being made an honorary member of the SIGNA EPSILON XI fraternity that I belonged to. Of course, the hidden joke didn't dawn on her until another student saw her on the campus at a Lutheran student social and asked her if the SIGMA EPSILON XI on her sweatshirt stood for *SEX*? Oswanna was mortified and refused to even see me for at least a couple of months after that, but I wrote it off as simply a matter of her lacking a sufficiently broad enough sense of humor and quickly forgot about it as a promising joke that didn't quite pan out as expected.

Amazingly, many years later and long after having gotten out of the Air Force, I found Russ on the internet and reestablished contact with him briefly. He was still the same Russ, still a neurotic Woody Allen surrogate, but for all that just as likeable. For reasons I forget, we drifted apart soon after and lost track of each other. As for Oswanna, amazingly she later ended up coming to California, where she tried teaching school in San Francisco for a while. We got together occasionally, since by then I was relocated in the San Francisco East Bay (Berkeley) but there just didn't seem to be any real prospect of a solid long-term relationship between us, so she moved to Sacramento (CA), where she eventually married a sailor and had a family. As far as I know she is still there.

21) A winter's tale (about yellow snow)

I'll never forget one time when Mike, Russ and I drove out to Oswanna's family's farm on the south outskirts of town. It was deep winter, the snow was falling and the wind was blowing up a howling blizzard when we decided to go out to see her in my little blue VW convertible. As I mentioned earlier, the typical Minot snowstorm was more of a horizontal than vertical affair, since the unobstructed winds swept all the dry snow in a layer over the ground to a height of from thirteen to twenty-five feet. This meant that vision 'on the deck' could be totally whited-out and obscured, while just twenty-five feet higher the air was clear and the sun shining (albeit bleakly). For our part, there was so much snow already on the ground that it was just about all we could do, even in my stalwart little bug, to keep ploughing on through the drifts that clung to the roadway. Despite the bug's near-unstoppable snow-keeping ability, we all knew that to stop anywhere between town and farm would mean getting snowbound and temporarily marooned until the storm blew over. Thus, we kept driving, despite the fact that Russ and I had had several beers and were feeling a dire need to take a whiz (Mike, as a priest in training didn't drink anything 'harder' than root beer). I had let Mike drive, so Russ and I were passengers in the cramped bug, but since our respective bladders threatened to burst on the next sharp impact with a bump on the roadway, in our increasing desperation we finally hit upon a plan to relieve ourselves without necessitating a stop.

Forcing the bug's right-side door open against the howling wind-stream as a shield, first Russ and then I managed to shoehorn ourselves into the right front seat in succession and stand in the open doorway to direct a steaming jet of yellow fluid out onto the roadway. And this at a speed of about 35-40 mph in an almost total whiteout! It remains one of my finest performances to this day, I think, calling for a mix of good balance, reckless daring, and precise aim that I doubt I could ever repeat again. Mike's performance as 'pilot' on this mission was also flawless and after a short interval we managed to reach the safety of Oswanna's farm where she wondered how we could be so crazy as to attempt a passage in those conditions (after all, even the farm animals had had enough intelligence to stay safety out of the storm and in the barn; those that didn't and ended up grazing near the road into Oswanna's farm might have been momentarily attracted by two neat little lines of yellow snow that pretty much led right up to a point shortly past the entrance, by her gate!).

22) Elvis spotted in a flying saucer at Minot AFB again (again!)

Since we were 'townie airmen', assigned to the hospital in Minot and not located directly at the base (12 miles north of town), we were totally unaware of some mysterious goings-on out there that to this day challenge explanation. While Mikie, Frenchy and I were taking care of cranky old Norwegian vets (and seriously ill base personnel who had been sent to town), our awareness of all things considered classified on the base was considerably lessened, compared to that of our cohorts stationed at the base clinic. In addition to the base's 450th Bomb Wing, MAFB also hosted the 91st Strategic Missile Wing, a three-squadron strength unit comprised of nuclear-armed and combat ready Minuteman II intercontinental ballistic missiles (ICBM) on constant alert. This large ICBM complex joined two others situated on the northernmost frontiers of the country as part of the nation's 'TRIAD' nuclear deterrent force (sub-based missiles, land-based missiles, and nuclear bombers). Our 91st SMW birds, the solid-fuel Minuteman II ICBM (with an 8,000-mile range and armed with a 1.2 megaton single thermonuclear warhead), lurked in reinforced concrete prairie dog holes that had been designed to resist the near-direct hit of a Soviet thermonuclear missile and (in addition to their own highly secure perimeter defenses) were protected up topside by a very elaborately configured security force of mobile Air Police strike-teams. In the event that an unauthorized object (person, vehicle, aircraft, etc.) was detected within a certain radius of each silo, one of these teams would respond with extreme haste to intercept the intruder using both ground vehicles and helicopters. Above each silo complex elaborate sensors and surface detection systems were monitored by those below in the command and launch centers. These systems were also backed up by sensitive surface scan radar and motion detection arrays, leaving absolutely no chance that anything would get within several hundred feet of the silos' outermost perimeters without being detected.

According to authenticated reports and recorded documentation, the 91st SMW was visited by unidentified flying objects (yes, *UFOs*) several times throughout 1967 and 1968. In each of these instances, flying objects were picked up in the immediate vicinity of the silos, hovering or maneuvering close to the ground (in a non-aerodynamic manner, meaning they weren't conventionally winged airplanes) above them. Beams of light were directed by the objects at several of the silos and in at least one instance the *unimaginable* occurred as a result*: several of the missiles in their concrete silos went on full pre-launch mode entirely by themselves* (that is, the launch control officers had not initiated any launch actions themselves). Given the extremely complex series of command sequences and authorizations (both electronic and sequential) that a pre-launch mode requires, it is entirely impossible that these situations could have been either accidental or human-initiated.

Security teams actually approached the hovering objects and upon arrival at the complex found the locked outer perimeter gates open. In addition to radar documentation, a number of confirmed direct sightings were recorded and to this day there is no possibility that these objects were anything *other than* unidentified flying objects. More information about these sightings may be viewed here, for those interested: http://www.ufocasebook.com/minotafb.html and http://ufocasebook.com/minotafbufo1968.html . A separate article I wrote on the subject of unconventional flight propulsion systems makes mention of this incident and may be viewed here: http://www.authorsden.com/visit/viewarticle.asp?id=50806 .

So highly classified were these incidents at the time that I wasn't even personally aware of them until many years later, despite the fact that our medical group had direct responsibility for taking care of the medical needs of the 91st SMW launch crews and support personnel, and despite the events described having occurred when I was assigned to the 862nd MG at the time. Given the enormous range of possibilities concerning the existence of UFOs and all the swirling controversy that has forever surrounded the subject of space aliens and ET life in the universe, there is a strong tendency by most to simply dismiss 'hardened factual' instances such as those that occurred at MAFB back in 67 and 68 as simply the result of fanciful imagination. In this instance, however, as in so many thousands of others (as any research into this topic will quickly demonstrate), there is simply no possible dismissal of what happened as 'fanciful'. These totally mystifying but well-documented incidents remain unexplained to this day.

23) North Dakota learns about California style 'beatniks'

Back at the hospital in town, life for us continued with a fairly tolerable regularity. Once a week in the evenings we'd meet at the local Lutheran Church, situated just across the street from the college campus, for socializing with the women students and there would be the occasional party to attend (all strictly sans ETOH, of course, since these were all good little God-fearing girls from good little God-fearing families). Naturally nothing would have pleased us more than to get into a few sets of knickers, so it was often quite frustrating to have to put on halos and assume a more appropriately 'godly' demeanor, but persevere we did (without much luck).

Since the war was in full swing overseas, peaceful resistance was a frequent theme of some of the social gatherings and one or two of the parties we attended reflected unconstrained war-protest sentiment. People would come dressed as what they imagined San Francisco's beatniks looked like, with berets, turtlenecks, shades, peace symbols, bongos, etc. Of course, it was all pretty *hoakie*, given the fact that most folks in NoDak hadn't the most remote idea what REAL San Francisco Bay Area beatniks looked like and besides, the beats were almost totally extinct by 1968, having yielded to the growing hippie movement, with its iconic MJ and LSD substances. Nevertheless, they were known as 'beatnik' parties.

One of the most convincing of our group of male regulars at these LSA parties was a Lakota Sioux fellow named Phil. Phil was also a very, very smart young man, possessed of the sort of dark good looks that predictably set Scandinavian girls' heart rates a tick faster. Slim, but well-muscled and possessed of a naturally cool demeanor, Phil played the bongos with some skill and could also play the guitar. No *'kumbayaer'* Phil, and if he had been in California, he undoubtedly would have been right at home, riding the crest of the popular hippie movement wave. Strangely, Phil lacked any sort of connectivity with his Native American ancestry and if one didn't know his Lakota Sioux family name was *Mahpiyawakankidan* (*Sacred Cloud Worshipper*), one would think he was merely a smoothly acculturated Italian. With his impressive looks, keen intellect, and social adroitness, Phil would have perfectly fitted right in at any Bay Area (or Italian) coffeehouse. Being cool and with local connections, Phil would show up from time to time with a vampish female on his arm and smoking funny looking (and curiously smelling) cigarettes. Innocents that we all were, it wasn't until a few years later that I came to recognise these *Cheech and Chong* specials of Phil's as that evil scourge of J. Edgar's minions (LoL), *MJ.* [Sadly, super-cool or not, I am told that Phil ultimately succumbed to the bias and prejudice directed towards those Native American ancestry by WASP NoDaks and ended up prematurely dead from drink and substance abuse.]

But even if we were entirely devoid of any factual knowledge about REAL drugs, we were an inventive group at those parties and there was always a platter or two piled with simulated LSD (that took the form of a small red dot made from food color dye on the sugar cubes). The girls called it *'LSA LSD'* which usually gave our chaperone Pastor Jurgenson mild palpitations whenever he reflected on what his parishioners might think of what his youthful congregation members were up to. It was all in good, harmless fun of course since the mid-60s were still relatively innocent, compared with the far more harmful pop-culture social excesses of later decades that followed.

24) Hauling 'A' with Heine, the wunderauto

In the spring, another good airman friend of mine (who had a bright red 1963 VW convertible) would join my own blue 62 ragtop bug for a two-car convoy to the nearby shores of *Lake Sakakawea*, hauling a carful or two of the Minot college girls along for a day in the sun. There were small sailing dinghies available for sailing (Lido 14 Class) at the lake and the fishing was also great, if you liked great big lazy lake carp. Sometimes during the winter snow melt-off, these huge carp would get trapped in little drying rivulets and you could just wade in and catch them by hand (some 22 inches long and larger). To me, a person whom the fish usually avoided as often as the girls, that was quite a unique experience!

Having a ragtop VW bug in North Dakota was rare enough, but seeing two together sailing down the prairie roadways in 1967 was somewhat of a sight to behold. The fact is that, appearances to the contrary, the soft-top VW beetle was actually far *better* insulated than its hard-top counterpart, so in addition to the excellent snow-tracking and cold-weather characteristics of our '*Strength-Through-Joy*' wagons, they were also warmer in the winter. [As a note of explanation, the VW beetle was originally named the *KDF wagon* under Hitler's Nazi regime. That was an acronym for *'Kraft durch Freude'*, or KdF, attributable to the fact that as originally envisioned by Dr. Porsche and *der Furher*, German citizens would all subscribe to a mandatory savings program that would when completed result in their having purchased their own beetle. This program was known as the 'KdF' program, hence the original name of the vehicle.]

My own blue 62 soft-top bug was named 'Heine' (after the German poet) and it was the first thing I acquired after arriving at Minot. My very first car had been the lime green '40 Chevy Master Deluxe Coupe I mentioned earlier (as having been barely able to wheeze its way to the beach) that I had picked up for $50. Having had to leave it home when I enlisted, I gave a lot of thought to what sort of car I would get at my newly assigned base before passing by a local Minot used car dealership and spotting the blue bug. It was a 62 model and the asking price, used, in 1967 was $600. Although a considerably daunting sum for someone making only $125 a month to contemplate, I was fortunate enough to get an HFC (*Household Finance Company*, a franchised high-rate of interest private loan business) loan for the full amount and soon took charge of the small beast. It seemed to be in great condition with only about 60,000 miles on the clock, so Heine and I began a happy association that would last until I traded it in on a new 69 beetle (big mistake, as it turned out) a while later. While installing a battery warmer wrap under the rear seat (where the battery was located, being a rear-engined vehicle) I was briefly startled to find at least a bucket full of oats, wheat, and barley. Asking the dealer about this, I was told that the car had formerly been owned by the son of a local Lakota Sioux chief who had used it to haul feed for his sheep around in. I guess it's a good thing he didn't use it to ferry the sheep themselves, thinking this all over.

Heine the VW ragtop gave me excellent, uncomplaining service while in the US Air Force, regardless of whether I was freezing my ass off in North Dakota or roasting under the merciless Arizona sun and I really *should* have kept it, since a regarded it with about as much affection as a favorite dog. Unfortunately, after getting out of the Air Force and returning to the *Peoples Republic of Berkeley*, I decided to trade Heine in on a late model VW. Originally intent on getting a new 1969 VW ragtop, they had none available at the Berkeley VW dealer, so I let the salesman sweet-talk me into getting a beige hard-top instead. True to VW's rep, it ran perfectly, as smooth as a Swiss watch, but I soon got tired of it since it had none of the little quirks and endearing rattles that I had come to regard as 'personality' in my blue 62. For some reason I've never been able to either understand or explain, I actually enjoy having a few quirks in my vehicles; something about *karma*, I guess.

However, being very protective of it and trying to guard the new car against any possibility of damage on the crowded Berkeley streets, I was in the habit of leaving it parked safely at home by the curb, in the street in front of my apartment, and used a small motorcycle to get to and from work. Only a week after I had bought the new bug, I returned from work to find that some truck had passed too close to it and left a huge crease along the entire left (driver's) side, gouging a one-inch deep gash in both front and rear fenders! Since the fenders on old VW bugs project a good 6 to 8 inches beyond the doors, it is all too easy to overlook the fact that the lower-situated fenders are closer to one's passing vehicle than might otherwise be apparent and in a somewhat higher American full-sized truck, well...so much for my protective precautions! I felt like my girlfriend had been raped!

25) And now a serious note about the ravages of war

But I digress. Most of our patients at John Moses were, as mentioned, elderly Norwegian World War One veterans, many suffering from serious diseases and almost all of them crotchety, cranky, and sour dispositioned old men in their 80s and 90s. Since we were in our early 20s, there wasn't much real understanding between us and them. We did what we had to do and provided reasonably good medical and nursing care for them, but for my part and despite being a military person myself, I hadn't had the foggiest notion of what their World War One service had actually been like. At that point in my life I was far less historically aware than I am today, naturally enough, and had not yet undergone later years of academic study in history.

Although my father (who had passed on when I was age four) had been a *Spanish American War* veteran (too young to enlist as a private soldier, he had been a drummer boy for Teddy Roosevelt's regiment, back in 1898), the First World War was something that lay far beyond my understanding then. It had been simply another forgotten 'war' to me, *ho-hum.*

Reflecting on that today, it is amazing what a contrast there was between the conditions those First World War vets served under and those imposed upon us in the Air Force of the 60s. Reading later about the indescribable horrors of static trench warfare and the unimaginably terrible violence they suffered on the muddy French lines, I am always impressed by the fact that although the conduct of war has been steadily and increasingly refined since 1900, no matter how one considers it, war...any war at all, no matter how or where...is contemptible and lamentable. Unfortunately for them, in the early 1900s technology first began to make the mass killing of millions of soldiers possible, with the result that veterans of that war suffered in ways we can't even imagine today.

Looking back on the history of warfare, any modern student of history has to be profoundly struck by the unceasing brutality of armed national conflict throughout the ages. As science and technology grew from the age of the industrial revolution onwards, the means of inflicting death and destruction have kept proportionate pace, accordingly. With new weapons and more effective means of killing the enemy a given, over any period of time, one cannot but wonder how modern human sensibilities can tolerate the perpetuation of warfare. When the atomic age produced thermonuclear weapons capable of destroying the entire world many time over, some dared to hope that humanity had *finally* reached the point where a liberating epiphany of sorts was about to occur to humanity's collective consciousness. That hope has, of course, been long-since dashed as nations found ever-increasing and more efficient means of continuing to wage war just short of launching an Armageddon of nuclear holocaust. Today these 'means' take the form of so-called 'limited warfare', guerilla and terrorist resistance, and 'limited tactical action', but they are just as deadly in entirely new ways.

While wars still kill and maim combatants, the means employed to kill have simply become more technique-intensive, more highly technology-driven and more surgically precise. As medical science kept pace with weapons sciences, and as the effectiveness of medical treatment and casualty evacuation became more sophisticated, greater assurance of life-preservation became a byproduct of modern war-fighting, but at the same time that survival became more likely, permanent maiming and disfigurement arose as the new casualty norm. Today, in Afghanistan, improvised explosive devices are a whole new and terribly destructive force to be reckoned with, combining the worst features of traditional mine-warfare with the unpredictability and uncertainties of new guerrilla terrorist tactics. From my viewpoint, witnessing a whole new generation of partly dismembered, but still living bodies return home—life preserved, but forever severely disabled—my shame over being a member of the supposedly intelligent species that permits such outrages is intense.

26) Gavrilo blows it big-time

Back in the days of the First World War (1914 through 1918), weapons technology outpaced medical science by an order of magnitude, given the abrupt assumption of hostilities after Serbian assassin Gavrilo Princip shot the Austrian Crown Prince in Sarajevo. By the time the war finally ended in an armistice in 1918, monster long-range artillery had been developed that could send 14 inch (naval sized) high explosive shells down on an entrenched and helpless enemy more than 24 miles distant. The terrible devastation of new chemical and biological weapons had also been introduced, and the machine gun provided an entirely new way of efficiently mowing down an enemy by the thousands at a time. New tactics, such as using progressive heavy artillery bombardment (known as 'creeping barrages') followed closely by massed infantry attacks, came into use, and entirely new armored weapons such as the tank came into being, as well. Against all of these things there was little or no defense back in the First World War and as a result of this, the veterans we took care of had all suffered to some extent or another from all of those horrors, many from mustard and phosgene gas exposure (against which rudimentary 'gas masks' initially provided only partly or an incompletely effective defense), a great number from 'shell shock', and worse.

Additionally, many of our old vets at John Moses had sustained severe psychological injuries resulting from their exposure to trench warfare and their experiences contending with the sight of seeing their mates atomized all about by unceasing high explosive shelling. *'Shell-shock'* was the original term used to describe what we today understand as *'Post Traumatic Stress Disorder'*, but it was rather incompletely understood in those days and in far too many cases the psychological damage was left untreated, left undiagnosed (and therefore untreated), or simply dismissed as inconsequential. Then too, far too often PTSD was felt to be the result of cowardice or mere fearfulness, with the result that soldiers suffering from such devastating mental injuries were frequently regarded as shirkers and cowardly slackers, and sent right back to the line.

Over the years following their service in the trenches of World War One, many of those with lingering psychiatric effects simply worsened until finally, although they were committed to our hospital for quantifiable physical disease and old war injuries, most also suffered secretly from severe psychiatric illnesses associated with the war in addition to any chronic or long-term war-related physical ailments.

27) Private Parts gets his orders

Thus, as mere kids ourselves, we medics were largely unsympathetic to the cranky moods and demanding attitudes of ourf charges and certainly hadn't the slightest understanding of what they might have originally suffered or gone through in that most terrible war. Considering that the United States hadn't even gotten into the battles in Europe (effectively speaking) until the last stage of the war, the emotional and physical devastation suffered by our American troops paled by comparison with that suffered by the French, British, and German soldiers, since they had had to endure all this for almost *3 full years before* the US became involved in the conflict. Today, one reads the histories and accounts of participants that survive and one can only imagine at the cumulative effects on the soldiers (and civilians) of those three nations and the horrors they faced.

Reading any history of that first great world conflict, euphemistically known variously as *'The Great War'*, the *'First World War'*, and *'the war to end all wars'*, one reads the statistics and figures that after the passage of time all wars are reduced to (long after, of course, all the intensely personal suffering and anguish has long since passed and been forgotten) and tries (unsuccessfully for the most part) to garner a small bit of comprehension about what it must have been like. While some understanding may be gained through voluminous reading, it amounts to only the merest of a small fragment of awareness of what the actual fighting must have been like.

Although by no means reflective of the *true* depth of the irredeemable tragedy that the First World War engendered, a few statistics may be helpful to understand the magnitude of some of the carnage that prevailed. By conservative estimate, over *ten million* (10,000,000) men were lost on the actual battlefields, concurrent with an equally high number of unknown civilian mortalities. That doesn't take into consideration the millions upon millions who were either seriously injured and survived, or those who received disabling injuries that were not immediately life threatening (traumatic loss of limbs, permanent lung disease and/or vision problems resulting from exposure to war gases, etc.). *Perhaps the starkest statistic is the fact that over 20,000 British soldiers alone were killed on the first day in the First Battle of the Somme, and on average more than 6,500 soldiers were killed on each and every day throughout the full five-year period the war encompassed...*

When one takes a modern war, such as Korea, Vietnam, or the actions in Iraq and Afghanistan, circumstances and degrees of suffering pale by comparison. Although the death rates and overt loss of life for the latter wars are far lower than those arising in the First or Second World Wars, the emotional (and often physical) trauma suffered is still substantial. One of the main mitigating factors between the two eras is the fact that America as a nation has sunk far deeper into the familiar softness and comfort of our modern, technology-enhanced materialist culture, with the development of a consequently far less firm resolve and diminished fortitude to undergo deprivation beyond a certain point than has obtained in past decades. Thanks to the vicarious voyeurism enabled by modern, live media reporting, the loss of a few dozen of our soldiers today produces the same level of intense grief and emotional angst that the loss of *thousands* of World War One soldiers created among families back then, but this neither dismisses nor reduces the impact of war, no matter where it takes place, or in what era.

28) 'Maturity' is a synonym for getting older

Back in Minot, at John Moses Air Force Hospital, I had at the time none of these more recent awarenesses to help temper my youthful empathy beyond that which my normally somewhat pacific disposition supported and my intense opposition to the then-current war in Vietnam had, in my understanding, almost no association at all with the personal sacrifices all those old Norwegian vets had made in the First World War. I guess that's partly because I wasn't entirely anti-war (opposed to war in *any form* or manner), but simply (situationally and circumstantially) against that specific war being fought in Vietnam. My distaste for ALL war and national conflict didn't come about until sometime later, when I had read far more widely and gained a much broader and complete understanding of exactly what politically motivated armed conflict is all about.

Accordingly, I led two separate and compartmented lives during my Air Force service in North Dakota, one working as a medical orderly in a hospital full of old vets whom I had little concern for and *another* as an idealistic young anti-war protestor in uniform after duty hours. The great but perhaps unavoidable tragedy of that may be that I hadn't yet put all the pieces of the life puzzle together, but this is almost always the way life is. Life is a continuing experience that one may think of as an emotional and intellectual savings account. As the years go by, one's understanding grows commensurate with one's experiences and an equal ability to reflect intelligently upon them. Regrettably, by the time one is better able to put all those pieces of life's puzzle together meaningfully, the opportunities for making use of what is gained from them and bringing about meaningful change has diminished proportionately, until finally one is almost at the end of life and realizes with a sense of profoundly hollow sadness that nothing will *ever* really change. Human beings are doomed to a cyclical life experience, each generation not listening to the previous one and repeating the same mistakes over and over and over, until...*dare we hope for it?...*some major error in strategic planning occurs at the top of some superpower's food-chain or another and suddenly the human race (along with all its tendencies to squabble and violently disagree) will finally be vaporized out of existence. *Poof!* We should be so lucky...

29) Wars suck, but bicycles are kinda neat

Ah well. Meanwhile life goes on...barely. One of the many things I developed a taste for while serving in NoDak was bicycling. There was an old hole-in-the-wall Schwinn bicycle shop across the street from the Lutheran Church and just down the street from the campus. They had a nice array of Schwinn '10-speed racers' there, one in particular catching my eye: a *Schwinn Continental Super Sport*. By today's standards it was a fairly heavy beast and the quality none too great (not up to Italian or French expectations), but it was affordable and I soon discovered the delights of taking drives along some of the rural roads bordering Minot's city limits. Taking a knapsack in hand, I'd make a leisurely run out to the orchards on the north end of town and just cycle aimlessly down the rural country roads for a few hours until it was time to get back to town. There were apple trees along the way and on a hot summer day nothing was more personally satisfying than pulling over after a sweaty hour or so and decamping under an apple tree by the side of the road, to watch the world go by. While munching on an apple (I am guessing Adam rather innocently had the same pleasant feeling, when offered one by Eve), it was all too easy to forget crotchety old vets and ignore the possibility that at any given second, due to a sudden sharp international disagreement between the US and the USSR, the drowsy, bucolic calm of Minot's summer fields could be shattered by multiple rising intercontinental missiles exploding forth from their subterranean holes below, or that the hazy blue skies above could at any second erupt with a dozen explosive nuclear suns having a brilliance greater than the mind can conceive. The contrast between boy, bicycle, tree, and apple couldn't have been less distinct at such moments, but the possibility of a nuclear war breaking out was all too real to dare contemplate seriously at such a perfect moment; thus, after a leisurely respite of cheese, French bread and an apple, I would pedal back to the hospital attitudinally re-equipped to battle bedpans and renew my fight against the next day's small stresses and strains.

A few of the small, uncomplicated pleasures of those times occasionally return to my mind's eye, when I think back on those days. Some of those special little moments would occur while sitting at a nurses' station late at night, listening to the winter winds howl along the window ledges, moaning past the window panes and whining with a most animal-like plaintiveness. Closing one's eyes to blot out the dingy institutional yellow of the ward's walls, it was easy to think about the great frozen expanse of snow-draped landscape that lay just outside the window and seven stories beneath, as if it were a location off in Russia somewhere. There was something magical about that thought, very evocative and melancholy simultaneously, but I was given to abundant imagination anyway. The resulting mood reminded me strongly of the scenes in David Lean's cine masterpiece, *Dr. Zhivago*, in which he and *Lara Feyodorvna* have sought refuge in an old family *dasha*, far out in the snowy rural wastes surrounding Moscow, late at night. In one especially memorable scene, the windows of their frozen sanctum are frosted over with hoar crystals and the temperature outside is far below zero as Zhivago and Feordorvna huddle for warmth by the light of a single candle. Gazing at each other over the guttering of a half-burned candle with unspoken passion, it is a particularly evovative romantic moment in that movie. Although there was precious little romance at the dimly lit nurses' station that I was charged with watching over, a vestige of that mood was still vaguely palpable, lurking just beyond the mind's full grasp and captured in the vocalizations of the icy draughts playing outside the frost-covered windows.

30) Sodding off on 'All Souls Day'

Another time, at Halloween and late at night during a fairly stiff snowstorm, Mike and I had just finished up printing yet another issue of our war protest broadside (which we distributed at the USO and covertly passed out on the base whenever circumstances allowed) and on a whim, as we closed up and left, grabbed a large carved jack-o-lantern someone had left at the USO and placed the pumpkin on top of my VW bug's roof. The lit candle inside faced rearward, since the wind would otherwise have blown it out, and thus decorated I drove my beetle slowly back down the city streets to the hospital. It made quite an interesting spectacle, I'm sure, but there were few others out and on the road to see it. As our luck would have it, one of the few spectators happened to be a Minot policeman in his patrol car and we were soon pulled over. Although I can't imagine a LEO writing a ticket for something like *'illegally driving with lit Halloween jack-o-lantern on roof of car'* (since as we all know there are so many laws both enforceable and unenforceable on the books that no truly *legitimate* cause is ever required, should an officer decide to make a stop), we *were* pulled over. He had little sympathy for bored US Air Force enlisted men and clearly possessed no sense of humor at all, but he did let us off with a grumbled warning to get *'that blasted pumpkin'* off our car and go home. That was the extent of this real-life Washington Irving Halloween moment. Not half as dramatic as the one experienced by *Ichabod Crane* with his headless horseman pursuer, however. Someone had probably stolen his doughnut back at the precinct house.

31) Mike learns about 'marital bliss'

Not long after this, Mike met his first wife, Diane, who was a local townie and a cadet in the Minot Civil Air Patrol Wing and they soon married and moved into private quarters in town. Diane was very likely taken by Mike's unique combination of Rasputin-like and saintly qualities and of course they didn't grow them like Mike up in NoDak, so perhaps it is understandable that she fell under his spell quite rapidly. Besides, she understood the whole military *schtick*, being a CAP cadet and all, and read science-fiction a lot; for whatever the reason, they seemed to hit it off as well as anyone had a right to respect. For his honeymoon, Mike loaded Diane up into his beaten-up old Volvo 544 sedan and they *amscrayed* off to a small hotel in the nearby rural town of *Max* (yes, that's its real name: beautiful downtown *'Max'*). Max had, in the last 2000 census, a population of 278 humans, uncounted numbers of cats and dogs, and probably *several millions* of prairie dogs claiming residence within its municipal borders. In 1966 it had to be at least a third *less* populous. Of course, Frenchy and I felt we had to commemorate the occasion of Mike & Diane's honeymoon departure for Max by smearing a huge hunk of ripe Limburger Cheese on the manifold of the Volvo's engine, a rather large and almost unforgiveable lapse of decorum on our part (at least regarded as such by Mike and Diane, who had to live with the unbelievably *TERRIBLE* stench both up and back from their conjugal getaway).

Diane was also originally attracted to Mike because she read and enjoyed sci-fi almost as much as he and I did, so it initially seemed a match made in heaven. Geeks in love? Despite this shared interest, living with a saint has never been easy, however, and especially one with Rasputin-like overtones of mystic presence that tended to predominate at odd moments. Accordingly, the bloom soon faded from the blossom, so to speak; I later came to find out (after leaving for a different duty assignment) that Mike and Diane had parted permanently after only a couple of years together.

32) Minot AFB bids me a fond 'adieu'

Eventually, after nearly a full two years of similar misadventures and other post-adolescent experiential anomalies (of which this is a good example) that cemented our friendship and highlighted our mutual efforts to help bring the war in Vietnam to a close, I was finally given orders to report to a new duty station in Arizona (Davis-Monthan AFB, as part of that sprawling base's 803rd Medical Group) and Mike, Frenchy, Russ and I all parted company. Still, given the close bonds we had developed during our time together at Minot, we remained in touch over the years and in 1969, after I had returned to the *Peoples' Republic of Berzerkeley* in California, I shortly found Mike established in that city as well, it being the really happening West Coast place for peaceniks and radical-fringers and all. Russ returned to New York City, where he was reabsorbed into Woody Allen's alternate universe dimension once again. Of Frenchy, I heard no further word after I left Minot.

Not long after coming to Berkeley, Mike became involved with the Eastern Orthodox Church, soon becoming a priest in that religion and found his strong sense of rather eclectic mysticism quite at home within Orthodoxy's holy embrace. Although Mike and I lived in the same urban area, we really didn't cross paths much and after a year or so Mike relocated back to Portland, Oregon, where his younger sister lived. I was devastated to learn that after leaving Berkeley Mike had been diagnosed with a form of fatal leukemia that claimed his life a few years after that disclosure. Mike was truly one of the most unique and genuinely good, caring human beings I have ever had the honor and good fortune of knowing and it seems ironic that his life was ended prematurely (doesn't it always, when good people demise prematurely?). Sadly, I did not learn of his passing until a year after the fact and I greatly regret not having known of his condition until it was too late to get back in touch.

I remained in Berkeley, went to work for several hospitals in the East San Francisco Bay Area, and continued following my own path through life. But that is another (equally long-winded) story and probably good for at least another 50,000-word tangential excursion on paper. In summary, my introduction to Minot, to North Dakota, and to that entire Mid-West part of the United States, was an enormously rewarding and fulfilling one. I look back on those days of my earlier youth as part of a unique and richly memorable experience growing up to maturity. While I don't claim to have ever fully matured (I'm still a kid in my 60s, but aren't we all?), it certainly filled out a very important part of my attempt to grasp and understand a small portion of what the life experience is all about. 41 years later, I still have no greater clue about what matters most in life or what it all means, but like any good journey, the 'getting here' part of the trip has not been boring!

[Note: At this point, Porky Pig was supposed to pop up here and say *"Buda-buda-buda that's all, folks"* but I think they've sent him off to Afghanistan to entertain the troops in that unhappy war, with Miss Piggy. Oh well. Considering the history of humanity's perverse love affair with organized death and destruction, perhaps there really is no such aspect of war as *"...that's all, folks!"*, anyway. *D'ya think*?]

ABOUT THE AUTHOR

Kalikiano Kalei, who has never been without dogs in his life, for the past 17 years has shared life exclusively with Siberian Huskies. Although self-admittedly an 'Omega' personality, he has always fitted into his family's pack quite well. He is the author of several other books, including two collections of poetry, lives in Sacramento, California and takes absolutely *nothing* seriously except *everything*. Shown above are *Raki* (left) and *Laika* (right).

www.ingramcontent.com/pod-product-compliance
Lightning Source LLC
Chambersburg PA
CBHW071855090426
42811CB00004B/614

* 9 7 8 0 6 9 2 9 6 2 8 6 2 *